PRINCESSES of the LATER MIDDLE AGES

This book is dedicated to my parents:
to my dad John, you are my hero;
and to my mum, Angela, my cheerleader…
With all my love

PRINCESSES of the LATER MIDDLE AGES

ROYAL DAUGHTERS OF THE PLANTAGENETS

SHARON BENNETT CONNOLLY

PEN & SWORD HISTORY
AN IMPRINT OF PEN & SWORD BOOKS LTD.
YORKSHIRE – PHILADELPHIA

First published in Great Britain in 2026 by
PEN AND SWORD HISTORY
An imprint of
Pen & Sword Books Ltd
Yorkshire – Philadelphia

Print ISBN 978 1 03619 218 1
ePUB ISBN 978 1 03619 220 4
ePDF ISBN 978 1 03619 221 1

A CIP catalogue record for this book is available from the British Library.

Typeset in Times New Roman 10/13 by
SJmagic DESIGN SERVICES, India.
Printed and bound in the UK by CPI Group (UK) Ltd.

The Publisher's authorised representative in the EU for product safety is Authorised Rep Compliance Ltd., Ground Floor, 71 Lower Baggot Street,
Dublin D02 P593, Ireland.
www.arccompliance.com

For a complete list of Pen & Sword titles please contact
PEN & SWORD BOOKS LIMITED
George House, Units 12 & 13, Beevor Street, Off Pontefract Road,
Barnsley, South Yorkshire, S71 1HN, England
E-mail: enquiries@pen-and-sword.co.uk
Website: www.pen-and-sword.co.uk

or

PEN AND SWORD BOOKS
1950 Lawrence Rd, Havertown, PA 19083, USA
E-mail: uspen-and-sword@casematepublishers.com
Website: www.penandswordbooks.com

MIX
Paper | Supporting responsible forestry
FSC® C013604

Contents

The Normans and Angevins

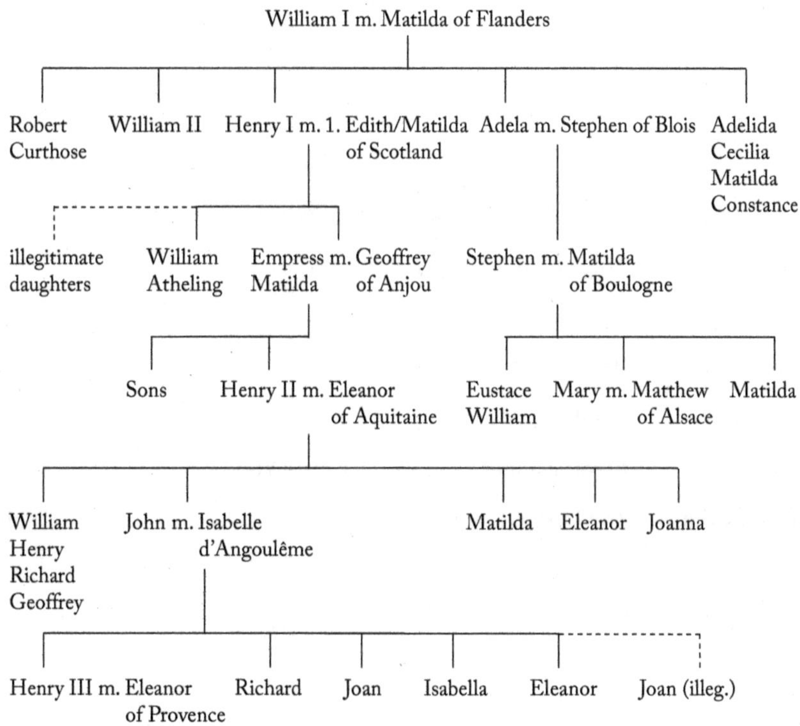

The Plantagenets

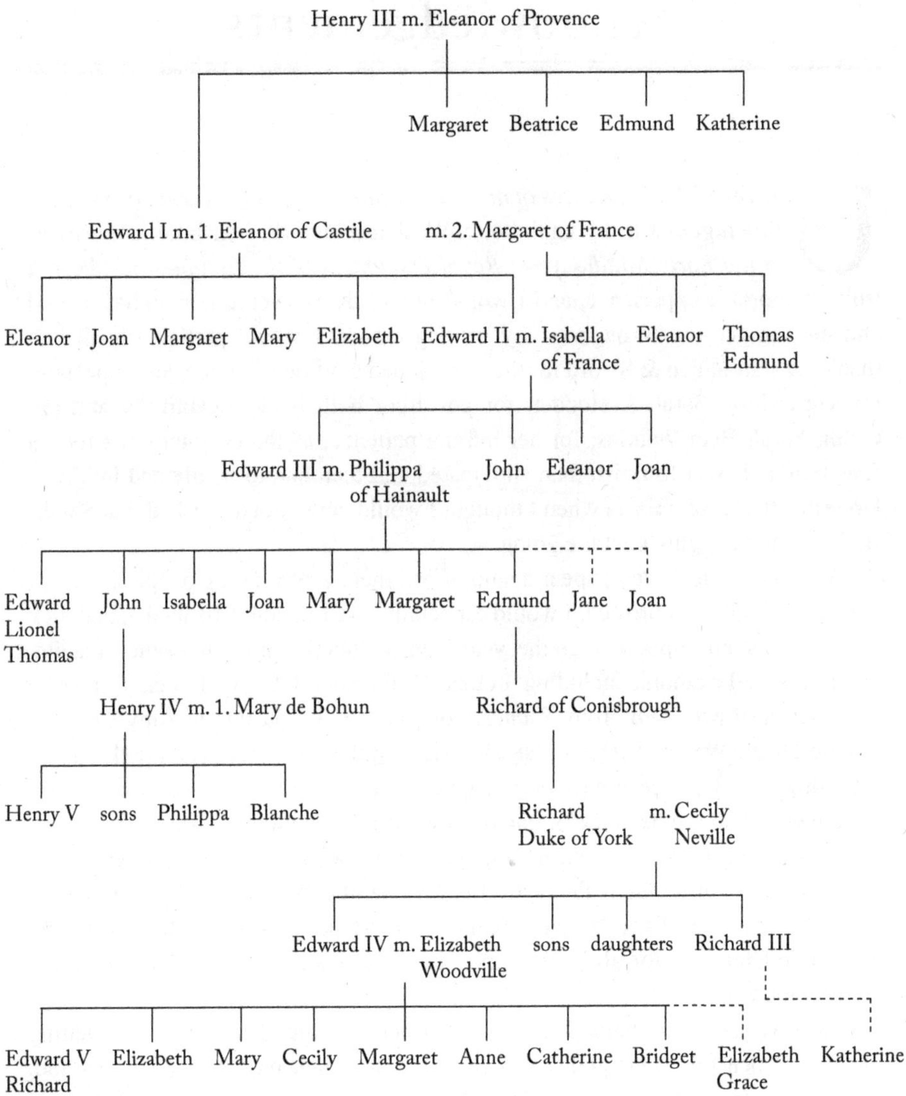

Acknowledgements

Unbelievably, *Princesses of the Later Middle Ages: Royal Daughters of the Plantagenets* is my tenth book. Writing it and its sister book, *Princesses of the Early Middle Ages: Royal Daughters of the Conquest* has been a truly memorable experience, and I would like to thank everyone who has helped and encouraged me throughout my writing career. I would particularly like to thank the staff at Pen & Sword for their continued confidence in me, and especially my copyeditor, Sarah J. Hodder, for polishing both books beautifully and my editor, Sarah-Beth Watkins, for her infinite patience, as the original book took a few months longer to finish than anticipated and then had to be divided into two. Honestly, there were times when I thought I would never get it finished, but Sarah-Beth's gentle nagging kept me going.

Although writing can appear a solo effort, there are so many people involved before the book is published. I would especially like to thank Elizabeth Chadwick for her constant support over the years. Many thanks, also, to some amazing historians and authors, including Louise Wilkinson, Danna Messer, Catherine Hanley, Carol McGrath, Tony Riches, Toni Mount, Linda Porter, Amy Licence, Kristie Dean, Wendy J. Dunn, James Wright and Janina Ramirez for the many little snippets of advice and encouragement. And to Gemma Hollman, for clearing up a query I had on the name of one of Edward III's daughters-in-law. The online author community has proved invaluable to me. So, I would like to extend my gratitude to Cathie Dunn, Paula Lofting, Samantha Wilcoxson, Lynn Dawson, Virginia Crow, Melissa Speed, Eleanor Swift-Hook, Patricia Bracewell and Stephanie Churchill for all your support and encouragement with this book and the previous ones.

I reserve a special 'thank you' for my partner in crime, Derek Birks, for getting me into podcasting. Our podcast, *A Slice of Medieval*, has been great fun and, hopefully, entertaining. And we have had such incredible guests, like Bernard Cornwell, Helen Castor, Scott Mariani and Ian Mortimer, to give us their own insights into history.

I must also express my gratitude to readers of my books and blog – *History ... the Interesting Bits.com* – for their wonderful support and feedback. And to my friends on social media who are always there to give me encouragement.

And thank you to the various historical sites I have visited over the years of research – York Minster, Lincoln Cathedral, Lincoln Castle, the British Library, the National Archives, to name just a few – and all the wonderful staff who have been happy to talk about all things medieval.

I would like to say an extra special 'thank you' to Sasha, Gill and Kai at Lindum Books in Lincoln for hosting my author talks and being a huge and constant support for nearly a decade. I am grateful to everyone at Gainsborough Old Hall, Conisbrough Castle, Lincoln Castle and Lincoln Cathedral Café for being my places of refuge when I needed to get away from the computer. They are my havens from writer's block. A thank you must also go to my friends closer to home, particularly Sharon Gleave, Jill Gaskell, Rosanna McGlone, Libby Millard and Andrea Raee and all my local friends, for dragging me out for a coffee every once in a while.

I reserve a special thanks to my family, especially to my mum and dad for all their love and encouragement, and for their own passion for history. And to my husband, James, thank you for putting up with all the history nerdiness. I could not have done it without all of you. The biggest thank you has to go to my research assistant and son, Lewis Connolly, who has grown up travelling to various wonderful places with me in the process of making each of my books a reality. He has turned into a fabulous sounding-board for my ideas and arguments. A chip off the old block, if ever there was one, he is well on the way to becoming an excellent historian himself and I really value the many history-related conversations we have on a daily basis.

And last, but by no means least, I will always owe a debt of gratitude to the great historians throughout history to the present day, who have gallantly edited and translated the chronicles of the medieval era, so that they are accessible and readable for all of us who have an interest in the period, but very little understanding of Latin. Every effort has been made to ensure the accuracy of this book. However, any errors that may occur are entirely my own.

Introduction

Princesses of the Later Middle Ages: Royal Daughters of the Plantagenets is the second part of the book that was designed to be *The Medieval Princess* – except it turned out to be a much bigger project than I ever anticipated and was far too long for one book. So, out of one project, *The Medieval Princess: Royal Daughters from the Conquest to the Wars of the Roses,* I have two books. *Princesses of the Early Middle Ages: Royal Daughters of the Conquest* was the first instalment, looking at the daughters of Harold II, William the Conqueror and England's kings from 1066 to the end of the reign of King John. I should have known, of course, that I could not fit all these amazing women into one volume, after all, my inspiration for the books was Mary Anne Everett Green's comprehensive, six volume series *The Lives of the Princesses of England.* I owe a huge debt of gratitude to Mary Anne for the work she did in bringing these women into the light.

The inspiration for this book, and its sister, is rather odd. It comes from a meme that appears on social media every once in a while, which is something along the lines of 'My daughter wanted me to treat her more like a princess. So, I married her to a stranger to strengthen the alliance with Poland!' This is, essentially, the vision we have of a medieval princess. She is a pawn, nothing more than a bargaining tool in the world of international politics as far as her parents were concerned. As Helen Castor writes:

> Royal brides – a rarefied kind of human freight, each delicately wrapped in her jewelled trousseau – were transported hundreds of miles over land and sea in bodily service to their country, to marry men they barely knew or had never met. The transaction might cement an enduring political relationship, or it could prove to be a fleeting aberration, a deal done in a moment of cynical manipulation or unwarranted hope – but, whether they found themselves cherished or isolated, these young women were unlikely to see home and family again.[1]

But was that really the case?

In *Princesses of the Early Middle Ages,* these royal women appear to have had two options: to marry or to become a nun. The two daughters of King Harold II, who was killed at the Battle of Hastings in October 1066, did not have the guidance of their father when their fates were decided, but they were influenced by the time in which they lived. Growing to adulthood in the aftermath of the Norman Conquest one of the sisters, Gytha, left England with her paternal grandmother and was eventually married to Vladimir II Monomakh of Kyivan Rus, a union most likely arranged by her Danish cousin, King Swein Estrithson. Gytha's sister, Gunhild, remained in England in the convent at Wilton, which was patronised by her aunt Edith of Wessex, Edward the Confessor's queen. There is some doubt whether Gunhild was ever intended for convent life. Wilton was an abbey renowned for the education of young noblewomen who did not necessarily go on to take their vows. And Gunhild certainly did not. She appears to have led a rather unconventional life as the concubine of first Alan the Red and then his brother, Alan the Black. Whether she ever married either brother is still disputed.

Harold's daughters may not have had the guidance of their father, but his shadow, as the defeated and dead king of England, must have been long. It would certainly have affected their marriage prospects. Marriage with Gunhild or Gytha did not bring an accompanying alliance with England. And Gytha's status as a member of the Danish extended royal family was only significant enough to bring her a marriage with the son of a younger son of a dynasty at the far reaches of Europe, notwithstanding that circumstance and family deaths made Vladimir II Monomakh far more influential than could have been foreseen at the time of the wedding.

With daughters of the Norman kings, there is little evidence that the girls themselves were consulted on their futures. And that was especially so if they became nuns, as they were often dedicated to the Church in their infancy. Of William the Conqueror's four known, undisputed daughters, two married French lords – the counts of Blois and Brittany – one was dedicated to the Church as a child and the fourth joined a convent after several failed marriage proposals. King Stephen also dedicated his youngest daughter to the Church, sending her to a convent when she was just 6 or 7 years old. Although she took to convent life, Mary (or Marie) was violently dragged from it when she became the last surviving child of King Stephen and therefore Countess of Boulogne in her own right. As Stephen's heir, she was rich and valuable, and way too dangerous to be allowed to remain unmarried, even if she was a nun. She had a claim to England's throne and that claim needed to be controlled and contained. Interestingly, after she had provided her husband with two daughters to continue the family line, Mary was finally able to obtain a divorce and return to the cloisters, leaving her husband, Matthew of Alsace, to raise the children.

As the only legitimate daughter of Henry I, Stephen's predecessor, Empress Matilda was never destined for a convent. Indeed, she achieved the heights few princesses would ever reach, as Holy Roman Empress. And she so nearly became England's first crowned queen regnant. But despite being proclaimed Lady of the English in 1141, Matilda was never able to consolidate her position as England's ruler. And, although she did not have a daughter of her own, the empress's three granddaughters, the daughters of Henry II and Eleanor of Aquitaine, fulfilled what has come to be seen as the traditional role of a princess, marrying into foreign lands to forge alliances that are strengthened by that familial bond. King John's daughters, in turn, were destined for the same roles, marrying into Germany, Wales and Scotland. All except the youngest. Eleanor, who was a babe in arms when her father died. She was married at the age of 8 to William Marshal II, to bring that powerful magnate into the royal family. And her second husband, Simon de Montfort? Well, that was a love match which would causes its own problems, when family disharmony and political upheaval would result in the Second Barons' War.

Would the story of the princess in the waning of the Middle Ages be the same as had come before?

Technically, a princess is the daughter of a reigning king, although the term 'princess' was not used in medieval times; they were referred to as 'Lady'. But we shall use the term, to help distinguish between noble women and royal women. Princesses of England are often shadowy figures, hidden in the background – we may have the story of their lives, but not their thoughts or feelings. As we shall see, royal parents took great care in the raising of their daughters. Princesses led pampered lives, but they were also nurtured, educated in languages and diplomacy. They were raised in the knowledge that they would be an ambassador for their country – for their father, brother or nephew. They would be the personal link between two kingdoms, between their country of birth and the country of their husband and – God willing – children. But marriage was not just a means of producing children; it was their career. A princess was raised in comfort and privilege, but with a responsibility to the future – a duty and destiny imposed on them from the moment of their birth

Not all princesses were fortunate in their marriages and not all kings took as much care in their choice of alliance as one might expect. It would be the princess who would suffer. Alliances may shift. Kings may die. Or a king may see an opportunity at the expense of his daughter's peace of mind. But these were the exceptions. Time and again, we see the princess making a life for herself in her adopted country. Acting the diplomat. Acting as regent during her husband's absence, or for her son. The princess is often the link that maintains the peace. Some did not see their homeland again, maintaining family connections only through letters and gifts, and the sharing of news by ambassadors.

That marriage was a part of a peace treaty was a clear demonstration of intent on both sides, that they wanted a lasting peace. What more could a king do to show his wish for peace, than bring his enemy into the family?

Royal daughters were raised with a sense of duty and responsibility, to family and to country. It has long been the view that their duty was to 'smile and wave', or perhaps 'grin and bear it'. And to have children, of course. To produce that all important male heir who would one day be king, or lord, of the land. But their job was so much more! They were the senior diplomat of their homeland, providing that exclusive access to a king that only a wife can. They were the ties that bound royal families together or provided the closest bond between a lord and his king. And we will frequently see instances where a royal daughter will use her personal correspondence to mend a breach, share diplomatic news or act as a conduit between her husband and her father or brother.

The fates of these princesses varied greatly. Too large a number died tragically young, either as babes in the cradle, by succumbing to disease in adolescence, or struggling to bring their child into the world. Occasionally, we also meet a princess who escapes the future designed for her, – a princess who marries for love, or retreats into a convent. Some never left England's shores, their destinies to be the wives of their father's barons, to tie noblemen to the Crown in a personal alliance that would be hard to break, without causing dissent between husband and wife. And then there are those whose lives are irrevocably changed by the usurpation of the Crown or civil war. Lives changed for the better for the daughters of Henry IV; and for the worse for the children of Edward IV, suddenly affected by the taint of bastardy.

The first problem for any writer is answering the question of 'where to start?' As *Princesses of the Later Middle Ages: Royal Daughters of the Plantagenets* was originally the second half of one book, my question was 'where do I split the books?' I wanted a sensible breaking point, so that each book could work as a standalone. I also needed to make sure that both books were roughly the same length. A natural break, in my mind, was between Henry III's daughters and those of Edward I, but that would make the first book much longer than the second. Looking again, the natural break, which would also work with the word count, was actually between the children of King John and those of Henry III, which also has that invisible transition from the Angevin royal house of Henry II to the later Plantagenets. The last medieval princesses, of course, were the daughters of Edward IV, who bridge that other invisible divide, between the medieval and early modern eras, from the Plantagenet royal line to that of the Tudors.

Chapter One

Henry III: Cherished Daughters

Henry III had a rather dramatic childhood. His father died when he was just 9 years old, and the country was beset by civil war, foreign invasion and a rival king. The English rebels had invited the son of King Philip II of France to claim the crown from the hated King John. Louis had been proclaimed king in London but was never crowned. At John's death, the country was still riven by civil war and the Capital was firmly in the hands of Prince Louis. The Papal Legate, Guala Bicchieri, and William Marshal, Earl of Pembroke, were tasked with the guardianship of the young king and organising his coronation. Henry was knighted by Marshal on 27 October and crowned in Gloucester Abbey the following day; a chaplet belonging to his mother was used in place of a heavy crown. Guala oversaw the ceremony, allowing the bishops of Winchester, Worcester and Exeter to anoint Henry and administer the coronation oath. When William Marshal lay on his deathbed in 1219, he expressed a hope that God 'may grant that you grow to be truly worthy'.[1] He also warned the young king not to 'emulate some wicked forebear' and prayed that Henry would 'live not long but die before that happens'.[2] King John's mismanagement of the kingdom was still fresh in all minds and the barons were eager that Henry would learn from his father's mistakes.

In 1217, Henry's mother, Isabelle d'Angoulême, left England for her own domains in France. Isabelle shocked England, and probably the whole of Christendom, in 1220 when, in a scandalous *volte-face*, she married her daughter's betrothed, Hugh X de Lusignan. And then, instead of sending Joan back to England, as Isabelle had promised, the 10-year-old princess went from being Hugh's betrothed to being his prisoner. Joan was held hostage to ensure Hugh's continued control of her dower lands, and as a guarantee to the transfer of his new wife's dower. England, on the other hand, was withholding Queen Isabelle's dower against the return of Joan and her dower lands. After a few months of wrangling, Joan was eventually returned to England; Isabelle's dower, was not wholly resolved. Despite their rocky relationship – she once locked him out of the castle – Isabelle and Hugh had nine children together, including Aymer de Lusignan and William de Valence. Many of his Lusignan half-siblings would later cause problems for Henry III, after arriving in England to seek patronage and advancement from their royal half-brother.

In 1223, King Henry first asserted his right to personal rule. All royal castles were ordered to be surrendered into the king's hands, and while some constables were permanently relieved of their positions, others were back in their castles by Christmas. In 1225, a modified Magna Carta was reissued, and it is this version that remains on the statute books today. The king was still heavily reliant on his justiciar, Hubert de Burgh, however, and it was not until de Burgh's popularity began to wane, from 1227 onwards, that Henry really began to rule. The subsequent years were marred by political infighting, with Hubert de Burgh trying to hold on to what power he could, and Henry III attempting to assert his independence, building up his own coterie of household knights and political allies. De Burgh's dramatic downfall saw him imprisoned in Devizes Castle in 1232, only for there to be a thaw in his relationship with the king in 1234, when his enemies themselves fell from power following the Marshal War. This was a rather contained civil war led by Richard Marshal, younger son of Henry's former regent William Marshal, and encouraged by the Welsh prince, Henry's brother-in-law, Llywelyn ap Iorweth, also known as Llywelyn the Great.

From 1234 onwards, Henry firmly established his personal rule, initiating a period of political stability that lasted for over fifteen years. Finally turning his mind to marriage, he chose Eleanor of Provence. The daughter of Raymond Berengar, Count of Provence, Eleanor was well connected. Her mother's family were the counts of Savoy, and she was the younger sister of Marguerite, wife of Louis IX of France. Although she was connected, Eleanor was not a rich heiress – the dowry was eventually set at 10,000 marks, and that was never fully paid. Henry and Eleanor were betrothed at Canterbury on 14 January 1236 and were married at Westminster Abbey six days later, with Eleanor being crowned queen of England following the wedding ceremony. Henry was 28 years old; Eleanor was 12 or 13. Henry was probably the most cultured of England's post-Conquest medieval kings. His love of the arts saw him invest in silver, gold and enamel work, hangings and embroideries, and magnificent frescoes for the royal palaces. His greatest achievement is undoubtedly the rebuilding of Westminster Abbey, which he established as the royal necropolis and would be the site of his own tomb, close to the shrine of his patron saint, Edward the Confessor. It stands as a physical legacy of a most remarkable reign, and it still remains at the heart of the monarchy today.

Henry was the least martially-inclined of England's medieval kings, but that did not stop him getting drawn into conflict, both at home and abroad. The arguments over his mother's English lands continued and they were confiscated, for a short time, in 1221. In 1224, however, they were confiscated for good when Hugh de Lusignan allied himself with the French king, Louis VIII. In exchange for a substantial pension, Hugh and Isabelle supported a French invasion of Poitou (lands in France that belonged to the king of England, her son). They were reconciled with Henry in 1226, and Isabelle met her first-born son for the first time in more than twelve years in 1230, when Henry mounted a futile expedition to Brittany and Poitou. Isabelle and Hugh, however, continued to play the kings of France and England against each other, always looking for the advantage. In 1242, for example, when Henry III invaded Poitou, Hugh X initially gave support to his English stepson, only to change sides once more, precipitating the collapse of Henry's campaign.

Henry's foreign policy had initially centred on the recovery of the Angevin Empire, lost by his father, but his expeditions to Poitou and into Normandy had proved fruitless. He then expanded his horizons, marrying his sister, Isabella, to Emperor Frederick II. He also encouraged his brother, Richard, to accept the kingdom of Germany in 1257. And Henry accepted the crown of Sicily for his younger son, Edmund; the only problem was that the crown was offered by the Pope, with the proviso that Henry would send an army to wrest the island from Frederick II's son, Manfred. The enterprise was the proverbial money pit and Sicily was eventually conquered by Charles I, Duke of Anjou, brother of the king of France and husband of Beatrice of Provence – Eleanor's sister.

Henry's greatest enemy proved to be the man who would one day become his brother-in-law, Simon de Montfort. Simon became the leader of the faction opposed to the favours given to the king's family; first to the queen's Savoyard relatives and then to Henry's own half-siblings, the de Lusignans, who arrived in England following the death of their and Henry's mother, Isabelle d'Angoulême, in 1246. When Simon had first arrived in England, he and Henry had become firm friends. Simon de Montfort was a third son, whose prospects would have appeared bleak during his younger years. An opportunity arose for him through his father's claim to the earldom of Leicester, via his mother, Amicia. The continuing hostilities between England and France in the early years of the thirteenth century meant that Simon's father was never able to take possession of this inheritance. When the senior Simon de Montfort had died in 1218, he was succeeded by his eldest son, Amaury, who then transferred all or some of his claims to the earldom of Leicester to his younger brother, Simon, who in turn then departed for England to claim his inheritance.

Simon was able to gain control of his family's portion of the Leicester lands, although he was not able to obtain the earldom that went with them. In 1231, he did homage to Henry III for his lands, and he continued to rise through the ranks of the court throughout the 1230s. From 1234 he attended meetings of the great council, pursued diplomacy with Scotland and Wales, and acted as steward – a post traditionally held by the earls of Leicester – at Henry III's wedding to Eleanor of Provence in 1234, although the earldom had still not been conferred on him. Simon did make enemies, however; his closeness to Henry and the fact he was a foreigner did not endear him to his fellow nobles.

At some point after the mid-1230s, possibly at the wedding of Henry and Eleanor of Provence, Simon met the king's youngest sister, Eleanor, and the couple fell in love. Eleanor was the widow of William Marshal, second Earl of Pembroke and had taken a vow of chastity on Marshal's death in 1231, when she was still a teenager. With the king's permission, Simon and Eleanor married in January 1238 in a secret ceremony in Henry's private chapel. Due to Eleanor's status as a princess and her vow of chastity, and the fact that Simon was a foreigner and a minor noble, secrecy was essential. Simon and Eleanor's first child, a son named Henry, was born in November 1238, and in the spring of 1239, Simon was finally confirmed as Earl of Leicester.

Unfortunately, the marriage was to be the spark that would end Henry and Simon's friendship, and in August 1239, at the churching of Eleanor of Provence following the birth of Lord Edward, the king's eldest son and heir, Henry turned on his brother-in-law. He accused Simon of seducing his sister and defiling her before their marriage, of bribing the Pope and using the Crown as surety for his debts without the king's permission. Due to Eleanor's vow of chastity, Simon had been prevailed upon to journey to Rome in March 1238 to seek a papal dispensation for the marriage. He had borrowed a large amount of money for his trip from the queen's uncle, Thomas of Savoy, Count of Flanders, giving the king's name as security. The king only discovered this when Thomas later asked for his money back. With further borrowing and accumulated interest, by this point the initial £200 debt now amounted to £1400.[3]

Henry flew into a rage. He forbade Simon and a pregnant Eleanor from attending the queen's churching ceremony and the stunned couple had to flee London, taking a ship to France; so hasty was their departure that they were forced to leave their son behind, with his wet nurse. Robert Grosseteste, Bishop of Lincoln and a friend of Simon's, intervened on his behalf with the king and Simon was able to return to England in 1240, ostensibly to raise funds to go on crusade and to collect his eldest son. Simon and Eleanor were only fully restored to favour on Simon's return from the Barons' Crusade in 1242. In the same year, Simon campaigned in Poitou, and between 1248 and 1252 he was in Gascony, acting as Henry's seneschal. His financial worries were gathering pace, with his Leicester lands being insufficient to support his growing family and his wife's Marshal dower only being paid sporadically. To make matters worse, in 1252, Henry called Simon to Westminster to answer charges of brutal high-handedness in Gascony. Henry was thwarted by baronial support for Simon, who countered with arguments that Henry had contravened the terms of his commission and failed to support Simon financially.

As relations between the king and the barons caused tensions, Simon became involved in the baronial opposition to Henry III's unpopular policies. Magna Carta had set out guidelines whereby the king should be guided by his barons, and the barons expected to be consulted on his policies and actions. Increasingly acting on his own initiative, Henry was going against the various interests of the barons. In 1258, the Provisions of Oxford set up a new form of government, with a fifteen-man Privy Council established to advise the king and oversee the government's administration. The lands and castles that Henry had given to his Lusignan favourites were confiscated, and the banished barons were escorted to Dover and sent into exile. The Provisions were confirmed and extended in 1259 in the Provisions of Westminster, but were overthrown by Henry, with the help of a papal bull, in 1261.

In April 1260, it appeared that Lord Edward, just a few months shy of his twenty-first birthday, was preparing to oppose his father, the king, and several barons were summoned to London, armed, and given lodgings in the city; Edward, on the other hand, was denied entry. The crisis was averted when Edward reconciled with his father, and then travelled to the Continent to take part in tournaments. In May 1261 papal bulls, issued by Alexander IV, arrived in England, absolving the king, queen and the realm of their oaths to adhere to the Provisions of Oxford. Henry published the bulls at Winchester in early June. By the end of the year, resistance had collapsed and the king's opponents were pardoned for their actions. Simon de Montfort took his wife and children and left for the Continent, returning in April 1263.

Simon was now the undisputed leader of the rebel faction, who insisted on the enforcement of the Provisions of Oxford of 1258. Many of the barons had grievances to work through. There were violent clashes when Montfort's army attacked royalists and occupied the Welsh Marches. In May 1263, Montfort summoned his supporters to Worcester and told them to come armed for war. The king was in dire straits; his Savoyard allies were pursued and violated, the queen's barge was attacked, pelted with mud, rotten eggs and stones, as it approached London Bridge, and the king was isolated in the Tower of London, surrounded by a hostile mob. Eleanor of Provence was eventually able to reunite with the king in the Tower, but the experience had shaken her. On 15 July, Simon de Montfort's army entered London, with Montfort appearing at the Tower the next day to ask for Henry's submission; Henry had little choice but to agree. The king then rode with Simon to Windsor, where Lord Edward, now firmly on the side of his father, was continuing his resistance. The young prince relinquished the castle, if a little ungraciously, without a fight.

The king's brother-in-law now had control of the ministries of state and the royal castles of England. In August 1263, attention was turned to the marriage of the heiress Isabella de Forz, widowed Countess of Aumale. Perhaps with a view to reconciliation, Simon de Montfort and his handpicked council awarded Isabella's marriage to Henry III's younger son, Edmund, who was 18 years old at the time; Edmund would become Earl of Aumale and Devon and receive a rich endowment from the accompanying lands. On 23 September, the king and queen, together with their eldest son, Edward, travelled to France to meet with King Louis and to seek the French king's adjudication over the Provisions of Oxford. As attempts to control the king failed, Simon and the barons rose up in revolt and the Second Barons' War broke out. The rebels besieged Rochester Castle between 19 and 26 April 1264, but Montfort was forced to withdraw to London when the royalist army arrived to relieve the fortress. As the king proceeded to secure the submission of the Channel ports, Simon de Montfort, with reinforcements from his son Henry and the London irregulars, marched out of London and headed south, hoping to bring the king's forces to battle.

The two armies came face to face at Lewes in Sussex. On 13 May 1264, Simon de Montfort and his men formally withdrew their homage to the king, and on the morning of 14 May, the two armies arrayed themselves for battle, with Henry having the larger force, but Simon having the higher ground. Eager for the fight, Edward took the field in advance of Henry and charged the left of the baronial line – comprised of the raw troops recruited in London – before the rest of the royal army was ready. Inevitably, in the face of such a ferocious attack, the Londoners broke and fled, Edward and his cavalry hot on their heels. Henry was left with no option but to hurry to the attack, climbing the hill to engage Simon's centre. The royal left, led by the king's brother, Richard of Cornwall, engaged Simon de Montfort's right but faced stiff opposition and were pushed back down the hill. Despite attacking uphill, Henry's division held its own in the centre, until Simon sent in his reserve to tip the balance in the barons' favour. Simon's troops pursued the royalist forces into the town of Lewes, with Henry only just able to disentangle himself from the street fighting and seek shelter in the priory. By the time Edward and his cavalry returned to the field, the battle was lost. Edward tried to rally his forces for a fresh offensive, but his leading barons thwarted his efforts by riding from the field. Instead of pulling back and regrouping, Edward chose to fight his way to his father, who had set up a defensive perimeter at the priory. Father and son were trapped; the next day they agreed to surrender.

The king – and country – was now firmly in Simon de Montfort's control; Henry was little more than a figurehead with Edward held hostage for his father's good behaviour. The king was forced to pardon the rebel barons and reinstate the Provisions of Oxford. De Montfort then established a government based on the Provisions and in 1265 called the Great Parliament. But Simon's victory was short-lived. Henry's wife, Eleanor of Provence, was already in France trying to gain support for her husband's cause. She met with the lords who had escaped the battlefield at Lewes and learned of the disastrous battle. After advising the queen to gather a force for invasion, the exiled lords appealed to the King of France for aid for their cause. They returned to England at Whitsuntide in 1265, under the leadership of John de Warenne, Earl of Surrey, and William de Valence, Earl of Pembroke, and 'with a power of crossebowes and other men of warre'.[4] Warenne and Valence landed with a force of 120 men, both cavalry and infantry. Having escaped his captors while out riding, Edward met up with Valence and his men and attacked several towns in the Welsh Marches. On the night of 1–2 August, having ridden through the night from Worcester, they launched a surprise attack on Kenilworth Castle, Simon de Montfort's home, and captured a good number of Simon's noble commanders, men and equipment. The earl's son, the younger Simon de Montfort, managed to escape with a sizeable force.

On the morning of 4 August 1265, Edward appeared on the high ground, north of the town of Evesham. Mistaken in the belief that the royal army was a contingent of reinforcements being brought up by the younger Simon de Montfort, the Earl of Leicester was taken by surprise. Still in Simon de Montfort's custody, Henry had been brought to the battlefield. As soon as the king saw Edward, he abandoned Simon de Montfort, as fighting was breaking out on all sides. Henry, who was wearing borrowed armour, was almost killed by Edward's forces before they realised it was the king and escorted him to safety. The battle was a slaughter. Edward had decided that Simon de Montfort had to die and assigned men to that task.

In the aftermath of the conflict, Henry determined to take revenge on his enemies, ordering the sequestration of rebel lands, which triggered a wave of looting throughout the country. It was only in October 1266 that the papal legate was able to persuade Henry to pursue a less draconian policy. The resulting Dictum of Kenilworth allowed rebels to recover their lands in return for the payment of harsh fines. The Statute of Marlborough followed in 1267, effectively reissuing the Provisions of Westminster and limiting the powers of local royal officials and the leading barons, but without the restriction to central royal authority. Simon's widow, the king's sister, was allowed to leave England.

Although they had their disagreements, and war drove a fatal wedge between Henry and his youngest sister, Eleanor, Henry III had been close to his siblings and continued to foster such closeness within his own family when he and Eleanor of Provence had their children. Henry and Eleanor's relationship would be a partnership that lasted the rest of Henry's life. She would be his lover, friend and political ally throughout his reign, though her relatives seeking Henry's favour would cause resentment among the English barons. Their first child, a son, Edward – the future Edward I – was born in 1239, followed by four more children. A second son, Edmund, was born in 1245; he would be created Earl of Lancaster and his descendant, Henry IV, would eventually sit on the throne as the first king of the royal House of Lancaster. Another son, John, was born in December 1250 and died in August 1252. Of their three daughters, Margaret was born in 1240, Beatrice in 1242 and a final daughter – their last child – Katherine, was born in 1253.

Margaret had been born on 5 October 1240, at Windsor Castle, though there is some confusion around the date and some sources suggest she was born on 29 September.[5] She was named for her mother's older sister, Marguerite of Provence, queen of France as the wife of Louis IX, and for St Margaret, to whom the queen is said to have called out to during her labours.[6] When Margaret was just a few days old, Henry made her a gift of twelve ounces of gold, with the same being given to her mother, along with £127 to pay for the expenses of her confinement.[7] The pious king had a choir chant the '*Christus Vincit*' before him on the day of his daughter's birth, and ordered thousands of paupers be fed 'so that Omnipotent God deigns to prosper our state and that of our queen and people'.[8] The king also ordered that a Mary Mass should be celebrated daily for the little princess, while five candles should be burnt in veneration of the five joys of the Virgin.[9] Only a year younger than her brother Edward, the children were given their own establishment at Windsor Castle. As a result, the king and queen divided their time between Westminster and Windsor.

The young royals were attended by a host of nurses, valets, cooks, clerks and chaplains.[10] The nursery was also populated by many noble children, who would be raised alongside Edward and Margaret. Their household was managed by Hugh and Sybil Giffard, an English couple, and their clerk was a Savoyard named Walter de Day. The children also had two nursemaids, Alice and Sarah.[11]

In 1242, when Margaret was still only a toddler, Henry began negotiations with his erstwhile brother-in-law, Alexander II, King of Scots, for a possible marriage between Margaret and the Scots king's young son, also called Alexander. Alexander was a year younger than the English princess. At the same time, Henry was preparing to leave for Poitou for what would prove to be a disastrous military campaign against the French king, Louis IX. Before their departure, Henry and Eleanor took the children to St Paul's in London, where offerings were made at the cathedral. Edward and Margaret each presented a cloth of arras, while the king and queen each gave cloth of gold.[12] Leaving their two children in England, and seven months pregnant, Eleanor accompanied her husband to the Continent. Shortly after their arrival, the queen fell ill and retired to the castle of La Réole while Henry continued with his expedition. As a result, the Virgin's girdle was sent out to Bordeaux, from Westminster Abbey, to aid the queen in childbirth.[13] And it was at Bordeaux that their daughter Beatrice was safely delivered, on 25 June 1242, named after her maternal grandmother, Beatrice of Savoy.[14] It would be a month before the baby girl would meet her father, after his forces were routed by the French.

Showing that his children were in his thoughts even when at war, while Henry was in Gascony, the king wrote to Hugh Giffard at Windsor, instructing him to retain the services of Richard the Harper, to entertain the children, with singing, dancing and games.[15] The king also instructed that the children should be given the best wine available from the castle cellars, presumably watered down, after he had received complaints about the quality of the wine being served to them. Henry also ordered 'forty-seven ells of good linen-cloth, price 7*d.* an ell, to be bought for Edward our dear son and Margaret our daughter, to make sheets and coverchiefs'.[16] The children's expenses also included robes for their attendants, deer and lampreys for the dinner table and other luxuries.[17] The king, queen and baby Beatrice returned to England in September, landing at Portsmouth and passing through Winchester before arriving at Windsor on 6 October 1242, where little Beatrice, with her nurse Agnes, joined Edward and Margaret in the nursery.[18] Three years later, in 1245, they would be joined by a baby brother, Edmund.

By the time of Edmund's arrival, Margaret's future had already been decided. A treaty with Scotland in 1244 formally agreed the marriage of Margaret and Alexander. Preparations for the wedding were then brought forward following the death of Alexander II in 1249. Margaret's betrothed was now king of Scots. And Scotland had a problem. Alexander II had, apparently, made no provision for what would happen if he were to die before his son came of age. Malcolm IV had come to the throne at the age of 12, while Alexander II had been 16; neither had needed a regency, assuming full powers as king the moment they succeeded. However, Alexander III was still only 7 years old and in no way could be thought mature enough to rule without a regent or regency council. Scotland had never had a child-king. The laws of succession prior to the establishment of primogeniture, which was still in its infancy, had guaranteed that the crown would go to the senior adult male within the royal family. But the crown now passed from father to son and a regency was needed to rule until Alexander III was old enough to assume the responsibility. Initially, most of the officers appointed by Alexander II continued their duties into the reign of the new king; there was no clean sweep of officials in the new administration. The leading magnates distributed the responsibilities of regency amongst themselves. In this, the Scots appear to have closely followed the recent example of England following King John's sudden death in 1216 and the subsequent long minority of Henry III, who was only 9 at his accession. King Henry did not interfere but kept a close eye on events north of the border as rival factions vied for control of the regency council. As the king's justiciar, Alan Durward, husband of the young king's illegitimate half-sister, managed to keep the Comyn faction at bay for the early years of the reign. But by 1251, the regency government was having trouble containing the excesses of the Comyn family and their adherents, failing to prevent their attacks of churches and other lands.

King Henry was already unhappy with the Durward administration, which had revived the appeal to the papacy to allow for an anointing ceremony to be included in the coronation (something successive English kings were opposed to) and was also asking for Scottish Church taxes to go to Scottish crusaders, rather than Henry III's military enterprises. Henry wanted not only a more effective government in Scotland, but one that was sympathetic to English interests. According to John of Fordun, 'the magnates of Scotland saw the danger in the country being under the governance of a boy king, and that his councillors, who were perhaps the greatest men of the whole kingdom, were swayed by the advantages each one had to gain'.[19] In order to avoid the dangers of the self-interested magnates, and on the advice of the clergy, an embassy was despatched:

> to Henry, king of England, to the end that the treaty of peace formerly made between him and the late king Alexander might be renewed, and most firmly secured by an alliance through a marriage to be contracted between the young king Alexander and this same King Henry's daughter. So, when this embassy came to London, the king of England granted all their demands to their hearts' content.[20]

In return, Henry despatched his own embassy to Scotland, with an invitation and safe conduct, for the young king, along with his advisers and magnates, to meet with him at York over Christmas 'in order to settle the aforesaid business'.[21] With the royal families of both Scotland and England staying at York Castle over the Christmas period, the meeting between the two kings and their advisers resulted in everything being happily settled, at least to Henry's satisfaction. The kings and the lords of both kingdoms swore upon the most holy Gospels, to uphold the terms agreed upon. Negotiations were followed by the ceremonial events of the gathering:

> Alexander, king of Scotland, therefore, a boy of nine, there received the honour of knighthood at the hands of Henry, king of England, on Christmas Day, amid the greatest joy and good wishes of the lords of either kingdom; and, on the morrow – that is, on Saint Stephen's Day – the king of England gave his first-born daughter, named Margaret, in marriage to the king of Scotland.[22]

On knighting young Alexander, King Henry presented him with a silver-handled sword in a scabbard of silk along with a pair of silver-gilt spurs.[23] Twenty other youths were knighted alongside the Scots king. The next day, the wedding ceremony was conducted in private in York Minster, early in the morning, by the elderly Walter Gray, Archbishop of York. The gathering of vast crowds, there to see the great magnates of the two kingdoms in all their finery, necessitated the early start, to avoid a crush. The bride was escorted to the altar by her brother Edward and three of his companions, each dressed in expensive cloth of gold, embroidered with the three leopards of England.[24] Matthew Paris records the splendour and extravagance of the wedding banquets:

> And if I should expound more fully the abounding diversity of the banquets, the variety of changed robes, the pleasure of the applauders of jesters, the great numbers of those at table together, the

> extravagant narrative would arouse derision in the ears and minds of those who were not there.[25]

The feasting required the provision of 170 boar, 1400 deer, 7000 chickens, 10,000 haddock, 25,000 gallons of wine and about 70,000 loaves of bread.[26] Before returning home to Scotland, Henry agreed to pay Alexander 5000 silver merks as Margaret's dowry.[27] The celebrations were not without controversy, when Alan Durward was accused of attempting to betray King Alexander. According to the *Chronicle of Melrose*, the accusations arose out of a scheme by Durward to get the Pope to legitimise the daughter he had by his wife, Marjory, the young king's illegitimate half-sister. He 'and his accomplices, had despatched messengers and presents to the pope'.[28] Had he succeeded, then it would have meant 'that if any accident should happen to the king of Scotland, they should succeed him in the kingdom as its lawful heirs. Had he succeeded in this, he would without doubt have been a traitor towards the king and the queen'.[29] His ambitions were enough to cause the downfall of the Durward administration. Now with a vested interest in Scotland, for the sake of his daughter, its new queen, and son-in-law, Henry III intervened to reorganise the Scottish government, ousting Durward and his friends and installing justiciars, a chamberlain and a chancellor who were all Comyn adherents. The government had swung from one faction to the other and one wonders if Henry should have taken a little time to investigate further before choosing a side. The changes were done with the pretence that Alexander had made the decision himself as the Scottish magnates acquiesced to Henry's dispositions. Suggesting Alexander was perhaps more mature than you would expect of a 10-year-old, John of Fordun reported that:

> The king of Scotland, having, by the advice of the king and magnates of England, arranged and regulated everything with moderation, went home again with his consort, and, disguising his intentions, awaited better times for correcting excesses of this kind.[30]

The newly married children departed York for Scotland at the end of January, with little Queen Margaret, bidding a no doubt tearful farewell to her parents.[31] They travelled by Berwick-on-Tweed to Roxburgh and onto Linlithgow, where the party arrived in April 1252. From there, they moved on to Edinburgh Castle, which was to be the young couple's principal residence. The queen was also allotted two representatives, Robert de Noreis and Stephen Bauzan, to travel with her and look after her interests.[32] A doting father, Henry III had made provision for everything and on the return of the young king and his new queen to Scotland, their household was established along Henry's guidelines, the Scottish royal household becoming an extension of the English royal household, with frequent communication between the two.[33] Henry named Robert de Ros, an Anglo-Scottish baron, as guardian to his daughter and son-in-law, with John de Balliol, another Anglo-Scottish baron, being appointed sometime later.[34] Such appointments mirrored Henry's own childhood under the tutelage of two baronial guardians. Queen Margaret was placed under the supervision of Mathilda de Cantiloupe, who was a widow of one of the stewards from King Henry's own household.

Margaret was an unhappy little queen, lonely and suffering from homesickness. It is hardly surprising. She was 11 years old, miles away from her family, friends and the life she had known. Everything was unfamiliar. She detested the grim fortress that was Edinburgh Castle and did not like the Scottish weather. She had grown fond of King Alexander but was kept apart from him most of the time, Robert de Ros having strict instructions that the couple were not to sleep together at such tender ages, it being considered detrimental to the health of both bride and groom. The child wrote miserable letters home to England, telling her mother and father of her unhappiness. It must have been even more demoralising for Margaret to know that life in the nursery at Windsor was continuing without her. At Christmas 1253, Eleanor of Provence presented several brooches to a number of nurses in the children's household, including to Beatrice's nurse, Agnes.[35] Home must have felt very distant for Margaret when she heard the news that, on 25 November 1253, her mother had given birth to a daughter, Katherine, a little sister she might never meet. The news of the safe arrival of his 'fair daughter' was delivered to King Henry by his yeoman, William de Valers, who was rewarded with £15.[36] The little princess was baptised by her mother's uncle, Boniface, Archbishop of Canterbury.

In a small example of domesticity, Eleanor of Provence's wardrobe accounts for 1252–1253 record that the queen owned a mewed hawk and that she also bought falconry gloves for her daughter Beatrice and son Edmund.[37] Negotiations began in 1253 for the marriages of Margaret's closest siblings, Edward and Beatrice, with members of the Castilian royal family. Alfonso X, king of Castile, agreed to withdraw his claim to Gascony to seal the deal. Ahead of the marriage, Edward was to be endowed with lands to the value of £10,000 and Alfonso was to have the honour of knighting him.[38] Although the intended marriage for Beatrice did not materialise, Edward was married to Eleanor of Castile on 1 November 1254, at the Abbey of Las Huelgas in Burgos – the abbey where his great-aunt Leonor, Henry II's daughter, was buried.

Meanwhile, Margaret was increasingly unhappy in Scotland. Her parents petitioned for Margaret to be permitted to travel south to visit her mother, but the Scots refused to allow her to leave, presumably afraid that she would not be seen again if she were to go home. In 1255, Eleanor of Provence sent one of her own physicians to Scotland to visit her daughter. Reginald of Bath found the Scots queen to be pale and depressed, and:

> when master Reginald had learned the troubles of her mind and body he severely reproved her guardians and magistrates. And after disputes and words of bitter altercation and even of threatening, he accused all the nobles of the king and queen and the guardians of the kingdom as being guilty of treason, convicted and menaced them.[39]

After scolding the Scots for their treatment of their queen the unfortunate physician himself fell ill and barely had time to write to the queen of England before succumbing to his illness, saying:

> that he had come thither under an inauspicious star; for he had seen that their daughter was unfaithfully and inhumanly treated among those unworthy Scots, and because he had blamed them the Northerns had prepared for him snares of death.[40]

Margaret's position was made worse by the fragmentation of the regency council, which had again split into factions shortly after the return from York. Walter Comyn, Earl of Menteith, and his allies had managed to alienate much of their support in Scotland. In 1254, Simon de Monfort was sent north of the border on a secret mission, so secret we know not what it was, merely that the king had 'put certain secrets in his mouth'.[41] It may have been to do with Margaret as a year later, the king despatched another secret mission to Scotland. This time it was Richard, Earl of Gloucester and John Mansel who arrived at Edinburgh Castle without any forewarning and apparently disguised as members of the household of Robert de Ros. Once inside, they were joined by their own retainers, a handful at a time, until their entire force was within the castle, and they no longer had to fear being overpowered. Queen Margaret met with the earl and Mansel:

> with confidence, and complained grievously that she was unfitly guarded or rather imprisoned in that castle, a dreary and solitary place, wholly lacking wholesome air or verdure, as being near the sea. Nor was she permitted, so she said, to go about in her realm, or to keep a special household, or even the girls whom she desired to have, as attendants and chambermaids. Nor was the king her husband permitted to have conjugal access to her, or to rejoice in mutual embraces. And whether anything secret was added to her complaints is unknown.[42]

As Gloucester and Mansel had been listening to the complaints of the Scots queen, Durward and the Earl of Dunbar had staged a coup, seizing Edinburgh Castle, and therefore taking custody of the king. Margaret and Alexander, now 14 and

13 respectively, were reunited and, from this moment on, allowed to cohabit. Frustrated by the Scottish nobles, with the Comyn faction rejecting all proposals of compromise, Henry and his queen headed north. Staying at Wark on the Scottish border in September 1255, they were reunited with their daughter and her husband. Queen Eleanor was taken ill, and Margaret was allowed to extend her stay and remain with her mother as she recuperated. The two royal couples were frequently in each other's company for the next two weeks, with only nine miles separating the respective residences of the kings at Roxburgh and Wark. Margaret's younger sister, Beatrice, had also accompanied her parents, in what must have been a very happy reunion. Queen Margaret then spent some time at Morpeth with her mother and sister.[43] Henry and Alexander used the time to make arrangements for a new Scottish government. Henry joined Alexander at Roxburgh, where:

> he was met by the king of Scotland, who received him with the greatest joy, and brought him into the church of Kelso with a great procession. Here, after having held a conference, [Henry] entrusted the king and the realm to the earl of Dunbar and his adherents, and so returned to his own country after a kingly banquet had been served.[44]

An assembly of seventeen lay and eight ecclesiastical magnates was formed to approve the appointment of a new council of fifteen established to rule Scotland for the remainder of the minority of the young king; until he was 21, in fact.[45] At the same time, King Alexander issued a declaration promising to treat Margaret 'with matrimonial affection and every consideration befitting our Queen and the daughter of so great a prince'.[46] King Henry returned south on 21 September but Queen Eleanor, still not fully recovered from her illness, and perhaps a little reluctant to leave her daughter so soon, lingered a little longer, with Henry giving her £100 for her expenses.[47] When Queen Eleanor and Beatrice did return home, they received a marriage proposal for the 14-year-old princess, from Alfonso of Castile. He was rather insistent that Beatrice should marry his brother, Manuel, as part of the treaty that had seen Edward marry Eleanor of Castile. Henry was reluctant to send Beatrice to Castile as he was aware that the king of Castile could dispossess and disinherit anyone at his pleasure, including his own brother, which would leave Beatrice destitute and far away from home. Henry would not have that.

It cannot have been easy for England's king and queen, looking to decide the future of their unmarried teenage daughter, while at the same time worrying about the situation of their already-married daughter, Margaret. It should come, perhaps, as no surprise that the new administration in Scotland lasted barely two years. Tensions were fraught between the factions when in early 1257, Queen Margaret received a visit from her brother, Edward, possibly accompanied by his young wife, Eleanor of Castile. It must have been a pleasant interlude, considering the gathering storms. She and Alexander spent August in England, attending the festivities of the Feast of the Assumption at Woodstock before continuing to London, where they were entertained by John Mansel.[48] The purpose of the visit may also have been to provide strength and comfort to Margaret's parents in their grief. Her baby sister, Katherine, had been born in November 1253 and suffered from a degenerative disorder of some kind. She was placed in the care of Alexander Parker and his wife, Amice, who were granted 'land in Old Wyndesor' in 'reward of the good service rendered by the said Amice in the education of Katharine the king's daughter' in April 1255.[49] Katherine was deaf and mute and by the age of eighteen months was being cared for, at least for some of the time, away from the royal nursery, at Swallowfield in Berkshire. Described as 'speechless and helpless, but very beautiful in appearance', her parents doted on her; Henry once ordered one of his men to capture a roe deer for his little daughter to play with.[50] She was in residence at Windsor in March 1256 when the king had a silver image of a woman, St Katherine, made. It was to be offered at the shrine of St Edward the Confessor 'for Katherine the king's daughter who has recently been ill'.[51] Three days later, the little princess was recovered, and the queen sent a messenger to the king with the news. Henry rewarded the man with a robe.[52] When she died in May 1257, her parents were sick with sorrow. The queen, in particular, was 'so overcome with grief that it brought on a disease, which was thought to be incurable, as she could obtain no relief either from medical skill or human consolation'.[53] Henry also fell ill.

The tragic little princess lived for a little over three years but had been a much-loved member of the family. She was laid to rest in the newly rebuilt Westminster Abbey. The king had an elaborate tomb built for her, with a silver effigy on top, adorned with gold and 180 precious stones.[54] It would have been a comfort to Queen Margaret to be able to spend some time with her parents so soon after such a sad loss but her visit south was a short interlude and respite from the problems at home. Once back in Scotland, Walter Comyn and his supporters 'seized the king at night as he lay asleep in bed at Kinross, and shamefully took him with them before dawn to Stirling on the morning after the feast of St Simon and St Jude in 1257. They also seized by force the king's great seal'.[55] Queen Margaret was also taken into custody – she was 'removed and guarded carefully, lest she should take after her father'.[56] According to Matthew Paris, they 'upbraided the queen moreover in that she had incited and summoned her father to come upon them as an enemy with his army, and do lamentable destruction'.[57] The growing political unrest in England, which was inexorably moving towards civil war in the contest between Henry III and Simon de Montfort, meant Henry was only able to aid his son-in-law in a limited capacity.

Alexander III, now 16, was becoming increasingly independent and self-confident and himself summoned a parliament to meet at Stirling in mid-April 1258. It took months to hammer out a settlement, but by September a unified council was established, with four each from the Comyns and Durward, alongside the queen mother, Marie de Coucy, and her husband, Jean de Brienne; this council survived until Alexander fully established his personal rule in 1260. As the young king was becoming more confident, and growing into his authority, Alexander travelled to England. He was able to press a beleaguered Henry III for payments of Queen Margaret's dowry, amounting to some 4000 marks – the payments being, by then, over nine years in arrears. Queen Margaret arrived a few days after her husband:

> very near to her confinement, coming for the sake of visiting the king and the queen and England, and, God willing, to be delivered there near to them. And she was conducted by the venerable man bishop [Henry] of Whithorn. And her younger brother Edmund met her; and she was received in formal procession at St. Albans in the hour of vespers, and honourably entertained. In the morning she set out for London. And when she was received, there were there at the same time three kings and as many queens: and who could without admiration think of their splendour and nobility? And when the queen had been presented to her parents the bishop, loaded with precious and diverse gifts, returned to Scotland as quickly as he could.[58]

Queen Margaret was five months pregnant when she left Scotland, so not that close to her confinement. She had not even informed the Scots council of her condition before leaving for England, lest they insist that she stay in Scotland until after the birth. It is understandable that Margaret would want to be near her mother when giving birth to her first child. Queen Eleanor may have wanted to spend time with both her surviving daughters, given that Beatrice would soon be leaving England with her new husband. During treaty negotiations with France in 1258, Eleanor's sister Marguerite, Queen of France, had suggested a marriage between Beatrice and John, the son of the Duke of Brittany. Negotiations started in earnest in May the following year. The Bishop of Brienne represented the Duke of Brittany, who requested the return of the honour of Richmond as part of the marriage treaty. Richmond had been held by the dukes of Brittany for many years but confiscated from John's father, and given to Peter of Savoy, the queen's uncle. While the wrangling over Richmond continued, Henry agreed to give the married couple the revenue of the county of Agenais, which was to revert to Henry under the new treaty with the French.[59]

Beatrice accompanied her parents to Paris for the Christmas season, where her future husband and his parents were also guests of the king and queen of France. The wedding date was set for 14 January 1260, at Compiègne, but was delayed following the tragic death of Louis, the son and heir of King Louis of France and nephew of Queen Eleanor. He was only 15. King Henry acted as one of the pallbearers for part of the funeral procession. Despite their grief, King Louis and Queen Marguerite attended the wedding just eight days later. The bride was 17, her groom just three years older. Instead of the newlyweds making their way to Brittany after the wedding, they remained in the company of Beatrice's parents. On 9 March, King Henry wrote to the Duke of Brittany from St Omer, to suggest that the couple continue on to England so that Henry could knight his son-in-law on St Edward's Day.[60]

Queen Eleanor, Queen Margaret and Beatrice were all present, then, when Beatrice's husband, John of Brittany and twenty-four other young men were knighted at Westminster on the feast of St Edward, 13 October 1260. The king, queen, their daughters and youngest son, Edmund, celebrated the Christmas season as a family at Windsor, there to await Queen Margaret's confinement. Alexander III was not in England for the birth of the baby. He had returned home in late 1260 to deal with the inheritance of the earldom of Menteith, in dispute following Earl Walter's death in 1258. Before he left, he exacted a promise from King Henry that he would not try to keep the Scottish queen in England after the birth. Henry agreed that Margaret and the child would be returning home forty days after her safe delivery, or by Easter at the latest. The king also promised that should his daughter die in childbirth and the baby survive, he would send the babe to Scotland.[61] The baby was a girl: 'That same year – on the last day of February, to wit – was born the king's first-born daughter, named Margaret, who was afterwards betrothed to the king of Norway'.[62] King Henry granted a pension to the man who brought him the news.[63] The little princess was christened on Easter Sunday, 24 April 1261, and she and her mother set off on their return journey to Scotland in late May. Perhaps learning from the lessons of the very recent past, arrangements were made for a regency council of thirteen named bishops, earls and barons, should King Alexander die before the baby was brought to Scotland.

Having said goodbye to Margaret and her new granddaughter, Queen Eleanor then had to prepare to say her farewells to Beatrice, who would finally make the journey to Brittany in July. Her husband had already departed England, having left to take part in a tournament in Paris, before heading back to Brittany, where he was waiting for Beatrice to join him. The queen gave her daughter seventy rings to give as gifts to the members of her new household. She also gave Beatrice a specially made illuminated book of hours, a very personal gift. The princess was to be accompanied across the Channel by a Savoyard protégé of the queen's, Eubolo Montibus, and would be met at Nantes by her half-uncle, Geoffrey de Lusignan. In early July 1262, Beatrice gave birth to her first child, a boy named Arthur after her father's ill-fated cousin Arthur, Duke of Brittany, who was killed by, or on the orders of, King John in April 1203. Beatrice's mother-in-law Blanche, Duchess of Brittany, wrote to Henry and Eleanor that Beatrice was ill but improving and that Arthur 'is a very good child, and very pretty, thank God'.[64]

In the same year, Henry received letters from both of his daughters. Having heard her father was ill, Margaret wrote him saying how she had herself suffered with news of his illness, but was improving on hearing news of his recovery.[65] Beatrice, on the other hand, was writing to her father on behalf of her aunt, her father's half-sister, Isabella de Lusignan, Lady of Craon. Isabella had been receiving an annual pension from Henry, but it had not been paid. Knowing how Henry indulged his children, she visited Beatrice to ask her to intercede:

> To the high lord and very dear father, if it pleaseth him, Henry by the grace of God, King of England, Lord of Ireland and Duke of Aquitaine, Beatrice his devoted daughter, wife to my lord John of Brittany, health and love as to her dear lord, with willingness to do his pleasure in all things.
>
> I give you to know, sire, that my aunt, the Lady of Croun [Craon], has come to see me, and has begged me to pray you that you would give her a debt which you owe her. And know, sire, that she has great need of it, for a daughter of hers who is married. Wherefore, I pray you, sire, that you, if you please, grant her this debt, and that you so act in this affair that she may perceive that my prayers have availed for her.[66]

There is no record of any further appeals from Beatrice on behalf of her aunt, so it may well be that her pleas were heard, and the Lady of Craon was sent her funds. This was not an isolated incident and appeals to one or more of the king's daughters appear in the records from time to time. Both Margaret and Beatrice sought to intercede for a man with their father when the queen of Scots was staying with her mother and sister in Northumberland. And there is record of Beatrice interceding with her father for one Ralp de Buylly in 1255. Buylly had been accused of the murder of a merchant for financial gain. Beatrice's pleas to the king saw the man pardoned and his confiscated goods returned to him.[67]

Beatrice and John were to have six children altogether. The eldest, Arthur, would inherit the Duchy of Brittany as Arthur II and would marry twice, first to Marie of Limoges and then to Yolande de Dreux, Countess of Montfort. Yolande was the second wife and widow of Alexander III (the husband of Arthur's maternal Aunt Margaret). After the birth of Arthur, another son, named John for his father and paternal grandfather, was born in 1266. He died unmarried. A daughter Mary was born in 1268; she married Guy IV of Châtillon, Count of St-Pol. Another son followed in 1269 – Peter – who was forced to sell his viscountcy of Leon to his brother Arthur after incurring massive debts. A second daughter arrived in 1271 – Blanche who was married to Philip of Artois. The last child was born in 1275. She was named Eleanor and became a nun, eventually becoming abbess of the great abbey of Fontevrault, where her Plantagenet ancestors, Henry II and Eleanor of Aquitaine, were buried, along with her great grandmother, Isabelle d'Angoulême.

Another surviving letter from Beatrice, written sometime between 1260 and 1268, (perhaps 1265 given the content), was of a more personal nature. It accompanied a letter written by her husband, which offered Henry military support, suggesting it was written during the Second Barons' War of 1264–1265:

> To the most excellent lord and father, if it pleases, to the venerable lord Henry, by the grace of God, illustrious King of England, Lord of Ireland and Duke of Aquitaine, his most faithful daughter Beatrice, consort of the Lord John, heir to the Duke of Brittany, send greetings with all reverence and honour.
>
> We rejoice to hear of your successes, of which your letters brought news and we report that our lady Duchess is in flourishing health, by divine favour, and because we always desire, with our whole heart, to know about you, we beg that you will frequently tell us how you are, let it be successful and pleasing, in order to increase our happiness. Be always strong in the Lord.'[68]

Beatrice and John appear to have had a contented marriage and resided mostly at the Breton court, though they also spent some of their time at Nantes. Beatrice enjoyed a good relationship with her mother-in-law, who wrote to King Henry sometime after 1265, that 'Madame Beatrice is very well and hearty'.[69] Beatrice and John then journeyed to England in 1266, when John was finally and formally invested with the earldom of Richmond, and paid his father-in-law due homage for it.[70] The earldom had been in the possession of Queen Eleanor's uncle, Peter of Savoy, and although Henry now invested John with it, the revenues were still claimed by Peter and it turned out to be an earldom in name only for Beatrice and her husband. The couple would return to England in 1268, not only to visit Beatrice's parents but also to procure permission and funds for John to take part in the forthcoming Crusade (the Ninth Crusade). Although he was seeking permission as Earl of Richmond, on a personal level he may also have sought the blessing of his father-in-law. In addition, Peter of Savoy had recently died, leaving the disputed earldom of Richmond to his niece, Queen Eleanor, who agreed to sign it over to her son-in-law, in exchange for the Agenais lands and revenues. So, Beatrice and John finally had lands to go with their titles. They were to remain in England for well over a year, with John occupied in raising funds for his Crusade. And it was in England, towards the end of the year, that Beatrice gave birth to her daughter Mary (or Marie). When the couple did return to Brittany towards the end of 1269, they left Mary and their younger children in the nursery at Windsor, to be raised alongside their cousins, the children of Beatrice's brother Edward, under the supervision of their grandmother, Queen Eleanor.[71]

Meanwhile, in Scotland, Alexander III's reign, once he reached his majority, saw a steady progress in growth, both politically and economically, which rendered the country robust, stable, and flourishing as the century advanced. This was aided by Alexander's consolidation of the western boundaries of the country. The Western Isles had long owed their allegiance to Norway, rather than Scotland, though Alexander II had died during a campaign to bring them into the Scottish kingdom. In 1263, King Haakon IV of Norway arrived in the region 'with eight score war-ships, having on board 20,000 fighting men' and 'took the castles of Bothe (Bute) and Man, and sacked the churches along the sea-board'.[72] The Norwegian king raided into Lennox and Loch Lomond. Alexander III mustered his army and marched against the Norwegians, confronting them just as their fleet was driven ashore by storms. After the ensuing Battle of Largs, both sides claimed victory, but the Norwegians had lost heart and Haakon sailed north to Orkney, where he died in December. Peace was agreed in 1266 in the form of the Treaty of Perth, 'which ceded the Western Isles to the Scottish crown in return for a down payment of 4000 merks, and an annual rent of 100 merks in perpetuity'.[73]

Whilst Alexander III was fulfilling his military duties as king, Margaret was performing her primary duty as queen. On 21 January 1264, she gave birth to a son, named after his father:

> In this year, upon the day of St. Agnes [21 Jan.], the queen of Scotland (being then at Jedburgh), gave birth to a son, who, at his father's desire, was named Alexander, when he was baptized by Gamelin, bishop of St. Andrew's. And it happened that on the same day upon which the king of Scotland was informed that God had given him a son, intelligence also arrived that the king of Norway was dead. Rejoiced by these twofold tidings of joy, the king gave thanks to God, who exalts the humble and humbles the proud.[74]

As the Scots rejoiced at the arrival of their prince, England was descending into civil war. King Henry and his son and heir, Lord Edward, were captured by the forces of Simon de Montfort, following their defeat in the Battle of Lewes on 14 May 1264. De Montfort effectively became the ruler of England, for a time at least, until he was defeated and killed at the Battle of Evesham on 4 August 1265. It must have been a worrying and stressful time for the Scots queen, her father and brother held captive while her mother travelled to France to elicit European aid for the struggle against de Montfort. As Edward was held in captivity, 'Oliver, the venerable abbot of Driburgh, was despatched to Edward, on the part of his sister, the queen of Scotland; and when his arrival was told to Simon, he conducted him into the presence of Edward'.[75] Unfortunately, we have no record of what was discussed in the meeting, though we can surmise that it was nothing dangerous as Simon de Montfort remained in the room all the time that Edward conversed with the abbot. Queen Margaret probably wanted to express her familial love and support to her brother. The conspirator in me does wonder if the queen's messenger was able to pass on some secret messages or personal letters, when de Montfort wasn't looking. King Alexander sent more practical support, in the form of a contingent of Scottish knights, prior to Evesham. The King of Scotland:

> from motives of sheer goodwill assigned three men from each hide to form an expedition to go to the aid of the king of England and his own kinsman [Prince] Edward. But when the downfall of Simon and his accomplices had become known, the Scots were generously sent away by the English prince and returned home.[76]

Lord Edward spent the next couple of years campaigning against the remnants of Simon de Montfort's forces and in 1267 was in Northumberland, where he captured John de Vescy at Alnwick Castle. Being so close to Scotland, it would have been remiss of him not to visit with his sister and brother-in-law. The family reunion appears to have been a happy one, as Edward 'turned aside to confer with the king of Scotland at Roxburgh. The king of Scotland and Queen Margaret, the sister of the said Edward, and almost the whole nobility of Scotland met him. After many expressions of joy and congratulation on both sides, they returned home happy'.[77] According to Bower, Edward was accompanied by his younger brother Edmund, and so the queen was reunited with both her brothers. It was a year for family reunions as 'Afterwards the king of Scotland, accompanied by the queen, went to York with a small select band of knights to console his father-in-law the king of England over his aforementioned tribulations and difficulties'.[78] The family gatherings continued as Christmas was spent at Berwick 'with almost all the magnates of his realm. Present also was Edmund, the younger son of the king of England, in order to have some talk with his sister the queen of Scots, and to provide companionship for the king of Scotland'.[79] There were more reunions in 1268, when Alexander's mother, Marie de Coucy, left her husband and returned to Scotland. The king arranged for her to remain in the country at her own pleasure, assigning her estranged husband an allowance from the dowager queen's revenues.[80] Almost two years later, in October 1269, Margaret and Alexander visited her parents in London to be present at a ceremony that would have been a highlight of Henry III's reign. They accompanied Margaret's father and brothers, Edward and Edmund, to Westminster Abbey as the relics of St Edward the Confessor were translated to his new shrine at the heart of the remodelled abbey.

Margaret was deeply affected by her father's death in 1272, her grief probably exacerbated by the fact she could not travel south to console her mother as she was pregnant. To add to her misery and stress, her brothers were taking part in the latest Crusade. Edward even had his wife, Eleanor of Castile with him: 'Queen Margaret of Scotland, deeply distressed by her various trials, chiefly by the death of her father and by anxiety about the return of her brother'.[81] No more children were born to the couple in the 1260s, though it is possible that Margaret suffered one or more miscarriages in that time. Her next child was born nine years after the birth of Prince Alexander, on 20 March 1273. Margaret was now in her early thirties, and the birth was a difficult one, from which she was slow to recover. The child, a boy named David, was said to be delicate.[82]

It was against this background of grief for her father, worry for her brothers and the trials of childbirth that a tragic incident happened while Margaret was staying at Kinclaven Castle that summer. The *Chronicle of Lanercost* recites the lamentable tale. The queen:

> went forth one beautiful evening after supper from Kinclavin [*sic*] to take the air on the banks of the Tay, accompanied by esquires and maidens, but in particular by her confessor, who related to me what took place. There was present among others a certain pompous esquire with his page, who had been recommended to him by his brother in the presence of his superiors. And as they were sitting under the brow of the bank, he [the esquire] went down to wash his hands, which he had soiled with clay in playing. As he stood thus bending over, one of the maids, prompted by the Queen, went up secretly and pushed him into the river-bed.
>
> 'What care I?' cried he, enjoying the joke and taking it kindly, 'even were I further in, I know how to swim'.
>
> Wading about thus in the channel, while the others applauded, he felt his body unexpectedly sucked into an eddy, and, though he shouted for help, there was none who would go to him except his little page-boy who was playing near at hand, and, hearing the clamour of the bystanders, rushed into the deep, and both were swallowed up in a moment before the eyes of all. Thus did the enemy of Simon and satellite of Satan, who declared that he had been the cause of that gallant knight's destruction, perish in sight of all; and the matron, led away unduly by affection for her parents, received rebuke for her selfish love, and showed herself before all men wounded to the heart by overpowering anguish.[83]

The unfortunate squire is said to have been given to Margaret as a gift from her brother, Edward, during his visit in 1267.[84] He claimed to be the one who had killed

Simon de Montfort, with his own sword, during the Battle of Evesham, renamed by many of the time as the Murder of Evesham. Maybe it was these claims that prompted the chronicler to call the young man 'pompous', seeing a certain justice in the squire's drowning. The same cannot be said for the poor, almost forgotten, young page who jumped into the river to try to save the young man. Queen Margaret was greatly distressed by the two deaths, probably compounding the grief over her father's loss. By referring to the queen's 'selfish love', the chronicler is making a veiled accusation that there was something more going on between Margaret and the unfortunate squire, but there is no suggestion anywhere else that Margaret was anything but loyal and devoted to her husband. Having just endured a difficult childbirth, one cannot imagine, either, that Margaret had the time or inclination to conduct a love affair with a lowly squire. Perhaps the *Lanercost* chronicler's imagination was running away with him somewhat?

Margaret's concerns for her brother, at least, proved to be unfounded. On hearing of his father's death, Edward, now King Edward I, left the Holy Land to return home. He took a rather leisurely and circuitous route, stopping en route to visit his domains in France and depositing his toddler daughter, Joan of Acre, with her grandmother, Jeanne de Dammartin, Countess of Ponthieu, where the little princess was to be raised for the next few years. It had been intended that Edward's coronation would be held on the Sunday after Easter, when 'Alexander king of Scots along with his wife and children was specially invited by Edward to be present at his coronation in London'.[85] The ceremony was delayed, however, by Edward holding a great council at Lyons. The English king finally landed at Dover on 2 August 1274 and on 19 August, Edward:

> was solemnly anointed and crowned on the 14th of the kalends of September by the Archbishop of Canterbury, Brother Robert Kilwardby. The nobles of the land attended the ceremony with a countless multitude, redoubling the display of their magnificence in honour of the new king. But my lord Alexander King of Scotland, who attended with his consort and a train of his nobility, exceeded all others in lavish hospitality and gifts.[86]

The new king had arrived in England with his wife, his son, Alfonso, his sister, Beatrice and her husband John of Brittany. Both sets of parents were reunited with children who had been in the care of their grandmother, Eleanor of Provence, at Windsor; Edward with his children Henry and Eleanor and Beatrice with her son John, nicknamed Brito in the family.[87] It must have been a happy family reunion, especially for Eleanor of Provence, with all four of her surviving children, Edward, Margaret, Beatrice and Edmund, together for the first time since 1260. It was a moment of joy before the grief of a series of family tragedies. Edward's son Henry took ill while staying with his grandmother at Guildford and died in the middle of October. Within a month, Edmund lost not only his wife, Aveline de Forz, but also the twin babies she was carrying. And then Margaret fell ill. Attending her brother's coronation was to be one of Margaret's last duties as queen and just six months later she became seriously ill during a visit to Fife. At the age of just 34, 'on the 26th of February, the said queen of Scotland, Margaret, King Henry's daughter, and this King Edward's sister, died at the castle of Cupar, and was entombed beside King David, at Dunfermline'.[88] The chronicler of *Lanercost* wrote a moving tribute to the English princess who had been queen of Scotland since the age of 10:

> She was a woman of great beauty, chastity, and humility – three [qualities] seldom united in one individual. When her strength was failing many abbots as well as bishops collected to visit her, to all of whom she refused entrance to her chamber; nor from the time that she had received all the sacraments from her confessor, a Minorite Friar, until her soul passed away, did she admit any other to discourse, unless perhaps her husband happened to be present. She left behind her three children – Alexander and David and a daughter Margaret, all of whom followed their mother in a short time, owing, it is believed, to the sin of their father.[89]

It is, perhaps, a blessing that Queen Margaret did not live to see the deaths of all three of her children in a few short years. Prince David had always been a delicate child and died, at the tender age of 8 years, at Lindores in June 1281. The young prince was buried among his ancestors in Dunfermline Abbey. His passing was lamented by John of Fordun as the start of Scotland's grief:

> David, moreover, had departed this life … at Strivelyn [Stirling] Castle, at the end of the month of June 1281, amid the deep wailing of all the Scots, and the still deeper wailing of the king; and he lies buried in the monastery of Dunfermline. His death was the beginning of Scotland's sorrows to come. Alas! woe worth the day, O Scotland! for, even though thou had known that so many days of mourning and tears were in store for thee, evils so great are hastening upon thee without fail. 'That, if thou knew, thou ne'er could think to bear them.[90]

Margaret, the Scots king's oldest child, now queen of Norway, died in childbirth on 9 April 1283. Her surviving daughter, Margaret, was to be Margaret and Alexander's only grandchild and she was recognised as Alexander III's heir following the death of Prince Alexander on 28 January 1284, at Lindores Abbey, just one week after his twentieth birthday, after ‘a lingering illness, with which he suffered a degree of mental aberration’.[91] It had been just fifteen months since the young prince’s wedding to Margaret of Flanders.

Queen Margaret’s death in 1275 was closely followed, just a month later, by the death of her sister Beatrice. The 32-year-old princess had recently given birth to her daughter, Eleanor, at Windsor and did not recover from the ordeal, dying on 24 March. She was buried at Greyfriars church, the church of the Franciscans, in London; her mother’s heart would be buried with her when Eleanor of Provence died in 1291. Beatrice died as Countess of Richmond, her husband only succeeding as Duke of Brittany on his father’s death in 1286. He survived his wife by thirty years, dying in 1305 in a tragic accident at the coronation of Pope Clement V; the duke was leading the Pope’s horse when a wall collapsed under the weight of the spectators, crushing John. He died four days later.

The pain of losing both her daughters in just a month, on top of all the other losses in recent years, must have been hard to take for Eleanor. She had suffered some sort of breakdown after the death of her little daughter, Katherine, in 1257 and now she had lost her surviving daughters.[92] It may be that the need to care for Beatrice’s newborn daughter offered some consolation and gave her something to focus on. Nonetheless, their deaths ‘left a deep sorrow after the great joy of the coronation, for they were ladies in the flower of youth, of high character and distinguished beauty’.[93] Eleanor of Provence and Henry III had achieved what few royal couples could. They had maintained personal, physical relationships with all their children throughout their lives. Although Margaret had made a dynastic marriage, it had been to Alexander of Scotland, so close to England that travel between the two royal courts was eminently manageable and frequent. And although Beatrice had married abroad, it was to the son of the Duke of Brittany, a duchy which enjoyed easy relations with England. Communication and travel between England and Brittany was well-established and made it easy for Beatrice to travel to visit her parents and take part in family events.

Chapter Two

Tragedy and Temper Tantrums

In the twilight years of his reign, as Henry became increasingly infirm, he focused on securing peace within the kingdom and his own religious devotions. Edward became Steward of England and played a more prominent role in government. Henry III died on 20 November 1272, while his son, Edward, was away on Crusade. At his funeral four days later the leading magnates of England swore an oath of loyalty to Edward as the new king. Edward – now Edward I – and Eleanor of Castile had been married since they were teenagers; Edward was 15 and Eleanor was 12 or 13. Edward's grief at her death in November 1290 is evidenced by the famous Eleanor Crosses – memorials that were erected at every point where the funeral cortège stopped overnight on the sad journey from Harby in Nottinghamshire to Westminster Abbey, where Edward's beloved queen was laid to rest. There were twelve crosses in all, starting with Lincoln, where Eleanor's body was taken after death, to be prepared for travel to London. Her viscera were removed and buried in Lincoln Cathedral, in a tomb close to the shrine of St Hugh. Her heart was buried at the Dominican friary in London – the Blackfriars – where her son Alfonso's heart had also been interred.

Theirs is one of the great love stories of the medieval era. But it was a relationship that was also marred by tragedy. Eleanor gave birth to as many as sixteen children but only five daughters and one precious son were still living at the time of her death. She had lost ten children, either at birth, in infancy or in the first ten years of their lives. Such grief is a burden no parent should have to carry. Eleanor was the daughter of Fernando III, King of Castile and his second wife, Jeanne (or Joan) de Dammartin, Countess of Ponthieu in her own right. Eleanor's father had died in 1252, and her mother returned to her own lands in 1254, leaving Eleanor in the custody of her oldest brother, King Alfonso X.

Edward and Eleanor were married at Santa Maria La Real (Las Huelgas) monastery, outside the city walls of Castile's capital, Burgos, on 1 November 1254. It was a political union; the first time they met was on their wedding day.[1] Part of the marriage agreement with Eleanor's brother was for Edward to be endowed with lands worth £10,000 a year by his father; this included the Duchy of Gascony and the Earldom of Chester. In return, Alfonso ceded all his rights to Gascony, disputed since the marriage of Henry II's daughter Eleanor to King Alfonso VIII, who claimed Gascony as Eleanor's dowry. Following the wedding, Edward and Eleanor spent just a week in Castile before the young prince took his bride back to Gascony, where the couple would spend the first months of their married life together. It may well have been at Bordeaux that Eleanor gave birth to her first child, a daughter who was born prematurely, arriving only seven months after the wedding. The records for this child are patchy, but reference is made to a daughter who died on 29 May, with no year given, and was buried in the Dominican priory in Bordeaux, when in 1286 or 1287 Eleanor provided a gold cloth as a mark of remembrance.[2] Eleanor is thought to have celebrated her thirteenth birthday in the same month her daughter was born, though the exact date is not known. She may still have been only 12 years old when she married and only 13 when she gave birth for the first time. Edward was 15. It must have been a heartbreaking time for both, having to deal with such a loss at a young age.

Eleanor first set foot in England in October 1255, accompanied by her new husband and her older half-brothers Sancho, archbishop-elect of Toledo and Don Enrique; 'This year, upon the Feast of Saint Eldreda [23 June] which was on a Sunday, the sister of the King of Spain, wife of Sir Edward, eldest son of his lordship the King, came to London, and a countless multitude of Bishops, Earls, Barons, Knights, and citizens, went forth from the City to meet her, as also his lordship the King, in person; the City of London being most nobly tapestried and arrayed'.[3] The city of London was 'handsomely hung with tapestry for the occasion'.[4] Don Enrique was to keep his sister company in England for the next four years, with Henry III paying all his expenses while he was in the country. His motives were not entirely in his care for the welfare of his sister. Enrique had led a rebellion against his brother, the king, in Castile and when he did leave England, it was not to go home but to North Africa where he became a mercenary.[5] Still, it must have been a comfort for the teenager, to have a big brother so close, whatever the reason.

After the brief mention of the daughter born in Bordeaux in 1255, no other pregnancies are recorded for Eleanor for nearly ten years. If there were more stillbirths or miscarriages in that time, they failed to come to the attention of chroniclers, and no mention of them are made in respect of masses being said in churches. The first named child we have is another daughter, Katherine, probably named after her paternal aunt born in the early 1260s and who had died at just 3 years old in 1264. This second Katherine's death is recorded in the Liberate Rolls with respect of an order for cloths of gold 'for the use of Katherine the deceased daughter of Edward the king's firstborn' dated October 1264.[6] The necrology of Canterbury Cathedral records the little girl's death as 5 September.[7] Unfortunately, her age is unrecorded but Eleanor of Castile's biographer, Sara Cockerill, suggests she was born in Gascony in later 1261 or early 1262; Edward's old nurse, Alice de Luton, was with Eleanor in France in the summer of 1262 and the most likely reason for this would have been to help look after a new baby.[8] Eleanor was six months pregnant at the time of little Katherine's death and another daughter, named Joan for her paternal grandmother, was born in December 1264 or January 1265. Given Eleanor went into confinement on 7 December 1264, and was churched around 3 February 1265, the baby girl was probably born in the last week of December, certainly no later than 3 January, given a woman's churching took place at least thirty days after the birth of a child. Tragedy struck again, almost exactly a year to the day after the death of Katherine, when Joan died at just eight months. The Close Rolls record the order for a gold cloth for the tomb of 'Joan, daughter of Edward, the eldest son of the king, recently deceased and buried in Westminster Abbey' dated to 7 September 1265.[9] Joan was buried in the same tomb as her older sister and her Aunt Katherine.

It cannot have been easy for Eleanor, dealing with such personal grief at a time of national crisis. Her husband, Edward, and his father the king had been captured after their defeat at the Battle of Lewes on 12 May 1264. They were separated and held prisoner, Henry in the custody of Simon de Montfort and Edward in the custody of Simon's wife, Eleanor – Edward's aunt. Edward had visited Eleanor and little Katherine at Windsor in the weeks before the Lewes campaign, with their daughter Joan being born nine months later. On 16 June 1264, the constable of Windsor Castle left the fortress, handing its custody to Eleanor, where she lived with her daughter Katherine and with Joan de Valence, wife of the Earl of Pembroke, who had fled to France following the defeat at Lewes. The next day, however, Simon de Montfort, in King Henry's name, instructed Eleanor to move her household to Westminster Palace and 'not to fail, as the king undertakes to excuse her to E[dward] her lord and will keep her harmless, and receives them into his safe conduct'.[10] Joan, who was heavily pregnant at the time, was ordered to 'some convenient religious or other place near those parts, until God delivers her of the off spring wherewith she is great'.[11] Edward was brought to Westminster in March 1265, amid negotiations for his notional release from custody. It is quite possible that he was allowed to see Eleanor at this time and meet his baby daughter.[12] Edward's release never did materialise, and he would not escape his uncle's custody until late May 1265. He would go on to raise an army and defeat de Montfort at the Battle of Evesham on 4 August 1265. Simon de Montfort and his eldest son, Henry, were killed in the battle.

In the aftermath of Evesham, there was still some mopping up of rebel enclaves to do and Edward could not rush back to his wife immediately. Although they had been kept apart at the time of Katherine's death, and Eleanor would have had to face her grief alone, it is possible that Edward and Eleanor were reunited shortly after Joan died and could console each other in their grief, as just a few weeks after Joan's burial Eleanor was pregnant again.[13] A son, John, was born at Windsor Castle on 13 or 14 July 1266. He was followed twenty-two months later by another boy, Henry, born on or before 6 May 1268. Edward and Eleanor must have breathed deep sighs of relief after both boys survived their first years. Their first surviving daughter was born on 17 June 1269, her father's thirtieth birthday, at Windsor and named Eleanor, for her mother and paternal grandmother. The king granted a reward to 'John de Beaumes yeoman of Eleanor consort of Edward the king's son for bringing the good news of the birth of her daughter Eleanor'.[14] Eleanor was placed in the household of her brother Henry, only thirteen months her senior, and was joined there by her cousin, John of Brittany (nicknamed Brito) who was a similar age. Each of the children had their own nurse; Eleanor's was Cecile or Cecilia Cleware. A rocker, an Alice de la Grave, or Alice de Leygrave, was employed to rock the cradles of all three children. She was probably only a girl at the time as the same woman appears in the records as the wet nurse of Eleanor's youngest brother Edward of Caernarfon, born in 1284.[15]

As the title of princess is a later creation, Eleanor was addressed as Lady Eleanor from birth. We have a few details of the nursery and nursery life. The children were bathed regularly and the women who assisted them were paid 3*d* a day. They were clothed in smocks and hose, no matter whether a boy or girl, and wore caps with peacock feathers, slippers, gilded buttons and furred gloves in winter.[16] Provisions included, for example, for 1269, wine, 400 pounds of wax, 20 pounds of pepper, 20 pounds of cumin and 10 pounds of ginger.[17] A year after Eleanor's birth, her father vowed to join his uncle, Louis IX, on Crusade. Eleanor of Castile would go with him, as would his brother Edmund and cousin, Henry of Almain. Arrangements were made for the children, who would be given into the custody of Edward's uncle Richard, Earl of Cornwall, though their daily lives were probably little affected by the arrangement. Eleanor was fourteen months old when her parents left England's shores; she would not see them again until she was five, in 1274.

Eleanor of Castile was pregnant when she departed on the Ninth Crusade on 20 August 1270 and gave birth to a short-lived daughter, whose name has gone unrecorded, at Acre, in the Holy Land, at the end of 1270 or beginning of 1271. Tragedy was also to hit the royal nursery back in England when John, the eldest of Edward and Eleanor's surviving children, died at the age of 5 on 3 August 1271, while residing at his great uncle's castle at Wallingford. News would have taken time to reach his parents, but little Henry and Eleanor would have noticed the absence of their big brother immediately. The following year, 1272, saw further loss in the deaths of two brothers; in April, Richard, Earl of Cornwall died at the age of 63 and on 16 November Henry III, the children's grandfather, died at the age of 65. With their parents still in the Holy Land, Henry and Eleanor were cared for by their grandmother, the newly widowed Eleanor of Provence.

By the time of King Henry's death, the Crusade was at an end. The crusaders had met with very little success and the nominal King of Jerusalem, Hugh III of Cyprus, brought it to a close by signing a ten-year truce with Baibars, the Mamluk leader, in May 1272. The couple could not return home immediately after the truce was signed however, as Eleanor had just recently been delivered of a daughter, Joan, and an assassin's attack had nearly cost Edward his life. Edward managed to kill his attacker but there is no truth to the oft-repeated tale that the dagger was poisoned, and that Eleanor sucked the poison from the wound. The knife that had been used was still kept in the treasury in England seventy years later.[18] So, they were forced to stay in the Holy Land a little while longer. Like her older sister, who had died so young, Joan was probably named for her maternal grandmother, Jeanne of Ponthieu. She was born in the spring of 1272 and would be known to history as Joan of Acre, due to her place of birth. Peter Langtoft, the author of a rhyming chronicle in the early fourteenth century, says that Joan was more beautiful than a hundred other women.[19]

Edward and Eleanor finally set sail for Europe in September 1273, taking their baby daughter home. They stopped in Sicily on the way, before spending Christmas on the Italian mainland. It was during their stay in Italy that English messengers arrived with the news of Henry III's death ten months before. As Henry III's eldest son and heir, Edward was now King of England. The news did not hasten Edward's return to England; he had known when he left that his father might die before his return and had made arrangements accordingly. Knowing England was in good hands, he and Eleanor continued their progress through Europe. They stopped off in Gascony, where on 9 October Edward made an agreement with Pedro, Infante of Aragon, for a future marriage between Pedro's eldest son, Alfonso, and Edward's oldest daughter, Eleanor, who was now 4 years old.[20] In late July and early August, Eleanor had been so ill that a wax candle was lit at a nearby shrine in the hope that it would aid her recovery.[21] And she did recover. Another marriage, for Henry of Windsor, was also arranged, this time with Jeanne (also known as Juana or Joan) of Navarre, heiress to Enrique I, King of Navarre. But when Jeanne's father died just a few months later, her mother, Blanche of Artois, sought the safety of the French court and Jeanne eventually married the son of Philip III of France, the future Philip IV. Jeanne would be the mother of Isabella of France, the future wife of Edward's oldest surviving son and successor, Edward of Caernarfon, Edward II.

Eleanor of Castile, now Queen Eleanor, was pregnant again and gave birth in Bayonne on 24 November, to a son named Alfonso, after the queen's brother, who travelled to Bayonne to attend the baptism as the little prince's godfather. Before finally making the crossing back to England, Edward and Eleanor also took the opportunity to visit Eleanor of Castile's mother Jeanne, Countess of Ponthieu, in France, staying through June and July 1274 and leaving their 2-year-old daughter, little Joan of Acre, to be raised by her for the next few years.[22] The couple finally landed on English soil, at Dover, on 2 August 1274 and were reunited with their two oldest surviving children, Henry and Eleanor, who would not even have remembered their parents, except maybe through the stories told by their grandmother, Eleanor of Provence. The two children would also meet their baby brother, Alfonso of Bayonne, for the first time. I can't help thinking it must have been a slightly awkward reunion, with both children and parents relying on the familiarity of formal ceremony to hide their discomfort.

Edward and Eleanor were crowned in Westminster Abbey on 19 August, with the usual level of grandeur and pageantry. Henry and Eleanor, and their cousin John of Brittany, had new robes for the occasion.[23] Two months later the king and queen were back at the abbey for Henry's burial. The 6-year-old prince had fallen ill while staying with his grandmother and siblings at Guildford in Surrey. Despite the efforts of his physician, Master Hugh of Evesham, the heir to the throne had died sometime between 14 and 17 October. A poignant entry on the payment of alms by Henry and Eleanor, which were made every Friday, shows Henry's name crossed out, and a sole payment of 8*d* by '*domine Alianore*' (Lady Eleanor).[24] Queen Eleanor was pregnant again at the time of Henry's death and gave birth to another baby girl, Margaret, at Windsor, most likely in March 1275. Her nurse was Cecile Cleware, who had previously taken care of 5-year-old Eleanor, and she was placed in the household of her brother, Alfonso, who was now fifteen months old.[25] Another sister, Berengaria, named for the queen's grandmother, was born thirteen months after Margaret on 1 May 1276 at Kempton, near London.

It was sometime around 1276 or 1277 that Eleanor, now the king and queen's oldest surviving child, joined the royal court. She had her own substantial household which included a chamberlain, a keeper of her hall, a valet of the bedchamber and many others. The royal court was itinerant, spending only a few weeks in one castle before moving onto the next, travelling throughout the south and midlands, though rarely the far north. In 1278, for instance, Eleanor met up with her parents' court at Devizes in Wiltshire, travelling with them to Glastonbury, where they celebrated Easter together before moving on to London in May.[26] That year, Eleanor was joined at court, at least for some of the year, by her younger sister, Joan. Joan had been escorted home by Stephen of Pencestre and his wife Margaret, in time for her wedding which was expected to take place in 1279. Her father was in the process of arranging a marriage for Joan to Hartman, the second son of Rudolf, King of the Romans, whose envoys had arrived in England in September 1277. Edward I offered a dowry of 10,000 marks for Joan, in return for Rudolf promising to give Hartman the revived kingdom of Arles, a large territory of the Holy Roman Empire comprising Switzerland and south-east France, including Provence. The match was proposed by the king's aunt, Marguerite of Provence, Queen of France. As the oldest of the four sisters, all becoming queens, Marguerite had expected to inherit her father's county, but he had left it to his youngest daughter, Beatrice, Queen of Sicily as the wife of Charles of Anjou. This smarted with the French queen who pursued a feud with Charles of Anjou, that lasted many years as a consequence. Negotiations went well, with the wedding date set for 8 September 1278.

The king sent his own envoys to Germany to finalise the details of Joan's dower lands and the provision that would be made should she be widowed; and to ascertain the character of Hartman, who was nine years older than 6-year-old Joan.[27] Rudolf proposed dower lands for Joan in Switzerland and agreed that he would do everything in his power to ensure that Hartman was elected King of the Romans, should he himself be elected Holy Roman Emperor. Unfortunately, Rudolf went to war with Bohemia in 1278 and the September wedding did not materialise. Hartman wrote to King Edward, saying that he would travel to England as soon as possible, and was due to arrive in June 1279 but came down with a serious illness and again had to delay. In the end, the wedding never happened, and Hartman was drowned in a boating accident in December 1281, when his boat hit a rock midstream.

Once back in England, Joan finally met her siblings, Eleanor, Alfonso and Margaret. Little Berengaria died on or before 27 June 1278, just a few weeks after her second birthday. Another daughter, whose name is unknown, was born in 1278 but died within hours of her birth. Following Joan's arrival, Joan and Alfonso were allowed to accompany their big sister, Eleanor and the royal court – for parts of the year at least. They would have been permitted to take part in the Christmas and Easter celebrations with their parents, as part of their education. Little is known of Joan's everyday life. She joined the court on an almost permanent basis once she was old enough to deal with the gruelling travel itinerary. Joan was supervised by a governess until her marriage in 1290; Edeline was the wife of Philippe Popiot, a knight in Queen Eleanor's household who had previously served the queen's mother, Jeanne of Ponthieu. Margerie, the wife of another of Queen Eleanor's knights, John de Hengham, also served in Joan's household.[28]

Although Margaret remained in the nursery, plans for her future were afoot. The king received envoys and a letter from Jan I, Duke of Brabant, talking of 'covenants of marriage between the very high lord, Lord Edward, by the grace of GOD king of England, on one side, and we on the other; that Jan [Johan], our eldest son, shall take to wife my lady Margaret [madame Margarete], daughter of the aforesaid king, when they are of an age to marry.'[29] Brabant was a large duchy with territory in modern-day Belgium and the Netherlands. Born in September 1275, Jan was just four months younger than his prospective bride. Duke Jan offered Margaret a dower of 3,000 *livres Tournois* annually, with the lands and rents listed in the agreement. Should Margaret be unable to marry Jan, for whatever reason, the next eldest daughter of the king would be substituted; the same was stipulated for Jan of Brabant, should he be unable to marry Margaret, his next eldest brother would do so.[30]

While the futures of his daughters were being considered and shaped in diplomatic negotiations, another daughter joined the nursery. Mary was born at Woodstock on 11 or 12 March 1279. Despite Mary being a popular name throughout the Christian world, it was an unusual name in the English royal family, only King Stephen had used the name previously. Just days later the queen heard of the death of her mother, Jeanne of Ponthieu, at the age of 60. As her last surviving child, Queen Eleanor inherited the county of Ponthieu and King Edward sent his brother Edmund of Lancaster, a powerful landowner in France as the husband of Blanche of Artois, Countess of Champagne, to secure possession of it. And just two months after Mary's birth, Edward and Eleanor left England to spend a month in Ponthieu, making arrangements for its administration as part of the English Crown. They also took the opportunity to meet up with King Philip III of France at Amiens, where the 1259 Treaty of Paris was ratified and, as agreed in the treaty, the Agenais was made over to Edward. Eleanor's claim to Ponthieu was recognised by Philip and the queen paid the king of France homage for the county.[31]

As you may have noticed, Edward and Eleanor were quite a nomadic couple, travelling among their domains, so their children were raised in the royal nursery, based largely at the royal palaces of Woodstock and Windsor. Visits from their parents were infrequent and from Edward, their father, even less frequent. The deaths of so many of their children before they reached adulthood has been suggested as a reason for Queen Eleanor keeping her distance from her children when they were young; however, it is just as likely that the simple fact Edward and Eleanor ruled a vast kingdom, including lands in France, meant their responsibilities necessitated long absences.[32]

By June 1281, as their daughter Eleanor turned 12, Edward was contemplating sending her to Spain, to conclude the marriage with Alfonso of Aragon. In the end, however, he delayed the marriage, claiming 'the queen her mother and our dearest mother are unwilling to grant that she may pass over earlier on account of her tender age'.[33] Eleanor of Provence and Eleanor of Castile had each been married at the age of 12; it is entirely plausible that both women wanted the youngest Eleanor to mature a little more before having to approach the marriage bed. Especially if Eleanor of Castile had given birth and lost her first child at the age of 13. No mother would want her daughter to endure such an experience. Eleanor was staying with her grandmother at Guildford in February 1282 when she wrote to Alfonso, explaining that she was using her grandmother's seal as she did not yet have one of her own.[34] Communication between the two kingdoms continued apace, still eager to conclude the marriage when the time was right. But Edward's attention was needed elsewhere, when he mounted a campaign in Wales. The king moved Eleanor of Castile, pregnant once again, to Rhuddlan, accompanied by their daughters Eleanor and Joan. Rhuddlan Castle had been 'civilised' for the queen's use with the addition of gardens, decorative seating and a fishpond to aid Eleanor's comfort. However, it was still Edward's headquarters, where troops were mustering, and messengers were coming and going at all hours – hardly the most comfortable and peaceful place for a queen to give birth. Unless a miscarriage or stillbirth has gone unrecorded, the queen had had a three-year break from the birthing chamber before the arrival of another daughter, Elizabeth, on or around 7 August.

Elizabeth would be the youngest surviving daughter of the king and queen's fifteen children – a sixteenth and final child, Edward (the future Edward II), would be born in 1284. Although the castle must have been bustling during Elizabeth's birth, one can imagine the rooms surrounding the birthing chamber were kept as serene as possible. Indeed, it seems Eleanor was allowed the 'lying-in' of a whole month following Elizabeth's birth with her churching at the end of it – a luxury that did not arise all that often for Edward's queen. Eleanor's wardrobe accounts show the queen purchased several small items for her baby daughter's use – a basin, some tankards, a storage chest and a bucket.[35] And, unlike her older siblings, Elizabeth remained with her mother during the first few years of her life. It is possible she was with her mother full time until the age of 2, or was at least visited regularly by Eleanor. Elizabeth was still with her mother when her baby brother, Edward, was born at Caernarfon. And when Edward was established in his own household, Elizabeth went with him. She spent most of her childhood in her brother's company; her education was supervised by her mother, often from a distance. Elizabeth is known to have had a fondness for books; books are recorded as forming part of her marriage goods on her first marriage, and the Alfonso Psalter was known to be in her possession at some time.[36]

The prospect of the younger Eleanor marrying Alfonso of Aragon was still under discussion in 1283. Eleanor's prospective father-in-law had laid claim to the throne of Sicily, in place of Charles of Anjou, following a rebellion against Charles known as the Sicilian Vespers. A native Frenchman, Pope Martin IV, had deposed Pedro of Aragon from both the Aragonese and Sicilian thrones. He wrote to Edward and expressed his 'surprise at his offering his daughter Eleanor in marriage to Alfonso, eldest son of Pere [Pedro], late king of Aragon, whom the pope deprived of his kingdom'.[37] The Pope urged Edward to renounce the alliance and coming marriage, and reminded him that Eleanor and Alfonso were related in the third degree and so would need a papal dispensation in order to marry, which would not be given. As such wranglings were going on, life for Eleanor and her sister Joan continued as normal, following their parents' court and attending masses daily. In September 1284, the royal family were visited by Margaret's future husband, Jan of Brabant, then 9-years old. The following year he moved to England permanently and was set up in his own household, with a chamberlain, marshal, cook, priest, clerk, kitchen staff and personal attendants. He was also entitled to three palfreys (horses), two coursers (horses for hunting), two pack-horses and dogs.[38] It was at about the same time that Jan's betrothed, Margaret, joined her older sisters at court and in the year 1285 accounts show the purchase of golden bowls and gold plates for Margaret's use, as well as two dozen gloves, pearls and basins, and new robes for Christmas.[39]

Edward and Eleanor travelled relentlessly, and not always with their children. Nevertheless, they did make time for their family, with weeks at Leeds Castle and Windsor built into their itinerary; such a holiday took place in 1285. A year after the death of 10-year-old Alfonso, the king took his family on a progress into Kent. Edward went on pilgrimage to the shrine of St Thomas Becket, at Canterbury, before spending a week at Leeds Castle with his family, followed by some hunting in Hampshire. It was at the end of this family holiday that they arrived at Amesbury in Wiltshire, where little Mary, still only 6 years old, was veiled as a nun; much to the delight of her grandmother, Eleanor of Provence, but to the consternation of her mother, the queen. Indeed, the *Chronicle of Nicholas Trivet* emphasises that Mary's veiling was done by her father, at the request of her grandmother, but only with the 'assent' of her mother.[40] It may well be that Eleanor had reservations about her daughter's vocation being decided at such a young age, or that she feared it was only being done so Mary's grandmother, Eleanor of Provence, would have a companion in the abbey. However, Mary's veiling had been in the planning for some years; Edward I had been in correspondence with the abbey at Fontevrault, the mother house of Amesbury, since 1282. Eleanor's reluctance, therefore, was probably more to do with when Mary was to become a nun, rather than the vocation itself; after all, the conventual life was considered a good career for a noble lady. The timing of her veiling may have been advanced not only by the failing health of Eleanor of Provence, but also by the imminent departure of Mary's parents. Edward and Eleanor were about to embark for the Continent and were expecting to be in France for a considerable time, years rather than months.

The actual ceremony must have been very moving. It took place at Amesbury Priory on 15 August 1285, where Mary was one of fourteen high-born girls who took their vows. The whole family was present to watch the ceremony, even her sixteen-month-old baby brother Edward. The king forgave the priory £80 owed to the Exchequer 'for love of his daughter Mary, whom he lately caused to be veiled in their house'.[41] Mary's cousin, Eleanor of Brittany, had taken her vows in March, shortly after her tenth birthday; Eleanor was the daughter of Edward I's sister, Beatrice, and would later demonstrate a great dedication to the religious life and eventually become Abbess of Fontevrault. After a long and eventful life, and with her health failing, the dowager queen took her own vows, retiring to the priory on 7 July 1286: 'My lady Eleanor, mother Queen of England, now, for Christ's sake, despised the withering flower of this world wherein she had formerly delighted, and on the feast of the Assumption was made a nun at Amesbury, where she had already dedicated her own daughter to God. For love of her my lord the King, her son, increased the wealth of that house with large rents'.[42] Henry III's queen died at Amesbury in June 1291.

Mary's life at the abbey was probably a very comfortable existence; in the year she was veiled, Mary was awarded an annual income of £100 by her father, rising to £200 a year in 1292, following the death of Eleanor of Provence.[43] As she was still only a child, the nuns at Amesbury would have been responsible not only for Mary's spiritual life, but also for her education. However, the cloistered life by no means meant that Mary was confined and separated from her family for any length of time. She made frequent visits to court throughout her life and was present for most family occasions. Having taken the veil in August 1285, Mary returned to be with her family in the autumn, to see the unveiling of the newly created Winchester Round Table and the creation of forty-four new knights by her father, the king. She visited her family again in March and May of 1286, each visit lasting about a month.

In the same year, Edward exchanged letters with Floris V, Count of Holland, discussing a possible marriage between Elizabeth, now 3 years old, and Floris's only surviving son, Jan, who was not yet a year old. It was agreed that the young boy would be raised in England. Edward agreed to pay another '50,000 pounds in black *Tournois*' for the marriage, promising £10,000 if Jan arrived in England before he completed his seventh year, and a further £10,000 when he did complete his seventh year.[44] The remainder would be paid when Elizabeth and Jan married. In return, Floris agreed a dower for Elizabeth of 6000 'black *Tournois*' in land annually. If Jan died when the marriage was still childless, a portion of the £50,000 would be returned to the king of England.[45]

The following year, Edward and Eleanor were to leave England for an extended visit to their French territories. They expected to be away for twelve months, but circumstances meant they would be away for more than three years. Edward had also been asked to negotiate peace over the throne of Sicily, claimed by both Alfonso III of Aragon and Charles of Salerno; each had succeeded their fathers in 1285. Edward had a vested interest in resolving the situation for the sake of his daughter Eleanor, who would not be able to marry Alfonso until he had settled his differences with the Pope. Before leaving, the king and queen made sure to spend time with their children, who would be staying in England, bringing Mary from her convent for the occasion. They went on a boating trip at Brentford, then made their way to Gravesend; the king and queen on a barge while the children travelled by ship. They said their goodbyes at Dover as Edward and Eleanor departed on 13 May 1286. It was when Eleanor of Provence and Mary returned to Amesbury that Henry III's queen finally took the veil.

For the other girls, the departure of their parents meant an end to the court's meanderings, and they would settle down to a less peripatetic existence, supervised by governesses and aristocratic ladies as they completed their education. The Wardrobe Book of Edward I suggests that the girls were all taught to read and write, with mention of the purchase of 'writing tablets for Eleanor the king's daughter'.[46] They would also have been taught to read Latin, so they could follow the offices of the Church, as well as the management of a noble household, rhetoric and diplomacy. The older girls joined the household of the two youngest royal children, Elizabeth and Edward, who were settled at their mother's palace of Langley – later to be known as King's Langley – in Hertfordshire. The royal siblings formed a court of their own, with noble companions of similar ages, the wards of their parents and the children of their parents' friends. They were protected by a sizeable force of armed guards, including seven knights and nine serjeants-at-arms. The total annual cost of the household exceeded £4000.[47] Even though they were miles away, their parents remembered their children, sending letters and gifts back to England on a regular basis; Edward sent Eleanor a coronet from Paris, a gold circlet set with sapphires, emeralds, rubies and pearls.[48]

The oldest of the royal siblings, Eleanor received petitions and interceded on behalf of those who asked. One such was a knight of the royal household, Eustace de Hache, who had failed to pay military service to his lord, because of his service at Langley, and was in danger of losing his estate. Eleanor wrote to her cousin. Edmund of Cornwall, regent in Edward I's absence, saying:

> To her very dear cousin, Lord Edmund, Earl of Cornwall, his cousin Eleanor, daughter to the King of England sends health and our dear friendship.
>
> Dear lord, since our lord the king has left us with Sir Eustace de Hache, our knight, and he is impleaded on many sides, and is so careful of the service of our lord the King that nothing avails him, since he cannot by any means depart from us, except by the mandate of our lord the King, we pray you, dear lord, since you are lieutenant of our lord the King, that you will command Sir William de Hamilton, by your letter, to let him [de Hache] have his warrant of essoin, so that he may not lose his land in our service, while our lord the King is out of the land. Dear lord, consent to do this for the love of us, so that he may feel our prayer avails for him. Dear lord, know that his day to have his warrant is this Tuesday next to come.[49]

Her petition failed but is evidence of her support for those serving the royal household.[50] Eleanor and Joan wrote jointly to the Bishop of Ely, John de Kirkeby, on behalf of Ellen, Lady de Gorges, who had been in the household of the princesses since their infancy. Ellen was the daughter and co-heir of Sir Ives de Morville and widow of Sir Ralph Gorges of Wraxall, who had accompanied King Edward on Crusade and died in 1271, possibly in the Holy Land. The letter concerned Ellen and Ralph's son, also called Ralph, his wife Maud, and John Lovel, a trustee of Maud, who were in a land dispute with Hugh le Despenser and another John Lovel. It seems likely that the Hugh le Despenser involved was the son of the Hugh le

Despenser killed fighting alongside Simon de Montfort at Evesham. At the time of the letter, 1386, his lands were still forfeit but Despenser would be made Earl of Winchester by Edward II and his son, Hugh le Despenser the Younger, would become the king's favourite in the 1320s – and come to a grisly end in 1326. They wrote:

> To the honourable father in God, Monsieur John, by the grace of God, Bishop of Ely, Eleanor and Joanna, daughters to the King of England, send health and true love.
>
> Dear Sire, since we understand that peace is not yet made between Monsieur Hugh Despenser and Monsieur John Lovel the heir, and Monsieur Ralph de Gorges and Sir John Lovel the bastard, for whom we have aforetime prayed you, we pray and require you again, as earnestly as we can, that you, if you please, will take trouble to keep accord with them. And because we see our good friend, Lady de Gorges, is so ill at ease in her heart that we have great pity for her, and should be most glad if she were alleviated of the great grief of heart that she has on account of the contest that is among them – therefore, dear sire, we pray you, if it please you, that you will make exertions that good peace be made, and that the thing be brought to a good end; and since we know well that you are empowered to adjust the fines of each party, we beg that you will do it, for the love of us. We commend you, dear sire, to God, who keep you, body and soul.[51]

The dispute appears to have been over some land in Somerset. The Lovel family were the lords of Cary, which was close to the Gorges lands at Wraxall; exactly what interest Despenser had in the lands is uncertain. The Despenser estates were primarily in the Midlands. The letter, however, is an indication of the interest the daughters of Edward I showed in the people who served them, and the care they had for those people, with touching references to Lady Gorges' heart and grief. It is also an indication that these young ladies were learning diplomacy and how to intercede in matters that concerned those around them from a young age; Eleanor was 17 years old and Joan just 14.

On a personal front, Eleanor's marriage to Alfonso was looking increasingly unlikely. Although Pope Martin IV had died, his successor was not happy with the treaty arrangements negotiated by King Edward, claiming they did not protect the papal states. He excommunicated Alfonso. As an English princess, Eleanor would not be able to marry an excommunicate, king or not.

Meanwhile, arrangements were moving forward for Joan to marry. Edward had finally settled on an English husband for her, Gilbert de Clare, eighth Earl of

Gloucester and seventh Earl of Hertford, also known as Gilbert the Red. Gilbert had been married to Alice de Lusignan, daughter of a half-brother of Henry III, in 1253 when Gilbert was 10 years old. The couple had two daughters but by 1267 were estranged. They separated formally in 1271, and the marriage was finally annulled in 1285.[52] Gilbert had been one of the leaders of the Second Barons' Revolt, alongside Simon de Montfort, until he became disillusioned and allied himself with Edward in the lead up to the Battle of Evesham. In offering Joan in marriage to one of the most powerful barons in England, Edward intended to bind Gilbert to the royal cause, thus weakening any baronial opposition. Once the annulment was achieved, Gilbert played the suitor to Joan, sending gifts of silk tunics with matching dresses for his future bride and her sisters, Eleanor and Margaret.

Now in her mid-teens, Joan was flexing her muscles while the king and queen were away, exerting her independence. She quarrelled with the steward to the royal children, Giles de Audenarde, and refused to deal with him, preferring to run up debts than ask him for money. She even wrote to her parents to explain her side of the story before Audenarde could tell his. Edward appears to have been indifferent to the quarrel and the queen paid off Joan's debts when she returned home.[53] On 13 August 1289, all five sisters were with their little brother Edward at Dover to welcome their parents home, after a three-year absence. The older girls, Eleanor, Joan and Margaret, now 20, 17 and 14 respectively, resumed their places at their parents' court, with Mary, Elizabeth and Edward visiting occasionally. And on 16 November 1289, Pope Nicholas IV issued the dispensation for Joan's marriage to Gilbert de Clare, necessary due to Joan's familial relationship with Gilbert's first wife, who was her father's first cousin. The wedding date was set for 30 April 1290.[54]

Mary would have seen quite a lot of her parents in the spring of 1290 as her father chose Amesbury as the location for a special meeting, convened to settle the arrangements for the English succession. Edward may have chosen the abbey so that his ailing mother could be present for the discussions. The Archbishop of Canterbury and five other bishops, in addition to Edward, Eleanor of Castile and Eleanor of Provence, were all present to formalise the settling of the succession on Edward's only surviving son, 6-year-old Edward of Caernarvon. Should Edward of Caernarvon die without heirs, it was decided that the succession would then pass to Edward I's eldest daughter, 'Lady Eleanor'.[55] Earl Gilbert, Joan's future husband, put his seal to a document supporting Edward's arrangements:

> 'And if by misfortune it should happen that GOD makes his commandment to our lord the king, and to his sons, and they have no heirs of their bodies, if the Lady Eleanor, eldest daughter of my lord the king above-mentioned, is alive, I will bear good faith to this same Eleanor, and to the begotten heirs of her body, and in no manner,

> not by force, nor by deceit, disturb her rights, nor her, nor the heirs of her body, should she have them, nor the kingdom of England nor the land of Ireland, according to the ordinance of our lord the king above-mentioned; which ordinance is:
>
> That our lord the king wishes and ordains that should Lord Edward [of Caernarvon], his son, or another son, should he have one, remain without heirs of his body; that therefore, after the death of our lord the king above-mentioned, the kingdom of England, and the land of Ireland, remain to Lady Eleanor, his eldest daughter, and the begotten heirs of her body.[56]

This was the first time an English king had proposed the succession of his daughter since Henry I had championed the cause of his daughter, Empress Matilda. Although the accession of Eleanor did not materialise, it is interesting to note that Edward thought his daughter capable and that he would rather she, or one of her sisters, succeed him than the sons of his brother Edmund. Eleanor of Castile was a distant mother when her children were young, but she seems to have developed closer relationships as they grew older, so it is not hard to imagine her taking the opportunity to spend time with 12-year-old Mary while these momentous events were taking place at the abbey. Mary was again with the court for the wedding of Joan of Acre to Gilbert de Clare, Earl of Gloucester and Hertford; Joan and Gilbert were married in a private ceremony at Westminster on 30 April. Joan was 18 years old and Gilbert 46. Although Joan's dress was second-hand, she was presented with gifts from her parents of a headdress from France and a matching 'magnificent zone [belt], of all gold with emeralds and rubies'.[57] With the promise of a position at the centre of royal politics, Gilbert relinquished his titles to the Crown; they were returned to him as a new grant that gave the lands and titles to the couple, jointly, as opposed to just Gilbert. As the *Lanercost* chronicler records, 'King Edward gave his daughter, the Lady Joan of Acre, in marriage to Gilbert Earl of Gloucester, with great celebration, that the bond of love should be more strongly knit'.[58]

Joan's temperament was said to be as fiery as her mother's. She refused to marry until she had the same number of attendants as her sisters. The king resolved the situation by hiring temporary servants, just until her wedding day. Joan's tetchiness was again in evidence during preparations for the wedding of her sister Margaret to Jan of Brabant, just a few months after her own. It was a much grander affair than Joan's wedding had been. Joan initially refused to attend, preferring to retire to Gilbert's estates. Edward and Eleanor retaliated by taking back seven dresses they were intending to give her and making them part of Margaret's trousseau.[59] Margaret also had a magnificent belt and a headdress of gold, set with pearls and rubies, with the royal leopards in sapphires. A second headdress was studded with 300 emeralds. Margaret was accompanied down the aisle by her sister Eleanor; although the oldest, she was still unmarried. Eleanor wore a gown decorated with over 600 silver buttons.[60] Given that Margaret was 15 and Jan almost 15, the young couple may have been allowed to consummate the marriage on their wedding night, but they would not initially live together as husband and wife. It was at the celebrations after the wedding that Archbishop Pecham preached the cross with Gilbert and Joan, along with many members of the court, swearing to go on Crusade to the Holy Land. However, events in Scotland changed Edward's priorities and the Crusade never happened; the death of Alexander III's granddaughter, Margaret, the Maid of Norway, in September 1290, left the Scottish throne vacant, and gave Edward the opportunity to extend his influence north of the English border.

The wedding celebrations would have been one of the last times the whole family was together. Eleanor of Castile died at Harby, near Lincoln, on 28 November 1290. Eleanor had been at the king's palace of Clipstone in Nottinghamshire when it was realised that her illness was probably fatal. Some of her children, Joan, Edward and Elizabeth, were summoned to the queen's bedside; although Eleanor and Mary are not mentioned, it does not mean that they did not visit their mother one last time. Indeed, still unmarried, Eleanor may have already been in her mother's company. Mary's deep affection for her mother was demonstrated in 1297 when she and her younger sister, Elizabeth, jointly paid for a special Mass in their mother's honour.[61]

Queen Eleanor would probably have died in the knowledge that her first grandchild was on the way, as Joan was three or four months pregnant at the time of her mother's death. Joan and Gilbert had four children together. Like her mother, Joan appears to have been pregnant most of her married life. Their eldest child, a son also called Gilbert, succeeded his father as Earl of Gloucester and Hertford, but was killed at the Battle of Bannockburn in 1314; he was married to Matilda, daughter of Richard de Burgh, Earl of Ulster, and sister of Elizabeth de Burgh, Robert the Bruce's queen. On 21 May 1291, Edward I gave £100 to the messenger who gave him the news of the safe arrival of his first grandchild.[62] Of Joan's daughters by Gilbert, Eleanor would firstly be married to Hugh le Despenser, the Younger, a favourite of her uncle, Edward II, who was executed in 1326. She then married William la Zouche de Mortimer, and died in 1337. Margaret was first married to another favourite of her uncle Edward II, Piers Gaveston, Earl of Cornwall, who was executed in 1312; she then went on to marry Hugh Audley and died in 1347. Their sister, Elizabeth, an influential patron of the arts, married three times: John de Burgh, Theobald de Verdon and Roger Baron d'Amory.

Gilbert could still find himself in trouble with the king at times, despite now being a part of the family. After becoming involved in a violent feud with Humphrey de Bohun, Earl of Hereford, in 1292 he was imprisoned and fined £10,000 to ensure his future good behaviour. The imprisonment was hardly onerous, as his wife was allowed to visit him and Joan even became pregnant during that time. Although the fine was never paid, Gilbert was eventually released. The following year, Gilbert and Joan visited Gilbert's lands in Ireland and in August a grant was made to 'Joan, countess of Gloucester, the king's daughter, of the custody, during minority of Gilbert, son and heir of Thomas de Clare, tenant in chief, of the lands late of the said Thomas, in Ireland, with the knights' fees, advowsons of churches, dowers when they fall in, wards, reliefs, escheats, and other things belonging to the said custody, but with the exception of those lands which Adam de Creting holds by the king's appointment of the said inheritance'.[63] The couple were only married for a little over five years before Gilbert's death, just weeks after the birth of his youngest daughter, Elizabeth. He died at Monmouth Castle on 7 December 1295: 'Gilbert, the great Earl of Gloucester, died after the festival of S. Lucia, a man prudent in council, puissant in arms and most spirited in defence of his rights'.[64]

One wonders how Eleanor felt, watching her two younger sisters marry while her own future was still uncertain. One week in 1291 saw two significant deaths, one for the family and one for Eleanor in particular. King Edward's mother, Eleanor of Provence, died at Amesbury on 24 June; she was in her late sixties. It had originally been intended that she would be interred in Westminster Abbey, in the chapel of St Edward the Confessor, close to her husband, King Henry III. But her place had been taken by Eleanor of Castile and so she was buried at Amesbury Priory and her heart was taken to London and buried at the Franciscan priory of Greyfriars.[65] Six days earlier, in Barcelona, Alfonso III of Aragon died after suffering from a high fever for ten days. He was 25. He and Eleanor had been betrothed since Eleanor was a toddler. She was now 22.

In the same year, at the age of 12, Mary took her final, binding vows at Amesbury Priory. Abbey life seems to have held few restrictions for her; Mary was regularly away from the cloister. She was frequently at court or visiting various members of her family. She was given an annual income of £200 by her father and on 2 January 1292, Edward gave a 'Grant to Mary, the king's daughter, nun of Fontevraud, dwelling at Aumbresbury, of 40 oaks (*robora*) yearly for her hearth in her chamber there, in the forests of Shut and Bokholte, to wit, one half in the forest of Clarindon, and the other in the forest of Lutegeresale, by the hands of the keepers thereof; also of 20 tuns of wine yearly by the hands of the bailiffs of Southampton'.[66] The discomforts of a cold and damp nun's cell were not for the princess. The following year, Mary is mentioned in a dispute between the prioress at Amesbury and the abbess of the mother house at Fontevrault. Although we do not, unfortunately, have all the particulars, the disagreement was over 'the promotion of the prioress in the monastery of Aumbresbury [Amesbury] and concerning certain other things pertaining to the jurisdiction of the monastery of fontévrault'.[67] The king was called upon to intervene and on 10 June he ordered 'the abbot of Stanle to deliver by chirograph the temporalities of Aumbresbury priory (lately taken into the king's hands because of contentions between the abbess of Fontevraud and

Margaret sometime prioress of Aumbresbury) to Joan de Jaynes, one of the nuns, whom the said abbess has sent to the king to be a prioress, and whom the king has admitted and accepted'.[68]

While Mary appears to have been making the most of her life as a nun, and Joan appeared to be content with her husband, Margaret and Jan showed no inclination of making a married life together. By the end of 1292, they were both 17 but still living separate lives. And when Jan departed for Brabant in 1294, to take up his duties as the new duke, following his father's death, Margaret remained in England for another three years, though Jan did visit often during that time. It was one of the risks for royal, arranged marriages, that a couple would turn out to be incompatible; they just had to make the best of it. Eleanor would have hoped that her relationship with her husband would be more satisfactory as she was finally married on 20 September, when 'In the twenty-first year of the king's reign, about the feast of S. Michael the king's daughter, Eleanor, was given in marriage to Henry, Comte de Bar, by whom he had a son, Edward, and a daughter whom Earl John de Warenne took to wife'.[69]

The county of Bar was geographically in eastern France, bordering Lorraine, but was a part of the Holy Roman Empire, rather than the kingdom of France. The wedding took place at Bristol and 'four harts and thirty bucks' were provided for the feast afterwards.[70] The happy couple stayed in England until the spring of 1294, leaving for Bar towards the end of April. The new countess was accompanied by her mother's household knight Sir Guy Ferre and Sir William Layburne, a baron from Kent, who were to examine the dower lands assigned to Eleanor and ensure their annual yield amounted to 15,000 *livres Tournois*, as agreed between Henry and Edward.[71] It was during the wedding celebrations on their arrival in Bar-le-Duc in 1294 that Eleanor's sister Margaret became Duchess of Brabant; her father-in-law was killed in the jousting.

Henry and Eleanor had at least two children. Their son, Edward, and daughter, Jeanne (Joan), were born in successive years, in 1294 and 1295, although there seems to be some confusion about who was the eldest.[72] It is said that a third child, Eleanor, married Llywelyn ap Owen of Deheubarth, but her existence seems to be a later invention. Young Edward would be heir to the English crown, after his uncle Edward of Caernarfon and his mother. And after his mother's death, he was second in line until the birth of his uncle, Thomas of Brotherton, in 1300.

Henry of Bar joined King Edward's war against France in 1297, leaving Eleanor in charge of the county, and the raising of their two young children. An army led by the Constable of France invaded Bar whilst Henry was fighting in Champagne: 'By force and by fire [the French forces] devastated the land of the Count of Bar'.[73] Eleanor hastily recalled Henry and the count returned to drive off the French army, then headed north to help fight off the French invasion of Flanders, leaving Eleanor in charge of Bar once again. King Edward spent Christmas 1297 in Flanders, accompanied by his daughters Margaret and Elizabeth. Margaret's husband, Jan, joined them, as did Eleanor. There is no mention of the children, but this may have been an opportunity for Edward to spend some time with his little grandchildren, Edward and Jeanne. Eleanor gave her father gifts including a comb, a silver enamelled mirror and a pricket (a spike for holding a candle).[74]

Having returned to the war, Count Henry was captured by a French raiding party at Comines, near Lille, leaving Eleanor with the informal regency of Bar, looking after her children, and raising the ransom that would inevitably be demanded for Henry's release. Henry was still languishing in his French prison when Eleanor died on 29 August 1298, of some unrecorded injury or illness.[75] According to the *Flores Historiarum*, the body of the English princess was brought back to England and buried in Westminster Abbey, London. Eleanor's children remained in Bar, in the charge of Henry's councillors, who were still negotiating for their count's release. Count Henry was eventually released in June 1301, following the intercession of an English embassy to France; under the terms of his release, the count was required to pay a hefty ransom, to relinquish parts of his province and to place the county under French feudal lordship.[76] The count returned to his two children, now 6 and 7 years old, and to his disgruntled councillors, angry at the terms to which the count had had to agree to obtain his freedom. The count's reunion with his children was brief, however, as he departed on Crusade the same year, never to return. Henry, Count of Bar, died in 1302, possibly as a result of injuries received in battle while fighting in Sicily. The count was succeeded by his only son, Edward, and the children were placed in the guardianship of a council of elders.[77] During little Count Edward's minority, the county of Bar was to be run by governors under the supervision of his grandfather, Edward I.

The last of the sisters to marry was Elizabeth, the youngest. She had been betrothed to Jan of Holland since 1285, when they were both still toddlers. Shortly afterwards, Jan had been sent to England to be raised and educated at the English court. In June 1296, Jan's father, Floris V, Count of Holland, had been murdered near Amsterdam. Jan was in England at the time of his father's death and Edward decided it was time to press ahead with the wedding, which was celebrated on 7 January 1297 at Ipswich Priory. Attended by nobles and knights from both England and Holland, the guests were entertained by a host of minstrels, including nine harpers, two trumpeters, two taborers (drummers), lute and vielle players, fools and acrobats.[78] Elizabeth was just 14 years old and Jan was about 13. It seems Elizabeth was very fond of her father – there is some suggestion, too, that she was his favourite – and she was loath to leave him, and England. The king himself threw Elizabeth's coronet into the fire during an argument with Elizabeth over her refusal to go with her new husband. The king had to pay 40*s* for a large ruby and a large emerald to be set into the coronet during its repair; presumably the originals could not be rescued from the fire. The princess wore a different coronet for her wedding, made of gold and costing £90.[79]

Jan departed England a week after the wedding, leaving his bride behind. It took several letters from Count Jan, and much cajoling from the king, to persuade Elizabeth to join her husband in her new country. In one letter, dated 9 October 1297, Jan wrote to Edward, saying:

> Very dear father, on other occasions we have requested of you that it might please you to send our dear consort to her land; dear lord, once again we humbly beseech you, for the great well-being of herself and of us and of our land and our people who very strongly desire to see their lady, our dear consort, that it might please you that you might arrange a certain day and a certain place where we can come to meet you, and that it might please you to bring our consort to her own country, as honourably as befits her.[80]

Even when she arrived on the Continent, landing at Flanders in August 1297, with her father and sister, Elizabeth was in no hurry to travel to Holland and be with her husband. It may be that she did not join Jan until March 1298, when her father returned to England without either of his daughters, Margaret and Elizabeth. In the event, however, the arguing proved unnecessary as Count Jan died at Haarlem on 10 November 1299. Elizabeth, a childless widow at 17, returned home to her father's court.

Meanwhile, Joan of Acre had taken her future into her own hands. As the land and titles to the earldoms of Gloucester and Hertford were held jointly with Gilbert, Joan remained in charge of the estates after Gilbert's death. The lands, spread across England, Wales and Ireland, produced an annual income of *l*6000 and the widowed Joan paid homage for them to Edward I, on 20 January 1296. Edward wasted no time in trying to find her a suitable new husband; his choice was Amadeus V, Count of Savoy. The betrothal document was dated 16 March 1297. However, it seems Joan had other ideas. In late 1296, she sent one of her late husband's squires, Ralph de Monthermer, to her father, the king, asking that he be knighted. Shortly after, in a secret ceremony in January 1297, Joan married the erstwhile squire, thus thwarting Edward's plans for her marriage with the Count of Savoy.

Edward was so furious that he ordered Ralph's arrest and had him imprisoned in Bristol Castle; he refused to receive Joan and confiscated all the lands and castles she had inherited from her late husband. The man appointed to take control of Joan's lands, goods and chattels, Malcolm Harlegh, was warned 'not to omit to do this as he loves himself and his own things and wishes to escape the king's wrath, certifying the king without delay as to how he has executed this order'.[81] Joan sent her three daughters by Gilbert to their grandfather to try to appease him – they were aged 4, 3 and eighteen months at the time. The Bishop of Durham also attempted to mediate. Edward soon mellowed, possibly when he discovered that Joan was pregnant with

Ralph's child. Monthermer was released and the de Clare estates were restored to the couple, although Tonbridge and Portland remained in the king's hands until 1301. The couple was officially pardoned, with Ralph performing homage for his lands on 2 August 1297 at Eltham Palace. He was first addressed as Earl of Gloucester and Hertford in May 1298 and would hold the title until Joan's death. Joan and Ralph had two sons and two daughters. Their eldest son, Thomas, was killed at the Battle of Sluys in 1340 and their second son, Edward, died in the same year. Of their daughters, Mary married Duncan, the tenth Earl of Fife, while Joan became a nun at Amesbury Priory in Wiltshire, the same abbey where her mother's sister, Mary, was a nun.

Mary's career in the Church was far from spectacular; although her royal birth gave her some influence, she never made high office and was never given a priory or abbey of her own. However, she was given custody of several aristocratic nuns at Amesbury, trusted to oversee their education and spiritual training. In 1293 Mary visited her brother, Edward, and in 1297 she spent five weeks at court, taking the opportunity to spend some time with her sister, Elizabeth, who had been recently married to Jan, Count of Holland, and was expected to leave England soon. Mary advocated for her convent, when the need arose, interceding with her father. In 1293, she wrote to the king:

> To the most high and noble prince, and her dearest and most beloved lord and father, my lord, by the grace of God, King of England, his devoted nun, Mary, wishes health, with all honour and reverence.
>
> Dearest sire, we understand that your escheators have seized and placed in your hands the manors of Leighton and of La Grave, with all their appurtenances, on account of the death of a guardian of the said places. And because you know that your ancestors gave them in perpetual alms to the convent of Fontevraud, we beg you, dearest sire, for God's sake and your soul's, that you will place the said manors out of all seisin, if you please, and command the escheators to go away without taking anything.
>
> And whereas my lord the Earl of Gloucester has also, for the same reason, seized the manor of Stanvele, may it please you to command the Earl and his people that they make take away their hands from the goods of my lady the Abbess, freely and without damage done. Do as much, most sweet father, for the love of me, that my lady the Abbess of Fontevraud may perceive in all things that I am a good attorney for her in this country. I commend to Jesus Christ the body and soul of you.'[82]

Mary had many cultural interests and was a patron of Nicholas Trivet, who dedicated his chronicle, *Annales Sex Regum Angliae*, to her. She was probably

Trivet's source for many of the details of Edward I's family and the inclusion of several anecdotes that demonstrated Edward's luck, such as the story of the king's miraculous escape from a falling stone while sitting and playing chess. He had stood up to stretch his legs when the stone from the vaulted ceiling landed on the chair he had just vacated.[83] The stories that Mary passed on to Trivet also serve to demonstrate that she was at court on a regular basis.

There was yet another royal wedding on 8 September 1299, when King Edward married Marguerite of France, who was forty years younger than the 60-year-old king. In fact, Marguerite was a number of years younger than two of her four stepdaughters and was a similar age to Mary. Edward and Marguerite would have three children together, including their sons Thomas of Brotherton and Edmund of Woodstock. A daughter, Eleanor, was born on 6 May 1306 and two days later was betrothed to Robert de Bourgogne, heir to the French counties of Burgundy and Artois. Following her father's death, the little princess was placed in the care of her half-sister, Mary, at Amesbury Priory, most likely to ensure she was well cared for and educated, with her half-brother, Edward II covering her expenses. She died around August 1311. She was only 5 years old and was buried at Beaulieu in Hampshire, Edward II paying £113 for her funeral and burial. [84]

Two months after her father's wedding, Elizabeth was widowed when Count Jan of Holland died of dysentery. Elizabeth was still only 17 and the couple had no children; which may suggest that Jan and Elizabeth had grown no closer once they started living as husband and wife, especially given she was to have eleven children with her second husband. We have little idea of what her life had been with Jan, or whether there was much affection between them, the lack of children could just as easily have been due to miscarriage or a still birth, neither of which are always recorded. With no children to keep her in Holland, Elizabeth returned home. The king sent two of his own officials to Holland in March 1300, to aid Elizabeth in gaining her rightful dower but even so, she would have problems receiving the revenue due to her for the rest of her life.

Almost exactly three years after the death of her first husband, on 14 November 1302, Elizabeth married again. This time there would be no arguments about leaving England as her husband was Humphrey de Bohun, fourth Earl of Hereford and Essex. Before the wedding, as had Gilbert de Clare prior to his marriage to Joan of Acre, Humphrey had relinquished all his lands and titles to the Crown, including that of constable of England. They were re-granted, jointly, to Humphrey and his new wife after the wedding. Elizabeth's second marriage appears to have been happy and successful. The couple were incredibly fond of each other and Humphrey and Elizabeth weathered the storms of change together. Humphrey had been a stalwart of Edward I's Scottish campaigns and in 1306 had been rewarded with the forfeited estates of Robert the Bruce. When Elizabeth's father died in 1307, Humphrey was initially a supporter of the new king, Elizabeth's brother and childhood companion, Edward II. He is witness to the document that created Piers Gaveston, Edward's controversial favourite, Earl of Cornwall. However, in 1310, he was named one of the Lords Ordainers, a council established to reform the king's household and government. He was stripped of his position as constable of England for refusing to accompany the king on his Scottish campaign of 1310–11 but was reinstated the following year. In 1314, Humphrey was one of the commanders of the English forces facing Robert the Bruce at Bannockburn. It is believed his arguments with his nephew-by-marriage, Gilbert de Clare, Earl of Gloucester, over who should have precedence in the battle formations, was a major factor contributing to England's defeat. Gloucester was killed in the fighting and Humphrey was captured by the Scots. As the brother-in-law of the king, he was the highest profile English prisoner. His freedom came when he was exchanged for Robert the Bruce's queen, Elizabeth de Burgh, who had been held captive by the English since 1306.[85]

Between 1303 and 1316, the couple were to have eleven children, including twin boys. Eight of the siblings survived childhood, six boys and two girls. Their eldest daughter, Eleanor, married James Butler, first Earl of Ormonde and, following his death, Sir Thomas Dagworth, who was murdered in 1350. Their youngest surviving daughter, Margaret, married Hugh de Courtenay, Earl of Devon, and lived until 1391. Two of their sons, John and Humphrey, would succeed, consecutively, to the earldoms of Hereford and Essex. William de Bohun, twin brother of Edward (who drowned in 1334) would be granted the title of Earl of Northampton by his cousin and close friend Edward III. The twin brothers had both been involved in Edward III's escape from Nottingham Castle and from the control of his mother's alleged lover, Roger Mortimer. Of the two remaining sons, Eneas died before 1343 and Edmund married Matilda, the daughter of Nicholas de Segrave, Baron Stowe. Sadly, Elizabeth died in childbirth on 5 May 1316 and her last daughter, Isabella, died with her. They were buried together at Walden Priory (Waltham Abbey) on 23 May. Humphrey survived his wife by six years; he was killed at the Battle of Boroughbridge in March 1322, fighting with the forces of Thomas of Lancaster against the king. Despite his will requesting to be buried beside his wife at Walden Priory, he was laid to rest at the Church of the Friars Preachers in York. Elizabeth and Humphrey were the ancestors of the Lancastrian kings through their great-granddaughter, Mary de Bohun, who married Henry Bolingbroke (the future Henry IV) and was the mother of six children, including two daughters, Philippa and Blanche, who we shall meet later.

After ten years of marriage, Joan of Acre had died at Clare in Suffolk, on 23 April 1307, from an unknown ailment, aged just 35. She was buried in the Augustinian Priory there, of which she was a benefactress, and where she had founded the Chapel of St Vincent. The earldoms of Gloucester and Hertford passed to her son by Gilbert (her son was also called Gilbert), and Ralph was given the title first Baron Monthermer in recompense. Joan may have been ill for some time, as there appears to have been some confusion in the reporting of her death. While Joan died at Clare Castle in Suffolk on 23 April 1307, her death had been prematurely reported to the king, her father, 300 miles away in Carlisle, on 1 April, or perhaps even earlier. It was on 1 April that Edward ordered all the archbishops, bishops, abbots and priors of England, and numerous others, to sing masses for the soul of 'Joan our dear daughter, who was countess of Gloucester, who has been commanded to God'.[86] On 6 May, still in Carlisle, perhaps having received the news that the initial reports were erroneous but that Joan had now died, the king ordered the churchmen that they should commend to God the soul of 'Joan, formerly countess of Gloucester and Hertford, our dearest daughter' as she had just died.[87] The ailing king himself would die just two months later, on 7 July – to hear such news, twice, must have been a cruel blow.

The financial provisions that had been settled on Mary by Edward I were amended in 1302, when she was given a number of manors and the borough of Wilton in lieu of the £200 she had previously been granted, but only for as long as she remained in England. Given that a proposed move to Fontevrault had been dropped shortly after the death of Eleanor of Provence, the likelihood of Mary leaving England seems to have been only a remote possibility. Mary had a penchant for high living; she travelled to court with an entourage big enough to require twenty-four horses. By 1305, despite her income, she was substantially in debt, with the escheator south of the Trent being ordered to provide her with £200 in order to satisfy her creditors. Mary also had a taste for gambling, mainly at dice, and her father is known to have paid off at least one gambling debt.[88] Following her father's death in 1307, her younger brother, now King Edward II, continued to support Mary financially and she still made regular visits to court. She would also intercede for her convent, on occasion. Around 1309, she wrote to her brother after the death of Amesbury's prioress, advocating for her favourite choice as replacement:

> 'To the very high and noble prince, her very dear lord and brother, my lord Edward, by the grace of God King of England, his sister Mary sends health and all manner of honour and reverence.
>
> Very dear sire, as a long time has passed since God did his will upon our prioress, we, after her death, sent in all haste to our dear cousin, the Lady-Abbess of Fontevrault, both on my part and on that of the convent, asking for a lady from this our convent, to wit, for the Lady Isabella, whom we understand to be well able and sufficient for the office, that she might be granted to us for our prioress. And we thought, dear sire, that she [the Abbess] would have willingly

> granted us our request, for she is bound to do so since she was brought up and veiled amongst us, as so she should neither wish nor permit that the church should be so long without prelates; but as yet we have had no answer, only we understand from certain people that she intends to send us a prioress from beyond the sea there, and a prior by her counsel out there. And know, certainly, my very dear brother, that should she send any other than one belonging to our own convent, it would prove matter of discord in the convent, and of the destruction of the goods of the church, which I know well, sire, that you would not suffer willingly and wittingly; wherefore I pray you, dearest lord and brother, and require you, both for the love of me and of our convent, which after God trusts surely in you – that you would please send word to my said Lady-Abbess, that she do not undertake to burden our church with any prioress out of the convent, nor with prior other than the one we have now, but that she would grant us her whom we have requested. Do this, most dearest brother, that our convent may receive your aid and sustenance in this case as they have always done in their needs. May Jesus Christ give you a long life, my dearest brother.
>
> Written at Swainton, in the Isle of Wight,
> the 9th day of May[89]

The Lady Isabella championed by Mary was Isabel de Geneville, and she was indeed appointed as prioress. Mary died sometime around 1332 and was buried where she had lived, at Amesbury Priory. She was a princess whose future was decided for her at a very young age. She doesn't seem to have excelled at the religious life in terms of advancement, in that she never achieved significant office, but she did make the most of the life chosen for her, making frequent pilgrimages and taking charge of the young, aristocratic ladies who joined the convent. Despite her dedication to the Church, she found her own path within it and seems to have achieved a healthy (for her) balance between the cloister and the court. There was, however, one moment of scandal; although it did not arise until more than twenty years after Mary's death. In 1345, in an attempt to escape an unhappy marriage, John de Warenne, Earl of Surrey, claimed that he had had an affair with Mary, his wife's maternal aunt, when he was 19 and Mary was 27 years of age. This would mean his marriage to Jeanne de Bar was invalid. This was indeed a drastic claim, given that Mary had been a nun since she was about 7 years old, and it was probably born out of desperation; John was becoming increasingly infirm and still had no heir to succeed him. It was a last-ditch attempt to marry his lover, Isabella Holland, and have legitimate children. It failed, though the earl's confession was presented to Pope Clement VI who:

> on 15 May, 1345, issued a mandate to the Bishop of S. Asaph to absolve John de Warenne, Earl of Surrey and Stratherne, Lord of Bromfeld and Yale, from excommunication, which he has incurred by inter-marrying with Joan, daughter of Henry, Count de Barre, whose mother's sister, Mary, he had carnally known. A penance is to be enjoined; and as to the marriage, canonical action is to be taken.[90]

Although it is highly unlikely that the claim was anything more than Surrey's desperate attempt to find a way out of his marriage, it cannot be ignored that Mary was frequently at court and such an opportunity may have arisen, hence the papal dispensation. No further action seems to have been taken with regards to the marriage. John's penance, however, appears to have been the generous donation of the manor of Hatfield to Roche Abbey:

> 1345. November 22. Westminster.
> Whereas the King's kinsman, John de Warenna, Earl of Surrey, holds the manor of Haytfield [*sic*] for life of the grant of Edward II … he may have licence to grant for his life to the abbot and convent of Roche, the advowson of the church of Haytfield [*sic*], held in chief, which church is extended, of the value of 70 marks yearly; and the King has assented to his petition. Also, as a further grace, the King has granted that the abbot and convent shall retain in frankalmoign the said advowson, which should revert to him on the death of the earl; and may appropriate the church whenever they deem it expedient to do so, to find thirteen monks as chaplains to celebrate divine service daily for ever in the abbey for the King, Queen Philippa, and their children, and for the earl; also for the soul of William, the King's son, who lately died in the said manor; also the souls of the progenitors of the King and of the earl.[91]

Edward I died just two months after the death of Joan of Acre and was buried in Westminster Abbey, next to his father, on 27 October 1307. Of his daughters, Mary and Elizabeth were present, along with little Eleanor, his daughter by Queen Marguerite. Edward II, the new king, was also present, as were his little brothers, Thomas and Edmund, and their mother. Margaret, Duchess of Brabant, who would be the last surviving of Edward I and Eleanor of Castile's daughters, was not in attendance. She did, however, travel the 140 miles to Boulogne, with her husband, to witness her brother's wedding to Isabella of France on 25 January 1308. It was the first time the siblings had met since 1297, over ten years earlier. The duke and duchess then crossed the English Channel to be present at the joint coronation of Edward and Isabella on 25 February in Westminster Abbey. Margaret would have most definitely enjoyed a happy reunion with her sisters, Mary and Elizabeth, who also attended the coronation, and she met, perhaps for the first time, her half-sister Eleanor. To mark the occasion, Margaret and Jan gave Edward a vial of the holy oil of St Thomas Becket, intending the king to use the precious gift during his anointing. But the king and his council decided against it.[92]

Margaret was widowed on 27 October 1312, when Jan II, Duke of Brabant, passed away at Tervuren Castle, aged 37. Her marriage appears to have been an unhappy one, with her husband having a string of mistresses and, as a result, a number of illegitimate children who were raised at court. The ducal court spent most of its time in Brussels, from where Jan issued 67 of his 137 charters. Charters were also issued from Leuven, Tervuren, Antwerp, Mechelen, Maastricht, Keulen and Nijvel, suggesting these were the towns frequently occupied by the ducal court and thus towns that Margaret would have been familiar with.

Margaret and Jan had one child, a son, who was born in October 1300 and would succeed his father as Jan III, Duke of Brabant, in 1312. He was 12 years old at the time. Rather than returning home, like her sister Elizabeth had done, Margaret remained in the duchy with her son. Shortly before his death, Duke Jan had agreed the Charter of Kortenberg, which would guarantee his son's succession and be used to establish a regency council to rule during the new duke's minority. Despite not being appointed to the regency council, Margaret would remain as her son's guardian. Though he was only 12, Jan was already a husband having married Marie d'Évreux, the 8-year-old daughter of Louis, Count of Évreux in 1311. Given their ages, we can assume that the marriage was not consummated for a number of years; this is borne out by the fact their first child, Margaret's granddaughter Joanna, was not born until 1322. Their second daughter, named Margaret for her grandmother, was born in 1323. Four more children followed, including three sons who all predeceased their father. Margaret spent twenty-two years as a widow, no doubt enjoying being a grandmother for the latter half of that period. Her familial connections with England, France and Spain helped to ensure Brabant maintained its position in European politics. She died sometime after 11 March 1333 and was buried in the Cathedral of St Michael and St Gudula in Brussels, but her tomb, and that of her husband are both lost.

Margaret was the last of the daughters of Edward I to die. She had perhaps, not enjoyed as happy a marriage as her sisters Joan and Elizabeth had done with their second husbands. But she had at least lived long enough to meet her grandchildren, a feat which none of her sisters had managed. The royal sisters had spent much of their childhood relying on each other, particularly when their parents were absent on their continental lands, or on Crusade in the case of Eleanor. They can often be seen together at their parents' court as they grew into teenagers. There was a closeness in the family that is not often seen among royal siblings, but that had been apparent also in the children of King John and of Henry III. It was a familial closeness that would be lacking somewhat in the children of Edward II, with Edward III going to war against the husband of his sister, Joan.

Chapter Three

No Comfort in Marriage

Edward II had been born as the fourth son of Edward I and Eleanor of Castile. Ordinarily, he would have had no chance of attaining the throne but by the time of his birth, two of his older brothers were long dead and the one nearest to him in age, 10-year-old Alfonso, would die just four months later. For many years, until the births of his half-brothers, Thomas and Edmund, born 1300 and 1301 respectively, Edward was his father's sole male heir. It was a heavy burden to bear.

Edward I and Edward II had very different temperaments and the son often did not live up to the expectations of his father. However, he did one thing his older brothers had not been able to do. He lived and he thrived. And he succeeded his father as king in 1307. The following January, the 23-year-old king married 12-year-old Isabella of France in Boulogne. They were crowned king and queen together, a month later, in Westminster Abbey. Edward's accession was met with great acclaim. His father was 68 when he died and had ruled for thirty-five years. Edward II was young, tall, strong and handsome. And he was an experienced soldier. With such attributes, his reign promised great things. It did not deliver.

Edward II is always ranked amongst the top three of England's most unsuccessful – or worst – kings. King John is the only one who takes the top spot more frequently than Edward. Edward II had a tendency to indulge his favourites. First, it was Piers Gaveston, who had been exiled by Edward I for his influence on the younger Edward when he was a prince. He was a focus of discontent for Edward II's vocal barons. And then it was the rapacious Hugh le Despenser the Younger. Edward had little taste for kingly pursuits, such as jousting in tournaments, but enjoyed pastimes that were considered eccentric for a king, including hedging, thatching, smithying, rowing and swimming. His military failures, including the defeat by the Scots at the Battle of Bannockburn, which saw Edward fleeing the field to avoid capture, added to his unpopularity. In 1315, Robert le Messager, a member of the royal household, remarked that 'it was no wonder that the king couldn't win a battle, because he spent the time when he should have been hearing Mass in idling, ditching, digging and other improper occupations'.[1]

Edward's wife, Isabella, was said to be a great beauty. She was born in 1295 as the only daughter of Philip IV (the Fair) of France and his wife Jeanne, queen of

Navarre in her own right. The early years of the marriage must have been difficult for Isabella. She was still very young, finding her way in a strange country with a husband who paid too much attention to one of his nobles. Piers Gaveston had now been given the title Earl of Cornwall, with lands and money and a marriage to the king's own niece, Margaret de Clare, daughter of Joan of Acre. Gaveston alienated practically the whole of the English nobility, who were wary of his influence over the king. They contrived to have him exiled once again, but again, Edward II brought him back. A set of parliament Ordinances of 1311, aimed at curbing the power and authority of the king, described Gaveston as 'evil'.[2] He was yet again sent into exile and his subsequent return, not authorised by parliament, galvanised the opposition. Gaveston was arrested at Scarborough Castle and taken south in the custody of Aymer de Valence, Earl of Pembroke and John de Warenne, Earl of Surrey, who had personally guaranteed Gaveston's safety. The party was intercepted by the Earl of Warwick, who took Gaveston to Warwick Castle and imprisoned him. Eight days later, Gaveston was put on trial before the earls of Lancaster, Hereford and Arundel, accused of treason and sentenced to death. Two days after that he was led out to Blacklow Hill, two miles north of Warwick, where he was run through with a sword and then beheaded, his body left where it fell.[3] Edward II was so distraught that he vowed Gaveston's body would not be buried until his murder had been avenged. The embalmed body was kept in the Dominican friary at Oxford for three years before it was finally interred in the friary at King's Langley in 1315.[4]

One result of Gaveston's death was that Isabella and the king drew closer. Their first child, their son Edward of Windsor, the future King Edward III, was born on 13 November 1312; he was created Earl of Chester eleven days later. Another son, John of Eltham, was born in 1316 and died of illness shortly after his twentieth birthday, whilst campaigning against the Scots. Edward already had an illegitimate son, Adam FitzRoy, although the identity of Adam's mother remains a mystery. He was born in the early 1300s, but died whilst campaigning in Scotland with his father, in 1322. Queen Isabella's property and income was increased in 1318, following the death of Edward's stepmother, Edward I's widow, Marguerite of France, on 14 February. Marguerite was Queen Isabella's aunt. Her dower lands now passed to the queen, giving her an annual income of £4500.[5] In addition to her dower, the king granted Isabella the county of Ponthieu, the town of Montreuil and fifty marks a week for her household expenses.[6]

Edward and Isabella's first daughter was born at Woodstock in Oxfordshire on 18 June 1318 and named Eleanor after Edward's mother, Eleanor of Castile. The king had been away on pilgrimage to Canterbury in the days leading up to the birth and only arrived at Woodstock on the day Eleanor was born. He gave Isabella 500 marks 'of the king's gift, for the feast of her purification after the birth of Lady Alienora, her daughter'.[7] The baby girl was placed in the household of her oldest brother Edward, along with her brother John of Eltham. In January 1319, while staying in York, King Edward made provision for John and Eleanor, assigning lands to cover their expenses:

> Jan. 16. Commitment during pleasure to Richard Damory and Robert de York. Mauley, steward of the household of Edward, the king's first-born son, and Nicholas de Hugate, keeper of the wardrobe of the same Edward, of the keeping of the castle and honour of the High Peak with the chace and other appurtenances thereof in the counties of Nottingham and Derby to the value of 291*l.* 13*s.* 4*d.*, and of 100*l.* of yearly farm which the abbot and convent of Hayles render at the Exchequer for the manor of Lichelade, co. Gloucester, and of 200*l.* from the issues of the castle, town and barton of Bristol, co. Gloucester, yearly by the hands of the keeper or farmer thereof, and of 31*l.* of yearly farm which the prior and convent of Bernewell render at the Exchequer for the manor of Cestreton, co. Cambridge, and of the manor of Macklesfeld, co. Chester, to the value of 175*l.* 8*s.*, and of the manor of Overton, co. Chester, to the value of 126*l.*, and of the manors of Rosfeyr, Dolpenmayn, Pennaghan and the commote of Meney in North Wales to the value of 170*l.*, all which the king granted at will to his son John and his daughter Eleanor for their sustenance, as is contained in letters patent made thereon; the king wishing that the said John and Eleanor stay in the company of the said Edward and at his expenses, as they have now done for some time; so that the said Richard, Robert and Nicholas answer for the issues in the wardrobe of the said Edward. By K.[8]

Sir Richard Damory had the guardianship of Edward of Windsor, while Sir Geoffrey de Scrope had been appointed, alongside John Stonor, as legal advisers to help in an investigation into negligence by the bailiffs of the prince's county of Chester. Nicholas Hugate was appointed as the prince's treasurer and keeper of his wardrobe.[9] The lands and manors had formerly belonged to the queen, and she relinquished them so that their revenues could be paid to Prince Edward's household to cover the expenses of his younger brother and baby sister. In return, Isabella was given the county of Cornwall by the king. The royal children were established at Wallingford Castle, where Eleanor was to be cared for by a nurse named Joan du Bois.[10] Within days of Eleanor's birth, Queen Isabella was on the move, leaving Woodstock on 27 June to accompany the king to a great council at Northampton, where a rather strange incident occurred. A man, known as John of Powderham, claimed that he was the rightful son of Edward I and that Edward II was an impostor. He asserted that, as a baby, he had been attacked in his cradle by a wild sow and that his nurse, too afraid to tell the king, had swapped the injured baby for a local child. Edward II was amused by the story and considered appointing John as a court jester; he also summoned John's parents from Exeter to ascertain his true background – he was a tanner. The king's nobles were not so amused at the attack on the royal dignity and John was tried and executed sometime between 20 and 24 July 1318.[11]

The king and queen departed for a visit to France in June 1320 but before leaving, Edward II assigned High Peak and the other manors he had given to his two youngest children, back to Queen Isabella. This suggests that John, who was almost 4, and 2-year-old Eleanor had left their big brother's household and joined the household of the queen. Given that the younger Edward was now 8, this makes sense. He was getting too old to be living in a nursery and was old enough to start his military training and education in earnest. Moving into their mother's household did not, of course, mean that the children were constantly in their mother's custody, just that she was the one responsible for their day-to-day management and the provision of clothing, sustenance and staff to care for them. They would have been too young to travel with their parents to France and would have stayed in England, under the supervision of nurses and governors.

A few weeks after her third birthday, Eleanor was joined in the nursery by a sister; Joan was born in the Tower of London on 5 July 1321. She was named for her maternal grandmother Queen Jeanne I of Navarre, wife of Philip IV of France. The king, also in London at the time of Joan's birth, but not at the Tower, granted an £80 respite on a £180 loan to Robert Staunton, the man who brought him 'news of her [Isabella's] delivery of Joan, the king's daughter'.[12] On 8 July, Edward arrived at the Tower of London to visit his wife and newborn daughter and stayed with them for several days. The Tower was in a rather dilapidated state, with holes in the roof. The rain dripped onto Isabella's bed as she was in labour. Furious, Edward dismissed the Constable of the Tower, John Cromwell, from his post. Little Joan was born at a time when her father was facing increasing opposition within the country. Calls for the exile of the hated favourites, the Despensers, father and son, saw an army led by Marcher barons surround the city of London, trapping Edward inside until he acquiesced to their demands. The king refused to accede to the pressure, until Queen Isabella, just weeks after giving birth, went down on her knees before her husband and begged him to send the Despensers away in order to prevent further violence. This act may well have been what finally drove a wedge between the king and queen, as Hugh le Despenser the Younger, on his return from exile a few months later, blamed the queen for persuading the king to send him away.

As the last of the children of Edward II and Isabella, it seems likely that the royal couple's relationship changed shortly after Joan's birth, their marriage heading for an irretrievable breakdown that would see the king deposed in favour of his son. Edward II was well known for having favourites. A few years after Gaveston's sticky end, Isabella's estrangement from her husband followed the rise of the new favourite, Sir Hugh le Despenser the Younger, and, by the time of Joan's birth, his influence on the king was significant and alienating powerful barons at court. In March 1322, those barons were defeated at the Battle of Boroughbridge, in Yorkshire, with many prominent lords killed, including the king's erstwhile brother-in-law Humphrey de Bohun, Earl of Hereford, the man who had been taken prisoner at Bannockburn. The leader of the insurrection, the king's cousin Thomas, Earl of Lancaster, was executed six days later at Pontefract Castle. The king's daughters Eleanor and Joan were, therefore, growing up in the midst of a period of great turmoil, not only within England, but within their own family. It is doubtful that, as they grew, the girls were unaware of the atmosphere, but Isabella and Edward were both loving parents and probably tried to shield their children as much as they could, ensuring stability in their everyday lives. Joan was soon placed in the household of her older siblings, and put into the care of Matilda Pyrie, who had once been nurse to her older brother, John of Eltham.[13]

Sometime before February 1325, Joan and Eleanor were established in their own household, under the supervision of Isabel, Lady Hastings and her husband, Ralph Monthermer. Isabel was the younger sister of Edward II's close companion, Hugh le Despenser the Younger, and this act has often been seen by historians as the king removing the children from the queen's custody. Although it could have been a malicious act, it must be remembered, however, that Ralph Monthermer was the girls' uncle-by-marriage through his first wife, Joan of Acre, Edward II's sister, and it was a custom of the time that aristocratic children were fostered among the wider family. The move may also have been done to ease the financial burden on Isabella.[14] She certainly saw nothing sinister in it at the time and made no objections to the arrangements. There is little extant evidence of Isabella's relationship with her three youngest children, other than the transfer of High Peak to her in 1320 to pay for the children's expenses, and a comment by the Mayor of London in the early months of 1323 stating that 'the queen and her children were dwelling' within the city.[15] Eleanor and Joan remained with Lady Isabel even after Ralph's death in the summer of 1325; however, the following January, they were given into the custody of Joan Jermy, sister-in-law of the king's younger half-brother Thomas, Earl of Norfolk. Joan was the sister of Thomas's wife, Alice Hales, and took charge of the girls' household in January 1326. They lived mainly between Pleshey in Essex and Marlborough in Wiltshire. One of the girls, though it is unclear which, spent some time at Ankerwycke in Buckinghamshire, staying with the prioress.[16]

As a consequence of the war with France, the little-known War of St Sardos, Queen Isabella saw her lands confiscated by the king, with Edward perhaps fearing that she would use her resources to support her brother, rather than her husband. According to the *Lanercost* chronicler, the king took action:

> to resume possession of the lands and rents which he had formerly bestowed upon the queen, and they allowed her only twenty shillings

> a day for herself and her whole court, and they took away from her her officers and body servants, so that the wife of the said Sir Hugh was appointed, as it were, guardian to the queen, and carried her seal; nor could the queen write to anybody without her knowledge; whereat my lady the queen was equally indignant and distressed.[17]

Despenser's wife was Eleanor de Clare, King Edward's niece, so it is questionable whether she was assigned to the queen as a jailor; it may be she was chief of the queen's ladies and acted as a companion and friend. However, it is clear that life in England was becoming increasingly difficult for the queen, due to the war with France. The dispute had arisen over Edward II's refusal to travel to France to pay homage to Charles IV for the counties of Gascony and Ponthieu, which Edward had inherited from his parents, Edward I and Eleanor of Castile, respectively. Charles sent an army into the counties to confiscate them from the English king.

The children, as was the fate of royal offspring through the centuries, were to play a part in their father's diplomatic plans. In an attempt to form an alliance against France in 1324/5, Edward sought marriages in Spain for three of his four children. Edward of Windsor, Edward II's oldest son and heir, was to marry Leonor, the sister of Alfonso XI of Castile. Eleanor was betrothed to Alfonso XI himself, who was seven years older than her. He had succeeded to the Castilian throne before he was a year old. Now 13 and no doubt advised and encouraged by his counsellors, Alfonso declared that he 'desires that his royal house shall be joined to the king's by a treaty of love by way of relationship'.[18] To which Edward II responded that 'The king rejoices greatly that providence has illuminated abundantly the boldness of Alfonsus's youth by gifts of virtues and natural and gracious good things, as widely diffused fame has made known and is as now spread to the ends of the world'.[19] Even Joan was not exempt, she was proposed as the bride for the grandson of James II of Aragon – the future Pedro IV. King Edward sent envoys to discuss the 'espousals ... of the king's daughter Joan with the first-born of Alfonso the eldest son of James king of Aragon, and the future heir of Aragon'.[20] The little prince was only two years older than Joan. All these plans would come to nought due to the king's deposition in 1327.[21]

On 9 March 1325, Queen Isabella departed England for France, to negotiate a peace settlement with her brother and bring an end to the War of St Sardos. Once at her brother's court, Queen Isabella:

> astutely contrived that Edward, her elder son and heir of England, should cross over to his uncle, the King of France, on the plea that if he came and did homage to his uncle for Gascony and the other lands of the king beyond the sea, the King [of France] would transfer to him all these lands from the King [of England]; and he [Prince Edward] was made Duke of Aquitaine.[22]

Passing French lands into the hands of the eldest son was an established tactic of English kings, in order to avoid paying homage to the king of France and therefore appearing subservient or inferior to their fellow sovereign. By 1326, the queen, Isabella, was living at the French court, along with her eldest son, Edward, refusing to return to her husband whilst he still welcomed Hugh le Despenser at his court. That summer, Isabella and her ally (and possibly her lover), Roger Mortimer, were to invade England and drive Edward II from his throne, putting an end to the proposed Spanish marriages. The king, captured and imprisoned in Berkeley Castle, was forced to abdicate in favour of his eldest son, who was proclaimed King Edward III.

We do not know when Isabella was reunited with her daughters. Worried about John of Eltham residing in temperamental London at the time of her invasion, she sent eight men-at-arms to ensure his safety and escort him to her in October 1326. Froissart suggests that Isabella was reunited with Eleanor and Joan at Bristol. However, he also claims that they were in the care of the Earl of Winchester or his daughter, Isabel Hastings, at the time when they had actually been living at Marlborough with Joan Jermy.[23] The following year, on 26 January 1327, the day after he had been proclaimed king, Eleanor and Joan joined their mother, Mortimer and the rest of the court in York Minster to witness the wedding of King Edward III and Philippa of Hainault. The king's sisters would have sat with their new sister-in-law – their new queen – to watch Edward participate in the celebratory jousts. It would have been a time of great rejoicing for the family, though the children may have felt the absence of their father.

On the deposition of Edward II, relations with Scotland became fractious. The teenage Edward III marched north and narrowly escaped getting captured or killed when the redoubtable Sir James Douglas raided his camp one night, before returning to Scotland. Once the king of England had returned south, the Scots crossed the border again and continued to harry parts of Northumberland, so 'ambassadors were appointed between the kingdoms of England and Scotland to arrange a temporary truce or confirm the former truce for thirteen years, or to come to any treaty for a perpetual peace if that could be done'.[24] With the advice of his mother and Roger Mortimer, the effective rulers of England, Edward 'was forced to release the Scots by his public deed from all exaction, right, claim or demand of the overlordship of the kingdom of Scotland on his part, or that of his heirs and successors in perpetuity, and from any homage to be done to the Kings of England'.[25] This would rankle with King Edward. By the 1328 Treaty of Northampton, it was agreed that:

> the aforesaid young king gave his younger sister, my lady Joan of the Tower, in marriage to David, son of Robert de Brus, King of Scotland, he being then a boy five years old. All this was arranged by

> the king's mother the Queen [dowager] of England, who at that time governed the whole realm. The nuptials were solemnly celebrated at Berwick on Sunday next before the feast of S. Mary Magdalene.[26]

With her father exiled or murdered (his fate remains a bone of contention to this day), Joan became the central part of another plan – that of peace with Scotland. The 7-year-old princess was to marry Robert the Bruce's only son and heir, 4-year-old David Bruce. The treaty provided that King Edward would supply an alternative bride, if Joan were to die before the wedding. Conversely, were David to die, Joan would marry King Robert's next heir instead – this would be the king's grandson and namesake, Robert Stewart.[27] There is no reference to the provision of a dowry in the treaty, but the Scots agreed to settle lands to the value of £2000 on Joan.[28] The English were so fearful that the Scots would renege on the agreement, given that the marriage could be repudiated any time before David's fourteenth birthday, that they stipulated that King Robert would pay a fine of £100,000 if the marriage ceremony did not take place before Michaelmas 1338.[29]

The treaty gave recognition to Scotland as an independent kingdom and agreed to the return of a number of items, precious to the Scots, that had been taken by the English in the recent wars. These included the Black Rood (a portion of the Holy Cross), the Ragman Roll (a document showing the individual acts of homage by the Scottish nobility to Edward I) and the Stone of Scone (the traditional stone on which Scotland's kings were crowned, and which had sat in Westminster Abbey since being brought south by Edward I). The people of London, however, 'would no wise allow to be taken away from them the Stone of Scone, whereon the Kings of Scotland used to be set at their coronation at Scone'.[30] The stone was only returned to Scotland in 1996. In return, King Robert was to make a payment of 30,000 marks in reparations for damages recently inflicted by the Scots.[31] The 1328 Treaty of Northampton was seen as a major humiliation by Edward III – and the 16-year-old king made sure his displeasure was known. However, he was obliged to sign it.

Although the Stone of Scone and Ragman Roll were not returned to Scotland, the marriage between Joan and David did go ahead, with a proviso that, should the marriage not be completed within two months of David reaching his fourteenth birthday, the treaty would be declared invalid. Neither king was present at the wedding celebrations. Wholly opposed to the marriage, Edward III refused to attend. Robert the Bruce stayed away also, claiming illness; the *Lanercost* chronicler claims that King Robert 'had become leprous'.[32] The children were married at Berwick-upon-Tweed on 17 July 1328, 'to the unspeakable joy of the people of either kingdom'.[33] Although the king was not present, 'the queen mother was there, with the king's brother and his older Sister and my lords the Bishops of Lincoln, Ely and Norwich, and the Earl of Warenne, Sir Roger de Mortimer and other English barons, and much people, besides those of Scotland, who assembled in great numbers at those nuptials'.[34] Despite the absence of the two kings, the wedding was a lavish occasion, costing the Scots king over £2500. In his *Scotichronicon*, Walter Bower described the wedding as 'an occasion of unutterable joy among all the people of both kingdoms'.[35]

Following the wedding, and nicknamed Joan Makepeace by the Scots, Joan was taken to Scotland to be raised alongside her child-groom. Her first stop was Cardross, where she and David stayed with King Robert for a short time. The little princess had been accompanied by a number of English ladies, most of whom returned to England at this point. Everything was to change for the two children the following year, when 'On the 7th of June 1329, died Robert of Bruce, of goodly memory, the illustrious king of Scots, at Cardross, in the twenty-fourth year of his reign. He was, beyond all living men of his day, a valiant knight'.[36] David Bruce, at the tender age of 5, was now King David II, and Joan was his queen. Joan and David attained the dubious record of being the youngest married monarchs in British history. They were crowned, jointly, at Scone Abbey in Perthshire, on 24 November 1331. David was the first Scottish monarch to have a coronation which included the anointing with holy oil, thanks to a bull of John XXII granted on 13 June 1329, something David's predecessors, Alexander II and Alexander III, had both argued for, but been denied:

> On the 24th of November 1331, David, son and heir of King Robert, was anointed king of Scots, and crowned at Scone, by the lord James Ben, bishop of Saint Andrews, specially appointed thereunto by a Bull of the most holy father John xxii., then sovereign Pontiff. We do not read that any of the kings of Scotland, before this David, were anointed, or with such solemnity crowned. The same day, John Stewart, Earl of Angus – Thomas Randolph, son and heir of Thomas Earl of Moray – and other nobles of the kingdom of Scotland, received the order of knighthood.[37]

It was also the first time a Scottish queen consort was crowned: 'In the same year and on the same day Joan of the Tower was crowned queen'.[38] Virtually nothing is known of Joan's early years in Scotland. We can assume she continued her education and maybe spent some time getting to know her husband, as the country was ruled by a series of guardians. Scotland, however, was in turmoil and Edward III was not about to let his sister's marriage get in the way of his own ambitions for the country. Unfortunately for Joan, Edward Balliol, son of the erstwhile king, John Balliol and his wife Isabella de Warenne, had a strong claim to the crown and was, as opposed to her young husband, a grown man with the backing of Edward III. He was crowned at Scone in September 1332. There then followed a tug-of-war for Scotland's crown, lasting many years. Edward Balliol had even proposed to King

Edward that Joan's marriage could be annulled, given the couple were still too young to consummate it, and that Balliol himself could marry Joan. Balliol must have been in his fifties by that time, and Joan was 10 years old. Luckily, nothing came of the suggestion. The war turned against David when his supporters suffered a heavy defeat at Halidon Hill in July 1333. The little king and queen had been staying in the relative safety of Dumbarton Castle, one of the few Scottish castles not in the possession of the English.

Ten months after the defeat at Halidon Hill, with the situation still precarious, Joan and:

> King David de Bruce, then a nine-year old boy, who was not strong enough to take revenge on his enemies, being only a child, retired to the kingdom of France with Rankin More and the queen under the supervision of his foster-father Sir Malcolm Fleming the keeper of Dumbarton, after the kingdom of Scotland had been put under Sir Andrew Moray as governor; and he was honourably received by the king and people of France.[39]

The departure of the King of Scots affected the morale of the forces he was leaving behind, but what choice did his guardians have? Exile in France was the better alternative to capture by the English.

Meanwhile, after attending the wedding of her younger sister, 10-year-old Eleanor of Woodstock returned south with Isabella. Instead of joining her mother's household, however, Eleanor had been placed in that of her new sister-in-law, Queen Philippa.[40] With the king and Joan already married, thoughts now turned to Eleanor's future. In 1329, discussions were underway for a marriage between Eleanor and John of France, the future King John II, son of Philip VI, which had first been suggested five years earlier; it was also proposed that John of Eltham would marry Philip's daughter Joan. Nothing came of the idea and in the following year, Eleanor's prospective bridegroom was Pedro, son of Alfonso IV of Aragon, which also came to nought. As negotiations proceeded, Eleanor enjoyed court life. In July 1330, she received a gift of elaborate Turkish clothes for the summer season, along with her mother and Queen Philippa.[41] Philippa had recently given birth to her first child, a son named Edward for his father and grandfather, and the court was in a festive mood. Later that year, at Nottingham, Edward III initiated a coup, overthrowing his mother, Queen Isabella and her ally Roger Mortimer, who had taken over the government of the kingdom after deposing Edward II. With a son and heir in the cradle and having just turned 18, Edward III was at last in command of his kingdom.

Sometime in the early 1330s, a petition was made to the king's council, requesting additional funds for the queen, and pointing out that the income assigned to her did not cover her expenses. The petition specified that the queen could not afford to buy food and clothes for herself and her household for the coming Christmas court, including for her sister-in-law, who is referred to as '*madame dame Elianore*'.[42] As a result of her pleas, the queen was given fifty pounds for Eleanor's expenses and granted the income of the county of Chester to support the households of her son and Eleanor.[43] The summer of 1331 saw a round of jousting tournaments across the south of England, during a visit of Philippa's mother, sister Johanna and her husband Wilhelm. At Cheapside, in the procession before the tournament, each knight led out a noble lady wearing a red tunic and white cap, led out by a silver chain. The king led out Eleanor, who had recently turned 13. The knights were masked and wore red velvet tunics with white hoods, the colours of Edward's personal saint, Saint George. They were dressed as Tartars. Each knight and lady, with her silver chain, rode down Cheapside, through cheering crowds, as the sun was going down.[44] It must have been quite the spectacle, and a memorable experience for the princess. It was even more memorable when the grandstand, holding the queen and her ladies, collapsed on the first day of the tournament. Philippa and Eleanor, luckily, escaped unharmed, though the queen's coronet fell from her head. Although others suffered injuries, there were no fatalities. A furious Edward was ready to hang the carpenters who had built the stand, until the queen intervened on their behalf and calmed the king.

In 1331, Eleanor's former nurse was awarded a pension of 30*l* a year as she was dismissed from the princess's service, no longer being needed.[45] Christmas that year was spent at court with her brothers and sister-in-law; the king gave both Eleanor and their brother, John of Eltham, a gold cup each as a new-year's gift.[46] And it was in early 1332 that the king appointed ambassadors, including the Bishop of Winchester, 'to treat for a marriage between the count of Gerle [Guelders] and Eleanor, the king's sister.'[47] Reynald II, Count of Guelders was a widower, of about 40 years of age, with four daughters. Eleanor was three weeks short of her fourteenth birthday when she married Reynald in the last week of May 1332. It had always been intended for Eleanor to marry the heir to a kingdom but plans for such unions with France and Spain had fallen through. In February 1332, Edward had agreed Eleanor's marriage to the Count of Guelders, a territory in today's Netherlands and close to the German border. The marriage was born out of a need for Reynald to form an alliance that would protect Guelders from France. The financial arrangements included Reynald assigning his bride lands to the value of 16,000 *livres Tournois* a year, to be enjoyed for life. The lands were to be placed in the hands of John of Shoreditch, Eleanor's procurator, within two months after her marriage. In addition, Edward was to provide his sister with 10,000*l*. sterling, 5000*l*. to be paid at the time of the marriage, and the remaining 5000*l*. to be paid in June of the following year.[48]

Eleanor was sent to her new life with 'a mantle cloak, and a hood of blue Brussels cloth furred with ermine, two pelisses, of green cloth worked with golden beads, a surtunic of cloth of gold, embroidered with the representation of a chase of hares and stags, a coronal composed of 260 large white pearls, another of 420 pieces of silver, and several zones [belts] wrought with pearls, silk and gold'.[49] Her bridal gown was a robe of Spanish cloth of gold, embroidered with silks of different colours, with a tunic and mantle of rich crimson velvet, embroidered with gold.[50] Her bridal bedding was of green velvet, embroidered in gold with the arms of England and Guelders, with curtains of silk from Tripoli and a coverlet embroidered with a hunting scene.[51] She was also supplied with a new chariot, horses, furniture for her hall and chapel, carpets, curtains, silver plate, dishes and a large quantity of spices. Everything was done to ensure that she was shown off as the eldest daughter of a king of England. Eleanor left England in early May and was accompanied by a large retinue, including her first cousins, the de Bohun twins, Edward and William, Eleanor Despenser, daughter of her aunt Joan of Acre and Queen Philippa's squire, Pamettus de Recte. Arriving at the port of Sluis on 6 May, she then travelled on to Nijmegen, where she and Count Reynald were married. Eleanor, not yet 15, gave birth to her first child, a son named Reynald, the following year. Another son, named Edward after her father, was born three years later.[52]

In 1338 there was a happy reunion when Edward and Philippa were staying in Antwerp; Eleanor and Reynald visited them there. Following the birth of their second son, however, the marriage came under strain. The count fell increasingly under the influence of his chaplain, Jan Moliart, who was also his chief adviser and chancellor. One chronicler suggests that Moliart had complete control over Reynald. He was accused of isolating the count and keeping him away from his wife, and of spreading rumours that Eleanor was suffering from leprosy. Moliart even looked into the possibility of repudiating the marriage. Banished from court, Eleanor lived in Rosendael Castle, probably with her youngest son, though whether or not she had custody of her oldest son is unknown. Incensed at her treatment, and the accusation of leprosy, Eleanor presented herself in front of her husband and his council, taking off enough of her clothing to prove that she was not afflicted with the dreaded disease.[53]

Afterwards, she established an independent household at Veluwe. She became a duchess in 1339, when Guelders was elevated to a dukedom in gratitude for Reynald's support of Emperor Louis IV in a power struggle in the German Empire. Four years later, Eleanor was widowed when Duke Reynald died, either from a riding accident in Arnhem or from falling off his chair and breaking his neck during Mass – reports differ. It had been an unhappy marriage, but Eleanor's widowhood would bring her even less joy. She acted as regent for her 10-year-old son, Reynald III, Duke of Guelders, but it was only a year later that the young duke declared that he had reached his majority. Mother and son were later estranged after Eleanor tried to reconcile him with his younger brother, Edward. During her regency, she did manage to have Moliart arrested and tried, testifying against him and again proving that she did not suffer from leprosy. Moliart was convicted and imprisoned. Retiring from public life, Eleanor used the title Lady of Veluwe, after the area she had been given as a widow's estate. She became a patron of various monastic communities favouring the Order of St. Clare. She eventually retired to Deventer Abbey, and when she died there in 1355, aged 36, Eleanor was buried in its church, Broederenkerk, which she herself had founded.[54] She did not live to see her younger son Edward depose and imprison his older brother in 1361. Reynald III was only released and restored to the title on Edward's death in 1371; his confinement must have been comfortable as he was said to have grown so corpulent that a wall had to be removed for him to exit his prison. He ruled for just a few months more before dying in December 1371. Neither Reynald nor Edward had a legitimate son to succeed him.

As Eleanor had endured a miserable marriage, her younger sister Joan's relationship with her husband was no less strained, and not helped by the animosity of their brother, Edward III. An ally of Scotland and first cousin of Joan's mother, Philip VI of France had given the king and queen, and their Scottish attendants, accommodation in the famous Château Gaillard, built by Richard the Lionheart, in Normandy. Although very little is known of Joan's time in France, David was involved in the failed negotiations between Edward III and Philip VI in 1335 and 1336, which were aimed at resolving the respective claims to the Scottish throne, of David and Edward Balliol. David is also thought to have accompanied the French king on campaigns in Picardy in 1339 and at Tournai in 1340.[55] Joan would have still been living in France when she heard of the demise of her older brother, John of Eltham, who had just turned 20 the month before his death in September 1336. John had been serving as one of Edward III's commanders in Scotland when he fell ill. It cannot have been an easy time for Joan, far away from family, with her brother fighting to dispossess her husband and, by extension, her. In 1341, it was finally deemed safe enough for the royal couple to return home and they arrived in Scotland on 2 June, where David and Joan were greeted with widespread rejoicing as 'all Scots were delighted beyond belief at his arrival, and held feasts with joy and dancing'.[56] The celebrations proved to be short-lived.

Scotland was still caught up in the dynastic wranglings of England and France as the Hundred Years' War gained momentum. The French asked for help in their conflict with the English, invoking David's obligations under the treaty of Corbeil, whereby, in return for French support, the Scots king had promised to invade England whenever the French king required it. David led his forces south into England. He fought valiantly in the disastrous battle at Neville's Cross on 17 October 1346, suffered a serious arrow wound to his face and was captured by the English; he was escorted to a captivity in England that would last for the next eleven years, save for a short return to Scotland in 1351–52. He had been released after reaching agreement with the English that should he fail to produce an heir, the Scottish crown would pass to a son of Edward III. As his heir presumptive, his nephew Robert Stewart, who had ruled Scotland in David's absence, had been outraged by the idea. The Scots parliament rejected the proposal and David, threatened with war by the English, was forced to return to captivity. Joan and David's marriage had proved to be an unhappy, loveless and childless union and, while a safe conduct was issued for Joan to visit her husband at Windsor for the St George's Day celebrations of 1348, there is no evidence that she took advantage of it. Although we know little of Joan's movements, it seems she remained in Scotland at least some of the time, possibly held as a hostage to David's safety by his Scottish allies.

As queen, Joan undertook her traditional duties of patronage, particularly with men of the Church. There are numerous examples, during 1349 and 1350, of the queen of Scots exercising her support of various clerics. On 4 June 1350, from Avignon, the Pope granted to, 'Joan, queen of Scotland, and William, bishop of Aberdeen. On behalf of William Boyl the bishop's nephew, scholar of civil law, for a dignity or office in the church of Aberdeen; notwithstanding that he has the vicarage of Samery, in the same diocese'.[57] And in the same year Alexander Bur, licentiate in civil law, received 'confirmation of the papal provision made to him, at the instance of the king and queen of Scots, of the canonry, prebend, and archdeaconry of Moray, now void by the death of Adam Perry; or for provision to him anew of the same'.[58] The queen also sought benefices for her secretary and her clerk, as well as the king's chaplain and almoner and the nephew of the Bishop of Moray.

It is highly likely that Joan visited David during his captivity in England, taking it as an opportunity to visit with her own family, including her mother. Queen Isabella is said to have supported Joan financially while her husband was imprisoned, feeding and clothing her. Joan does not appear to have taken an active role in the negotiations for David's release, despite her close familial ties to the English court:

> In the year 1357, about Michaelmas, King David of Scotland was released from prison, after having been, for twelve years, kept in close confinement in sundry places in England. There were given, for his ransom, 100,000 merks sterling, to be honestly paid within the ten years immediately following, without any treaty, dismemberment or subjection of the kingdom, or any exaction whatsoever. As security that the whole of this money would be paid to the king of England, the sons and heirs of nearly all the nobles and lords of the kingdom of Scotland were given, as hostages, into the hands of the English.[59]

When King David did return to Scotland in 1357, he was not alone. He brought his lover, Katherine Mortimer, with him. They had met in England, and it was said 'the king loved her more than all other women, and on her account the queen was entirely neglected while he embraced his mistress'.[60] Katherine exerted much influence over King David, infuriating the Scottish barons and in the summer of 1360, she met a grisly fate when she was stabbed to death on the road near Soutra, by men said to be in the service of the Earl of Angus.[61] David's association with Katherine appears to have sundered altogether his relationship with his queen. As David returned to Scotland in 1357, Queen Joan travelled south, receiving a safe conduct that Christmas from her brother, Edward III 'on business touching us and David' and again in May 1358 'by our licence for certain causes'.[62] Although the licences are understandably vague on the matter, Joan had, in fact, left David and Scotland: 'In 1357 the Lady Joan of the Tower queen of Scotland and sister of Edward de Windsor king of England made for England after seeking permission from King David her husband; and after spending a little time there as a pilgrim she died'.[63] Joan spent the rest of her life in England, living on a pension of £200 a year provided by her brother. The pension was paid quarterly and on 9 October 1359, it was paid 'To Johanna Queen of Scotland, by John Dodelle's hands, the quarter due her at Michaelmas of the 200*l*. a year granted her by the K. during her stay in England – 50*l*'.[64] Joan renewed family connections and was able to visit her mother and spend time with her, and nurse the dowager queen until Isabella's death in August 1358.

Although her health was failing, Queen Isabella was able to attend the great tournament, hosted by King Edward III at Windsor, for which Joan had travelled south from Scotland. It was part of a series of festivities following the return of the Black Prince from campaigning in France, with John, king of France, the prince's prisoner since his capture at the Battle of Poitiers in 1356. Held at Windsor on St George's Day, the tournament attracted nobility from Gascony, Germany, Hainault and France and was followed a few days later by the signing of the Treaty of London, between England and France. Despite their estrangement, as queen of Scotland, Joan occasionally acted on her husband's behalf. In February 1359, David acknowledged her assistance in the respite of ransom payments granted by Edward III, saying it was 'at the great and diligent request and instance of our dear companion the Lady Joan his sister'.[65]

Little is known of Joan's appearance or personality. Several years after her death she was described as 'sweet and debonaire, curtious, homely, pleasant and fair' by the chronicler Andrew of Wyntoun, although this description is standard fare for the time.[66] Having endured an unhappy marriage and having led an adventurous life, through no choice of her own, Joan of the Tower, Queen of Scots, died at the age of 41 on 7 September 1362, and was buried in the Church of the Greyfriars, Newgate, in London, where her mother had been laid to rest just four years earlier. Payments were made 'To Gilbert Prince painter of London, by his own hands for banners and other things bought from him for the exsequies of Johanna, late Queen of Scotland, as appears by bill of the late keeper of the wardrobe – 24*l*'.[67] A further payment is made when 'On 16th February following Peter of Preston of Scotland, is repaid 13 marks laid out by him in jewels bought for Johanna, late Queen of Scotland'.[68]

Joan of the Tower had been Queen of Scots for thirty-three years. She had never borne a child, nor is there any mention of her ever having become pregnant. So, on her death, David II was still without an heir of his own, other than Robert Stewart, the nephew he despised, who had six legitimate sons by 1362. Despite a second marriage to Margaret Drummond, David II died childless and was succeeded by his nephew as king Robert II. It is a sad testimony to the fate of princesses that both Joan and her older sister Eleanor endured unhappy marriages. Joan's was no doubt made worse by the animosity of her brother, while Eleanor's relationship with her husband was soured by his increasing reliance on an influential counsellor who actively worked to undermine the marriage. Both sisters had survived the misery of their parents' marriage only to find little comfort in their own husbands. At least Edward III had fared better in his relationship with Philippa of Hainault, finding both a lover and a partner.

Chapter Four

Precious Daughters

Edward III is arguably one of England's greatest medieval kings, reigning for fifty years. He started the Hundred Years' War with France and achieved some of its greatest successes and most famous victories, including Crécy and Poitiers. His marriage to Philippa of Hainault was a success, both personally and politically. They filled the nursery with boys and girls, princes and princesses, enough of each to guarantee the succession and make international alliances. Born Edward of Windsor in 1312, he was the oldest child of Edward II and Isabella of France. His birth, on 12 November, was announced to the city of London by his mother, the news greeted with great celebrations.[1] When the young prince was baptised four days later, the French delegation asked that he be named Philip, after the queen's father, but Edward II insisted that he be called Edward, after his own father, Edward I. He was established in his own household shortly after his birth and was given the county of Chester to support him financially. He was styled Earl of Chester from his infancy but was never named Prince of Wales or Earl of Cornwall, the titles that would later be associated with the heir to the throne. For four years, he was his parents' only child, until the arrival of John of Eltham in 1316. Of his sisters, Eleanor of Woodstock was born in 1318 and Joan of the Tower in 1321.

Edward's childhood had been overshadowed by the declining situation in England, caused by his father's over-reliance on favourites, and the abuses of one such favourite, Hugh le Despenser the Younger. This, in turn, caused a deterioration in the relationship between his parents, and the eventual departure of his mother to France. In March 1325, Isabella visited her homeland, ostensibly to negotiate a peace settlement with her brother, King Charles IV. Whilst there, it was agreed that Prince Edward should visit the French court, to pay homage to his uncle as Duke of Aquitaine and Count of Ponthieu, with which his father had just invested him. This was an old habit of English kings, passing on their French lands to their son, in order to avoid that awkward situation of the king of England having to acknowledge the king of France as his liege lord for his French lands. Once she had her son in her custody, Isabella refused to return to England and allied with Roger Mortimer, Earl of March, who had escaped from imprisonment in the Tower of London and fled to France. Isabella also refused to send her son back to England

and instead visited Hainault, where she negotiated Edward's marriage with Philippa, daughter of William, Count of Hainault, using the girl's accompanying dowry to buy mercenaries.

There were attempts to find a peaceful resolution, but they failed. Isabella refused to return to England if Despenser was still with her husband and Edward refused to send Despenser away. In September 1326, Isabella and Edward, with Mortimer and the English exiles, and about 1000 men, landed on the Norfolk coast. Their forces marched across the country to Oxford, meeting with little resistance. Once there, it was announced that Isabella intended to end the mismanagement of the realm. Moving onto Wallingford, she issued a proclamation on 15 October denouncing Despenser and his father, Hugh le Despenser the Elder. London rose in support on the same day, marking the collapse of Edward II's government. The king fled into Wales, and it was deemed that he had abandoned his kingdom. As a consequence, his son was proclaimed Keeper of the Realm at Bristol on 26 October. Edward II was then captured and forced to hand over the great seal before being sent to imprisonment at Berkeley Castle. The great seal was the key instrument of government and allowed Queen Isabella to call a parliament at which it was announced that Edward II had resigned his throne in favour of his son and Edward III was proclaimed king on 24 January 1327. He was crowned at Westminster Abbey on 1 February, by Walter Reynolds, Archbishop of Canterbury.[2]

The fate of Edward's father is hotly debated. He was either murdered at Berkeley Castle – although the official account says he died of natural causes – or was taken abroad and given into the custody of the papacy. Another scenario is supported by the famous Fieschi Letter, which reports that Edward escaped imprisonment and travelled throughout Europe. Edward met with a man claiming to be Edward II in Cologne in 1138; William le Galeys (William the Welshman) spent several weeks in the king's company. It is certainly an intriguing mystery.

Edward III was just 14 years old when he was crowned, and for the next three years was king in name only. The government of the kingdom was firmly held by his mother, and her ally and, most likely lover, Roger Mortimer. In between an expensive peace with France, which cost England £60,000 and a humiliating treaty with Scotland, in which Edward was forced to renounce his claim of overlordship of Scotland, and all the English had gained since the reign of Edward I, there was a happy occasion. Edward was married to Philippa of Hainault at York in January 1328.[3] The young couple were ideally suited in temperament and age; Philippa was perhaps eighteen months Edward's junior. She had a sense of humour, a love of romances and a sympathetic understanding of people. As a wedding gift, she gave Edward a collection of illuminated texts that would be inspirational for a young king, including the *Book of Julius Caesar* and the *Government of Kings*, in addition to a book of statues and one of music, with an illuminated picture of Edward holding a falcon.[4]

Edward had also had his first taste of military action in 1327, when he led an army into northern England against the incursions of the Scots. Having spent some weeks chasing after the Scots army, led by Sir James Douglas, the young king was very nearly captured when Douglas launched a nighttime raid on his quarters in Stanhope Park, before slipping away north.[5] The Treaty of Northampton was signed the following year. Edward not only had to renounce his overlordship of Scotland, but his sister, Joan, was betrothed to Robert the Bruce's only surviving son, David. The two children were married at Berwick in July 1328.

In the meantime, opposition to the rule of Isabella and Mortimer was gaining ground as they were proving to be just as rapacious as Edward II's favourites had been. Henry of Lancaster and the king's two uncles, the earls of Norfolk and Kent, were vocal in their criticism of the regime and it was only the intervention of the Archbishop of Canterbury that averted civil war. Acting to remove his enemies, Mortimer accused Edmund, Earl of Kent, of treason, after he attempted to free his brother, the former king, whom he believed was still alive. Kent was executed in March 1330. That October, a month shy of his eighteenth birthday, Edward instigated a palace coup whilst he and the court were staying at Nottingham Castle. Isabella and Mortimer were arrested, with the dowager queen being kept under guard for a time; she was later allowed to retire to Castle Rising in Norfolk, returning to court on occasion. Mortimer was not so lucky and suffered the traitor's death of hanging, drawing and quartering at Tyburn in London.[6]

By the time of his coup, Edward and Philippa already had a baby in the cradle, a boy named Edward – the future Black Prince – had been born in June. And, as Edward III was establishing himself as king, and restarting the war with Scotland, the little prince was joined in the nursery by a sister, born the day after his second birthday. Isabella of Woodstock is, to some extent, an exception to the traditional model of the dutiful princess. She appears to have been very close to her parents and spent most of her life at the English court. The eldest daughter and second child of Edward III and his queen, Philippa of Hainault, Isabella was born on 16 June 1332 at the royal palace of Woodstock. The queen had originally planned to have her confinement at the palace of Clarendon, which had been prepared for the event but appears to have changed her mind and moved to Woodstock.[7]

The princess was born into luxury. She had two cradles, one of which, the great cradle, was for state occasions. It was 'lined with taffeta, profusely gilded, and decorated with the arms of England and Hainault, and furnished, in spite of the summer warmth, with a coverlet composed of 670 skins'.[8] A tailor named John Bromley was appointed to her service before she was even a month old. It was in his creation of 'a rich robe of Lucca silk, with four rows of "garnitures", and edged with costly furs' that Isabella was dressed when she made her first public appearance, at the 'relevailles' or 'uprising' of the queen, when the baby was presented to the court.[9] Philippa's state bed hangings were decorated with birds and beasts and the arms of England and Hainault.[10] The queen's churching, on 19 July, the month following the princess's birth, was lavish indeed, with the church decorated in purple silk which was embroidered with birds, beasts, baboons and snakes. The church celebrations were followed by a grand tournament and a day of feasting, costing more than £292.[11] Isabella was then placed in the custody of Elizabeth de St Omer, who was already responsible for the care of Prince Edward. She and her husband were paid 25*l.* a year for the care of the royal children.[12] A damsel by the name of Joanna Gaunbun was employed as Isabella's rocker. She was given a pallet bed so she could sleep next to the baby, and paid 10*l.* a year. A similar amount was paid to Joanna Pyebrook, another maid in the princess's service. Both were to remain with Isabella for many years.[13]

In late 1333 or the early months of 1334, another princess had joined the royal nursery. She was known both as Joan, or Joanna, of the Tower and Joan of Woodstock, obscuring her place of birth but narrowing it down to the palace of Woodstock or the Tower of London, although the fact the queen's churching following the birth took place at Woodstock between 8 and 10 March suggests it was the former.[14] Joan was placed under the supervision of the widowed Mary de St Pol, Countess of Pembroke, a lady of learning who founded Pembroke College, Cambridge. The countess was assisted by Isabella de la Motte, a Frenchwoman whose lands in England had been confiscated as a consequence of the war.[15] By 6 March 1334, the children were 'dwelling' with the queen and she was given permission to 'order the household of the said earl [of Chester, her son Edward], Isabella and Joan at her will'.[16] The royal household, including the children, moved to York Castle for the summer to be closer to the king as he prosecuted his war against Scotland.

Even as her little sister joined the nursery, King Edward was contemplating his oldest daughter's future. In June 1335, he was considering a marriage alliance with Spain, with Isabella proposed as a bride to the heir to the Castilian throne. Further marriage proposals included the king's brother, John, for Mary, daughter of the lord of Coucy and 5-year-old Prince Edward with a daughter of the king of France, though worsening relations between the two countries ended that possibility. In fact, nothing came of any of these marriage plans but it does show that Edward was considering his children's futures and their value in marriage alliances.[17] Not yet six months old, little Joan escaped her father's marriage plans, but even before her second birthday, Edward was contemplating Joan's future. Arrangements were made for the little princess to marry Frederick, the eldest son of Otto, Duke of Austria, who was six years older than her. The king even agreed to send Joan to be educated at the Austrian court, though he delayed for a time, saying that he wanted to wait until he could escort his daughter himself.

Edward and Philippa had a large family, with at least twelve children (possibly more), of whom nine survived infancy. Philippa and Edward maintained close relationships with all their children throughout their lives. A second son, William of Hatfield, was born near Doncaster during the Christmas season of 1336 but lived only a matter of days or weeks, dying before 3 March 1337. He was buried in York Minster. It was the second loss for Edward in 6 months, with his brother John of Eltham having died in September 1336, aged only 20.

The children were maintained in some style in their household – they were supplied with their own plate and jewels, and provisions for their chapel, including priestly vestments and linen, and their own chaplain. New clothes were provided at every church festival (Christmas, Easter, Whitsuntide, etc), with robes of scarlet and grey cloth, trimmed with fur, and ornamented with buttons of gold or silver thread. There is a tale of the princesses' tailor having miscalculated their measurements and their dresses being too small for them as a result.[18] The king and queen maintained a close relationship with their surviving children and often travelled with them. When Edward left England in July 1338, Philippa and their daughters accompanied him. Isabella was 6 years old, and Joan was 4; each was given a pair of decorated silver basins by their father, in the days before they set sail.[19] And 'a certain pallet was provided for the Lady Joanna, the king's daughter, on her passage to foreign parts in a ship'.[20] The king wrote to Duke Otto of Austria, saying that he was bringing Isabella with him, which may be a scribal error, or an indication that Edward had changed his mind as to which of his daughters would marry Frederick of Austria; he does appear to have had a habit of changing his mind as to which of his two eldest daughters would marry whom – the same would happen in negotiations with both Castile and Flanders.[21]

Prince Edward, Duke of Cornwall, now 8 years old, was to remain in England as regent, though with capable officers around him to govern. The two girls were with their mother in Antwerp when the house in which they were staying caught fire during the night. The royal family had to seek shelter in the nearby abbey of St Bernard, the king and queen dressed only in their night clothes. It must have been a terrifying experience for the little girls, awakened from their slumber and forced to flee from the flames. Much happier events also happened while the family were staying in Antwerp; they were visited by the king's sister, Eleanor of Woodstock, and her husband, Raynald II of Guelders.[22] And whilst staying at the abbey of St Michael in Antwerp, the princesses welcomed their baby brother, Lionel, who was born in November 1338. Another brother, John, was born in Ghent, and thereafter known as John of Gaunt, in February or March 1340. It was in that same year that Isabella and Joan were sent back to England, with their baby brothers, making landfall on 5 August and lodged together in the Tower of London, possibly amid fears that they were potential kidnap targets for the French. Their travelling expenses for the journey are recorded as 57*l.* 14*s.* 2*d.*[23] The king and queen set up a single household for the four younger children, Isabella, Joan, Lionel and John, under the overall supervision of Isabella de la Motte, who had served in Joan's household for many years.

The wardrobe accounts of this time record the frequency by which the two princesses sent letters to their parents. Other recorded payments include a payment made by Isabella and Joan, in person, 'To John the bargeman, and his companion mariners, rowing in their boats the Ladies Isabella and Joanna, with their attendants, across the Thames, and leading them into the gardens, by their gift, with their own hands, September 17th 12*s*'.[24] They also gave a monetary gift to the valet of the Earl of Arundel, who had delivered the earl's gift of four 'beasts of chase'.[25] Entries also include coins for the girls to make as offerings to the Church and 'To Gerard de Gay, the minstrel of the king's children, in money given to him by them, and also for a winter coat, given him by their own hands, November 6*s*. 8*d*'.[26] Isabella also gave a winter coat to her valet, who would lead her horse when she travelled between London and Westminster. They gave winter shoes to many of their staff and helped to pay for the funeral of one of their kitchen staff.[27] The girls also received two young hares, as a parting gift from the Bishop of Carlisle after his stay.[28]

Such financial records can be tedious to read but give us an insight into the lives of the two young princesses. They were entertained by their own minstrel, were familiar with hunting, went for pony rides through London and entertained such distinguished guests as the Bishop of Carlisle. The girls also cared for those assigned to care for them, providing warm clothing, shoes and financial assistance. That they rode between London and Westminster, or crossed the river Thames by boat to visit gardens, demonstrates that the girls were not closeted away in a gilded cage, but that they were allowed to explore the world around them, albeit accompanied and protected. The accounts also give us an idea of the number and type of people who formed their household, including two chaplains, esquires, clerks of the pantry and butlery, a chief cook, a valet of the larder and kitchen, another of the hall and chamber, three damsels who were attendant upon Isabella, and two damsels for Joanna, each of whom would have had servants of their own. Entries also cover the type of equipment purchased for the princesses' household, including a ladle for pouring hot wax and hampers for storing their silver plate and dishes, from which they ate their meals. Their bedding was of green silk, with cushions of green velvet. The accounts also cover numerous entries for dresses, and other items of clothing for the girls.[29]

One lady who served Isabella and Queen Philippa, Joan Gambon, was well rewarded by the king and on 2 December 1339, at Langley:

> By letters patent the king lately granted to Joan Gambon, damsel of Isabella, the king's daughter, an annuity of 10*l*. at the Exchequer until he should grant her for life an equivalent of land and rent, and afterwards the said sum out of the toll of 12*l*. due from the town of Shaftesbury. As a further grace in consideration of her long service

> to queen Philippa as well as to his daughter he has granted to her for life the balance of 40*s*. over and above her annuity from the toll. By p.s.[30]

In June 1340, the king won a major sea battle against the French, off the port of Sluys in Holland. The king and queen returned home that December and the family were reunited, spending Christmas together at the Tower of London. Isabella and Joan were so taken by a group of four Augustinian friars, who had sung for the royal family on the feast of St John the Evangelist, 21 December, that they themselves presented the friars with alms. On 9 January, the king organised a special treat for his children in their own quarters. The king and the royal children were entertained by his own minstrel, Godenal, who was given 6*s.* 8*d.* by Isabella and Joan. The Christmas celebrations may have been too excessive, or perhaps winter bugs had been passed about the court as, shortly afterwards, Master Philip, a physician, was called to attend the princesses and make medicines for them.[31] In May of 1341, the king assigned the English revenues, lands and appurtenance of the late John III, Duke of Brittany and Earl of Richmond, to the support of his children, Lionel, John, Isabella and Joan.[32] The grant was reissued the following month to include Edmund of Langley, the latest addition to the growing family, born on or before 5 June 1341.[33]

Isabella and Joan made their first official public appearance the following year, at a tournament held by the king at Dunstable, dressed 'in robes so gorgeously embroidered, that eighteen workmen had been employed, for nine days, in their manufacture, under the supervision of John of Cologne, the king's armour-bearer, and eleven ounces of leaf-gold were bestowed upon them'.[34] The royal family grieved when the queen gave birth to another princess, named Blanche, at the Tower of London. The baby died shortly after birth and was buried in Westminster Abbey. Soon after, another little girl joined the princesses' household – Elizabeth de Burgh, who was a month younger than Isabella. Her father was murdered the year after her birth, and she was his only child. The sole heiress to the earldom of Ulster, she was betrothed to Prince, Lionel, and was to be raised alongside the king's daughters. In the same year, the king officially gave custody of all five of their younger children to Queen Philippa and thereafter they spent a great deal of time with their mother. The children also frequently resided at Chertsey Abbey in Surrey and in 1347 the abbot wrote to Edward III, complaining that 'the abbey is very often burdened with diverse charges by frequent visits of the king's children and the lengthy stay of them and their households'.[35]

From Isabella's infancy, Edward was making plans for her marriage. The 1335 negotiations for a marriage with Pedro, or Peter, the heir to the Castilian throne, fell through, though would be revived later with Joan as the bride. The following year, negotiations were opened with Louis, Count of Flanders, who had first sought the hand of Joan for his son, but then turned his attention to Isabella, though negotiations had stalled by 1340, amidst rumours that Edward was plotting with a brewer from Ghent to supplant the count with Prince Edward; the brewer was murdered in 1345. In 1344, as a new princess joined the nursery with the birth of Mary of Waltham, born at Waltham near Winchester on 10 October, a dispensation was sought from the Pope for Isabella to marry the eldest son of the Duke of Brabant, and her brother Edward to marry one of the duke's daughters – the dispensation being necessary as he was a descendant of Edward I through his daughter Margaret. Pressure from Philip VI of France and his wife, Jeanne of Burgundy, persuaded the duke to abandon the marriages. In 1345, Edward III opened negotiations with Alfonso XI, King of Castile, to arrange the marriage of Joan to Alfonso's son and heir, Pedro, who was a similar age to Joan.[36] An embassy had been sent to the Iberian Peninsula a year before, to negotiate alliances, and it may be that the possibility of a marriage had been raised then. Edward himself had first suggested the match way back in 1335, but Alfonso had not been receptive. The Flemings, in the meantime, tried to revive the match with Isabella, but were thwarted by the count, who sent his young son to the French court to be educated there. It was about the same time that, after a two-year truce, war resumed between England and France. Count Louis was killed the following year, fighting for the French king at Crécy.

Two months before the battle, in June 1346, Isabella, now aged 14, and Joan, aged 12, were in their parents' company when they petitioned their father to pardon a William de Bekethwait for the death of John de Beryer, which the king granted.[37] Earlier in the year, in January, the royal family had gathered at Leicester to attend the funeral rites of the king's second cousin, Henry of Lancaster, with the king buying black cloth for himself, his queen and their households for the occasion. The queen was in the early stages of pregnancy and gave birth to another daughter, Margaret, at Windsor Castle in July. She would have been celebrating her churching at about the same time Edward was fighting the battle at Crécy, in which 16-year-old Prince Edward had had his first taste of battle. Agnes Pore was appointed as nurse to the new princess, Margaret of Windsor, and £500 was assigned as expenses for the queen's churching.[38] Within months of the birth, Isabella accompanied her mother to Calais, where they were welcomed with magnificent court entertainments, even as the port itself was besieged by the English. Baby Margaret and her sister Mary, not yet 2 years old, remained in England, in the care of their nurses. The little girls were staying with their 7-year-old brother, Lionel of Antwerp, who had been appointed Keeper of the Realm in the absence of his father and older brother. The young royal siblings were staying at the castle of Beaumys in Berkshire when Margery de la Beche was kidnapped from the fortress. The widow of Nicholas de la Beche, Margery was abducted by a group of knights and forced to marry the ringleader, Sir John Dalton, despite her protestations that she was already married to Sir Gerard de Lisle. Another knight, Michale Poynings, was killed trying to defend Margery. Taking place before dawn on Good Friday, the attack was 'to the terror of the said keeper [of the realm, Lionel] and the rest of the king's children then with him there'.[39] It is highly unlikely the children were ever in any danger, but it must have been a scary time for the ones old enough to understand what was afoot on hearing the clash of arms and shouted warnings as they awoke from their dreams.

Joan would join her mother and sister in Calais in April 1347, but whilst she was still in England, Joan interceded on behalf of a Spanish sailor named Lupus Johannis, so that he be given permission to buy wheat in the west country and take it back to his homeland.[40] It was a small gesture, but one that demonstrated an interest in the people she was destined to rule as queen of Castile. The sisters often interceded for those they knew or had served them in the past. Sometime during their stay on the Continent, Isabella and Joan wrote to the chancellor in England, John Offord, requesting that he discharge from paying taxes, several men who had served them and 'our very dear lady mother the queen'.[41] Whilst the royal family was in Calais, the king revived the idea of Isabella marrying the son of the Count of Flanders, Louis II de Male, now count in his own right. Edward offered inducements to the leading men of Flanders to bring the marriage about. On persuading them that an alliance with England was preferable to one with France 'mightily rejoiced the king, for he imagined that by this marriage he would easily govern that country'.[42] The young count was not as easily persuaded as the lords of Flanders and was looking to marry a daughter of the Duke of Brabant, an ally of the French. Understandably, Count Louis pointedly refused to marry the daughter of his enemy, the man who had won the battle in which his father was killed. At which point, the young count was seized by his own men, adherents to the English alliance, and held captive until he acquiesced to the marriage, which he eventually did.

In March 1347, the king, queen and Isabella met with Count Louis at the monastery of Bergues where, presumably, King Edward assured the count that he had no hand in his father's death. Count Louis promised to abide by the marriage contract that had been agreed between the king and his father, promising to marry Isabella no later than two weeks after Easter. He also assigned the princess a dower of 10,000 Parisian livres annually, from lands in Flanders. In return, the king agreed to cede to Isabella the lands of Ponthieu, Montreuil, and Pervost Chatel. Edward further guaranteed to the young couple the sum of 40,000 golden deniers, as his daughter's wedding portion.[43] The financial arrangements made, Isabella and Louis were formally betrothed before the two parties separated to make the final preparations for the wedding. The count, however, was still held under guard, his nobles taking no chances that he would refuse to go through with the wedding. I am not exactly sure how successful anyone thought a marriage would be with the groom being forced to the altar at the point of a sword. As it is, we will never find out as Louis contrived to escape his guards when he was out hunting and rode fast and hard for the French court and the protection of King Philip VI and just months later, he was married to Margaret of Brabant.

What Isabella thought of being abandoned by her betrothed has gone unrecorded. She was 15 years old and had known since she could walk that marrying a foreign prince would be her fate. One can imagine she was embarrassed at the public humiliation, but she was probably indifferent to the loss of the count himself. They had met only briefly, so barely knew each other. And if he was the sort of man who would leave a girl at the altar, she was probably better off without him. So, life would continue much as it had before. Christmas 1347 saw the usual round of festivities, with King Edward ordering masks and costumes for the revelries at Guildford. Marriage plans for his children continued with Joan betrothed to Pedro, heir to Alfonso, King of Castile.[44] In May 1348, she attended a great tournament at Lichfield, along with her companion from the nursery, Elizabeth de Burgh and Elizabeth of Jülich, the bride of her father's cousin, John of Kent.[45] At the tournament, her father fought wearing the arms of Sir Thomas de Bradeston, one of the men who had been by his side in 1330, at the arrest of Mortimer. The king ordered robes of blue and white to be made for the occasion, for himself and eleven of his knights, the Earl of Lancaster and twelve of his knights and for the ladies, including Isabella.[46] She was also present for the tournament at Canterbury in mid-August, at which the ladies entered the city in masks. The king ensured that he, his family and his royal prisoners, captured during his campaigns in France and Scotland, were dressed splendidly.[47] As Edward III was celebrating his victories with great shows of pomp and pageantry, however, Europe was being gripped by a terrible disease. The Black Death was inexorably making its way across the Continent and would soon reach England's shores. Despite the reports, Edward had decided to keep the ports open. Trade was the lifeblood of England and ships were needed to maintain communication with the king's continental possessions. We can understand better today, in the wake of COVID-19, the difficulty facing Edward III, between keeping the population safe and maintaining the country's financial stability. Although keeping the ports open allowed the faster spread of the disease, closing them would not have prevented its arrival in England, not unless Scotland also complied, and the entire coastline of Britain was guarded. The Black Death's arrival on English shores was, surely, an inevitability. And in the mist of the disease spreading across mainland Europe, King Edward was preparing to send his daughter, Joan, to Spain, for her wedding.

Castile would be a useful ally in Edward III's wars against France. Negotiations had begun in 1344 and were now, finally, coming to fruition. In 1345, King Alfonso XI of Castile had sent a physician and a knight to the English court to inspect Joan and assure the king of the 'condition and manners' of the princess.[48] Alfonso had a complicated living situation, which would cause problems for Castile. He was married to his cousin, Maria of Portugal, by whom he had a son, Pedro, or Peter, of Castile, Princess Joan's proposed husband. Alfonso, however, preferred the company of his mistress, Leonor de Guzman, to that of his wife. He had ten children with his mistress, including his son, Enrique, or Henry of Trastamara, who was just a few months older than his legitimate half-brother, Pedro, later known to history as Pedro the Cruel. Alfonso's treatment of his wife and legitimate son, showing an obvious preference for his mistress, would foster a lethal animosity in the next generation. Pedro and Enrique would fight a bitter civil war, from which Enrique would emerge triumphant, with Pedro murdered at his half-brother's own hand. Such events were far in the future, but Edward III did recognise the influence of Leonor de Guzman at the Castilian court and wrote both to her and to Queen Maria on the matter of Joan's marriage. Edward also extracted guarantees from Alfonso, sending an envoy to Castile, Andrew Offord, who was an expert in law 'to obtain before all things sufficient security' that any son born to Joan and Pedro 'shall in any event' succeed to the throne after Pedro's death. Born in August 1334, Pedro was only seven months younger than his proposed bride.[49] Offord was also given a safe conduct to travel to Spain with the princess, when the time came. In the meantime, Pedro sent his own minstrel, Gracias, to England to perform for his fiancée. Gracias would then travel back to Spain in the princess's company.

Just weeks before her departure for Spain, Joan was in her father's company when she interceded with him, successfully, on behalf of the prior and convent of Plimpton. As a parting gift, when she was about to embark on the sea voyage that would take her to her new husband, the king gave Joan a brooch of rubies, diamonds, emeralds and pearls. Her brother, Edward, supplied her with three tuns of Gascon wine 'when she left for parts beyond the sea'.[50] Joan was accompanied by the Bishop of Carlisle and Robert Bourchier, who had once been Lord Chancellor of England. The king had ordered the preparation of forty ships for his daughter's journey and sent a message to the Castilian royal family on 1 January 1348 that Joan was about to depart. Her party was escorted to Spain by 130 archers from Somerset, Dorset and Devon. Sadly, she was never to reach her new homeland, nor meet her husband. Having left England's shores, her ship broke its journey in Gascony, at Bordeaux. The Black Death was at its height in the city and Baron Bourchier was the royal party's first victim. The 14-year-old princess was taken to Lormont, outside of the city, but succumbed to the disease on 2 September 1348. Remembered as 'beautiful in body, and abundant in moral virtues and grace', she was buried in Bordeaux Cathedral.[51]

The news will have reached England a matter of days later. Given that the king and queen had buried their baby son, William of Windsor, who had lived only a few months, on 3 September, the tidings of Joan's death would have compounded their grief. The king had certainly received the news by 15 September, when he wrote a poignant letter to King Alfonso, informing him of Joan's death. Written in Latin, it read:

> ...after much complicated negotiation about the intended marriage of the renowned Infante Pedro, your eldest son, and our most beloved daughter Joan ... we sent our said daughter to Bordeaux, en route to your territories in Spain. But see – with what intense bitterness of heart we have to tell you this – destructive Death, who seizes young and old alike, sparing no-one, and reducing rich and poor to the same level, has lamentably snatched from both of us our dearest daughter (whom we loved best of all, as her virtues demanded). No fellow human being could be surprised if we were inwardly desolated by the sting of this bitter grief, for we are human too. But we give thanks to God that one of our own family, free of all stain, whom we have loved with pure love, has been sent ahead to Heaven to reign among the choirs of virgins, where she can gladly intercede for our offence before God himself.'[52]

The king also wrote a letter to his daughter's fiancé, Pedro, on the same day, and another to Queen Maria a few days later.[53]

Isabella, aged 16, must have missed her sister terribly. They had grown up together and shared a household their whole lives. It is not hard to imagine the little conversations the sisters must have had as Joan was preparing to leave for Castile. Making promises to keep in touch, sharing concerns of how they would still think of each other, even though they were miles apart, wondering what married life would be like, hoping that Joan's marriage was as warm and loving as their parents'. Isabella still had two sisters at home, but Mary and Margaret had only just emerged from the nursery and were too young to be the friends and confidants of their big sister. However, despite the grief of Joan's loss and the tragedy of the Black Death overtaking the country, Isabella's future was still on the king's mind and in February 1349, he opened negotiations with Charles, the future Holy Roman Emperor who had been recently widowed, but nothing came of it. In 1351, aged 19, Isabella was to marry the heir to Lord Albret, who was some years younger than Isabella. There is some confusion, however, as to the groom's name. Some sources report it as Bernard, but Bernard was the second son, and it is highly unlikely that King Edward would agree to his oldest daughter marrying a younger son. It is more likely that Isabella was betrothed to the older son and heir, Arnaud. The king awarded Isabella and the groom 1000 marks annually 'in consideration of the marriage to be contracted between them'.[54] King Edward ordered five ships to take Isabella to her wedding in Gascony. Her trousseau included a mantle of Indian silk, furred with ermine; circlets of silk and pearls, decorated with a gold *agnus dei* set on green velvet; in addition to jewellery and dresses.[55] Her departure was set for a few short weeks before Christmas, but one week before she was due to leave, Isabella pointedly refused to board the ship waiting to take her to Gascony. If the younger son were Isabella's proposed groom, she may have seen the marriage as beneath her and although Edward would not leave his daughter destitute, her husband would only inherit his father's lands if his older brother died before having children of his own. Edward III does not seem to have been too perturbed by the cancellation of the wedding. He continued to support Isabella and described her as 'our very dear eldest daughter, whom we have loved with special affection'.[56]

Although Isabella's marriage plans fell apart, the king still had the future of his two younger daughters to attend to. In May 1353, Pope Innocent IV granted a dispensation for the marriage of Edward's youngest daughter, Margaret, to the little girl's second cousin, Jean de Blois, son and heir of Charles de Blois and Jeanne de Penthièvre, claimant to the Duchy of Brittany.[57] Charles had been held captive in England since 1347 and offered his son in marriage in return for his release, on top of a large ransom, of course. Charles was released but the king ultimately decided against the match, probably because Margaret's sister, Mary, had been betrothed to John de Montfort, the other claimant to Brittany, since she had been a babe in the cradle.

Edward continued to indulge his eldest daughter Isabella, she was with him almost constantly – far more than any of his other children. In 1354, Edward paid for a new balcony to be built outside Isabella's suite of rooms at Woodstock so that she would have a better view of the park.[58] Isabella continued to be an influential presence at court. In early July 1355, just before her father and four oldest brothers left England to campaign in France, Isabella, her mother and two of the king's leading magnates – and cousins – Henry of Grosmont, Duke of Lancaster, and William de Bohun, Earl of Northampton, worked in unison to persuade the king to grant a pardon to a knight named Sir John de Lyle, who had killed his fellow knight, Sir John de Goys. The pardon duly granted, the king's youngest son, Thomas of Woodstock, at only six months old, was appointed guardian of the realm as the king went off to war.[59] A month later, Isabella became an aunt when her childhood companion, Elizabeth de Burgh, the wife of her brother Lionel, gave birth to a daughter, named Philippa after her grandmother. And on 29 April 1358, Isabella is recorded as having made a visit to her ageing grandmother, Isabella of France, accompanying her father and the Earl of March; the dowager queen of England died later that year.[60]

The whole family came together at Reading Abbey on 20 May 1359 to attend the wedding of the king and queen's third surviving son, John of Gaunt to Blanche, younger daughter and co-heiress of Henry of Grosmont, Duke of Lancaster. The king paid thirty pounds for two silver buckles that Isabella would give to her new sister-in-law. While Blanche was also gifted three silver cups, in the name of

Gaunt's youngest brother, Thomas of Woodstock, and two youngest sisters, Mary of Waltham and Margaret of Windsor.[61] The day before the wedding of John and Blanche, another royal ceremony had taken place, with the betrothal of 13-year-old Margaret of Windsor to 12-year-old John de Hastings, Earl of Pembroke.[62] There seems to be some confusion as to whether Margaret and John were married at the ceremony, but their youth would suggest it was a betrothal, although there is no indication of a later wedding ceremony. Given their youth, it is unlikely the marriage was consummated at the time.

The three royal sisters were together again at court, with their parents, for the Christmas festivities in 1360 and in the spring of 1361 they all gathered at Newarke in Leicester for the funeral of the king's cousin and friend, Henry of Grosmont, Duke of Lancaster, who had succumbed to the Black Death. His wife, Isabel de Beaumont, died of the disease in the same year. Mary of Waltham was now 16 years old, and Margaret was 15. Isabella was 29 years old and still unmarried. The two younger sisters appeared less in the company of their parents than Isabella and Joan ever did, and were only given twenty marks a year, each, as pocket money. They visited court infrequently, although that is likely due to the continued threat of the Black Death, which made frequent recurrences for years after its arrival on England's shores in 1349. Sometime between March and July of 1361, Mary was married to John de Montfort. One of the claimants of the Duchy of Brittany, John had grown up at the English court, so the young couple would have known each other well. His mother, Joanna of Flanders, was held under house arrest at Tickhill Castle in Yorkshire, supposedly due to mental illness but it seems more likely that Edward kept her confined in order to increase his own influence over Brittany. Born in 1339, John was five years older than his bride. Mary would never be Duchess of Brittany. Indeed, she never even set foot in the duchy, as tragedy struck before 13 September 1361. A month before Mary's seventeenth birthday, the princess died. The king and queen's grief was further compounded just weeks later, when Margaret also passed away. The last mention of the youngest of the royal sisters is 1 October 1361. It is possible both girls had died during a resurgence of the Black Death. The royal princesses were buried together at Abingdon Abbey, where the queen commissioned a tomb for her daughters.[63] King Edward had windows erected to the memory of the princesses at King's Langley Priory.

Of the five daughters born to King Edward and Queen Philippa, now only the eldest, Isabella of Woodstock, was still living. And amidst the grief, there was one happy, if controversial, event when, on 10 October, Edward of Woodstock, known to history as the Black Prince, married his cousin Joan of Kent, in what appears to have been a love-match. It was certainly not the great dynastic match that one would expect of an heir to the throne. Joan had grown up in the royal nursery, alongside Edward and Isabella. She had been the subject of a bigamy scandal when married to William Montagu, Earl of Salisbury, only for Thomas Holland to claim

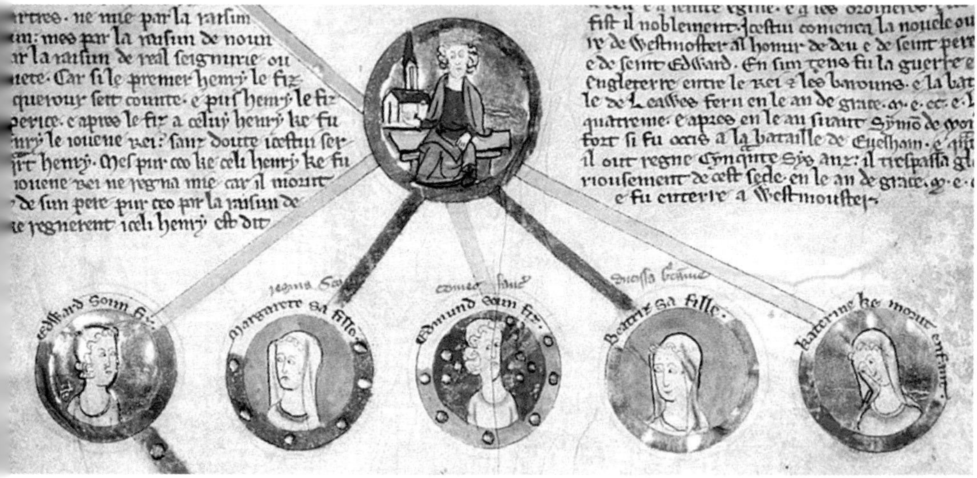

Above: Early chronology showing Henry III (top) and his children, (left to right) Edward, Margaret, Edmund, Beatrice, and Katherine, dated 1300–1308. (Courtesy of the British Library Catalogue of Illuminated Manuscripts)

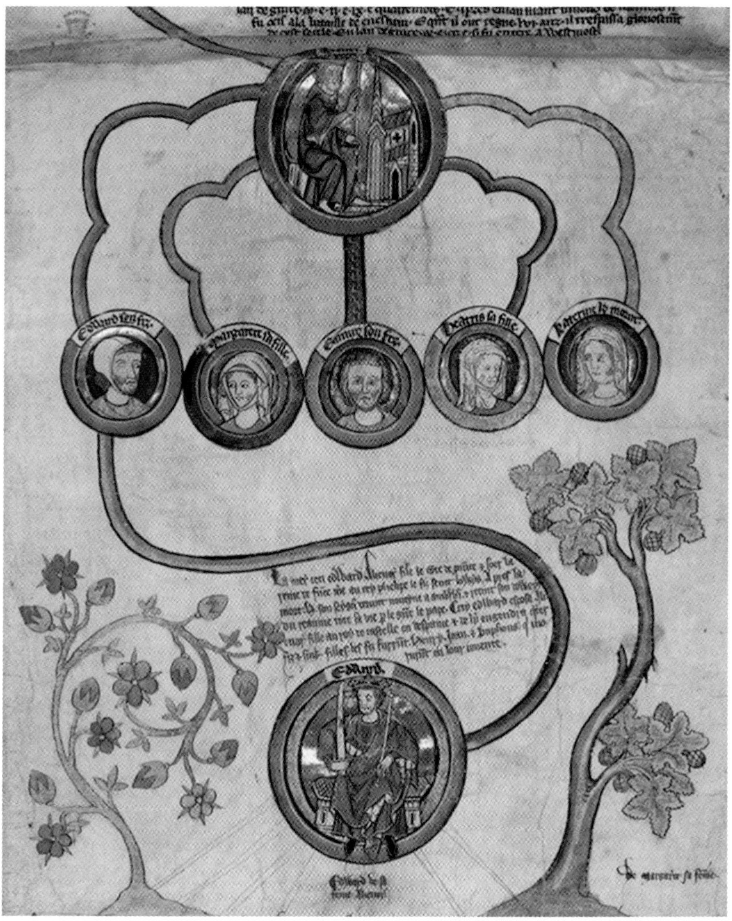

Right: Children of Henry III. (Courtesy of the British Library Catalogue of Illuminated Manuscripts)

Above left: Queen Margaret, daughter of Henry III and first wife of Alexander III. (Courtesy of the British Library Catalogue of Illuminated Manuscripts)

Above right: Beatrice of England. (Courtesy of the British Library Catalogue of Illuminated Manuscripts)

Below: Westminster Abbey, burial place of Katherine, daughter of Henry III and Eleanor of Provence. (Courtesy of Daniel Gleave)

Above: York Minster, scene of the weddings of Margaret and Alexander III and Joan and David I. (Author's collection)

Right: Edward I and Eleanor of Castile, Lincoln Cathedral. (Author's collection)

Above left: Eleanor, Countess of Bar. (Courtesy of the British Library Catalogue of Illuminated Manuscripts)

Above middle: Joan of Acre, Countess of Hertford. (Courtesy of the British Library Catalogue of Illuminated Manuscripts)

Above right: Margaret, Duchess of Brabant. (Courtesy of the British Library Catalogue of Illuminated Manuscripts)

Above left: Mary of Woodstock. (Courtesy of the British Library Catalogue of Illuminated Manuscripts)

Above middle: Elizabeth of Rhuddlan. (Courtesy of the British Library Catalogue of Illuminated Manuscripts)

Above right: Eleanor of Woodstock, Duchess of Guelders, at prayer, in the illustration for the Hours of the Holy Spirit in the Taymouth Hours. (Courtesy of the British Library Catalogue of Illuminated Manuscripts (London, BL MS Yates Thompson 13, fol. 18r))

Above: Tower of London, birthplace of Joan of the Tower, wife of David II. (Author's collection)

Right: Joan and David II with Philip VI in a miniature from *Froissart's Chronicles*. (Public domain)

Above left: Statuette of Joan, daughter of Edward III, on her father's tomb in Westminster Abbey. (Public domain image, via Wikimedia Commons)

Above right: Statuette of Mary, daughter of Edward III, on her father's tomb in Westminster Abbey. (Public domain image, via Wikimedia Commons)

Below: Windsor Castle. (Author's collection)

Above left: Portrait above Blanche's tomb in Neustadt an der Weinstraße. (Public domain)

Above right: Crown of Blanche of England kept at Munich Residenz. (By kind permission of Matthias Kabel)

Philippa, Queen of Denmark, Norway and Sweden. (Public domain)

The York sisters from the window in Canterbury Cathedral. (Public domain image, via Wikimedia Commons)

Above left: Elizabeth of York, Royal Collection. (Public domain image, via Wikimedia Commons)

Above right: Cecily of York, Viscountess Welles (Public domain image, via Wikimedia Commons)

she had been married to him first. Years of litigation, and Joan's own testimony, saw her marriage to Montagu declared null and void and she had enjoyed ten years of happy marriage with Thomas Holland before his death in December 1360.

Isabella had not been included in the flurry of royal marriages between 1359 and 1362. The king continued to support her, regularly giving her annuities and rewards and she appears to have been more in his company than any of her surviving siblings.[64] In 1355, she had been granted lands in Yorkshire and Lincolnshire, including:

> Manors and hamlets of Brustewyk, Bondebrustwyk, Skekkelyng, Little Humbre, Kayngham, Cleton, Skipsee, Outhorn, Withornsee, Lelle Dyke, Elstanwyk, Burton Pidesee, Preston, Sprotle, Hedon, Pauleflete, Skeftelyng, Kilnesee, Esyngton, and Ravenser, Yorkshire; and lands and tenements in Barowe, Lincolnshire (as U DCC/2/41). Also manors of Cosham, Wiltshire; Wedon Pynkeny, Northamptonshire; and Swalwefeld, Berkshire. With wardships and escheats in the premises. From Patent Roll, 29 Edward III.[65]

Isabella finally married on 27 July 1365, at Windsor Castle, at the comparatively late age of 33, in what appears to have been a love-match. Her husband, Enguerrand (or Ingram) VII Lord of Coucy, was seven years her junior, and a hostage for the fulfilment of the Treaty of Brétigny. He had been in the entourage of the captive king of France, John II, until the king's death the year before. Edward III is said to have approved of the match as he enjoyed family entertainments and Enguerrand had a fine singing voice.[66] The king and queen spent lavishly on their surviving daughter's wedding, with at least £4500 going to goldsmiths for the jewels and brooches given to Isabella. A further £100 was spent on the many minstrels who entertained the guests at the wedding celebrations.[67] On marrying Isabella, Enguerrand was released without ransom and on 26 November 1365, the king granted a licence for 'Ingram, lord of Coucy, and the king's daughter Isabel, his wife, to visit their lands and possessions in France; and grant that all children begotten between them, wherever born, shall enjoy their inheritance in England as if born in the realm'.[68] This last was probably added in the knowledge that Isabella was already pregnant with her first child, who was born in April 1366. Two daughters were born in successive years. Marie was born at the Château of Coucy, in France, and would later marry Henry of Bar. A second daughter, Philippa, was born at the royal palace of Eltham in 1367 or 1368, and would later marry Robert de Vere, Earl of Oxford and Duke of Ireland. Perhaps hoping that Enguerrand and Isabella would make their home in England, King Edward gave Enguerrand the earldom of Bedford in 1366 and, later, made him Count of Soissons. The marriage was not without its difficulties, however, and in later years the shine appears to have worn off. In 1368, Enguerrand left England for the Continent, going on to fight in Italy, while Isabella remained in England, attending the Christmas court, probably with her two daughters, at what would be her mother's last Christmas.

Queen Philippa died on 15 August 1369, at Eltham Palace in Kent. Isabella does not appear to have been in attendance on her mother at her death, although one of Isabella's daughters, most likely Marie, is recorded as having been provided with black cloth for her mourning clothes, by the king. The little girl, only 2 years of age, was accompanied by two nurses and three other female attendants, for whom the king provided more black cloth.[69] Isabella was probably in France with her husband and youngest daughter. It may well be that Marie had been staying with her grandparents and so was on hand to wear mourning and grieve her grandmother's death.

Enguerrand de Coucy renounced all his English titles following Edward III's death in 1377, choosing to give his allegiance to France. Isabella remained at the English court with her daughters, using the title of Countess of Bedford, even after her husband had resigned the earldom. She received robes as a Lady of the Garter in 1376. Edward's will gave to his 'very dear daughter' Isabella, an income of 300 marks per year, until her daughters were married.[70] In a charter dated 15 March 1379, Enguerrand and Isabella, together, swore allegiance to King Richard II, Isabella's nephew.[71] She died, in either 1379 or 1382 and was laid to rest at the Greyfriars Church in Newgate, London. Although it had turned sour, she had broken convention by marrying for love. In her stubbornness and outright refusal to marry her father's choice of husband, Isabella had been given greater control over her own life than most English princesses, before and after her. The marriage's later problems were a sad epilogue.

Isabella had remained at court even during the dark times, when Alice Perrers' influence over Edward III chased many others away. The king's mistress in his declining years, Alice Perrers was vilified by chroniclers for interfering in politics, benefiting herself and her friends and being an undue influence on the ageing, but much-loved, monarch. She was the mother of three children by Edward III, including two daughters. The origins of Alice Perrers are obscure; it has been variously claimed that she was the daughter of a thatcher, or a weaver. The chronicler of St Albans, Thomas Walsingham, claimed that she was of base birth, the daughter of a thatcher from Henneye.[72] Walsingham's chronicle was consistent in its criticisms of Alice and is not considered to be accurate. Alice Perrers had been involved in a number of disputes with the abbey of St Albans and Walsingham's animosity is evident in his description of Alice as extremely ugly and saying that she ruled the king with a clever tongue.[73] However, a recent article by W. M. Ormrod has led to renewed interest in Alice's origins. Ormrod argued that Alice may have been older than was previously believed and that Perrers was her married name rather than her maiden name. Alice had a brother named John Salisbury, and she was most likely from a family of London goldsmiths – the Salisburys – who provided jewels to the royal court. Alice then married another London goldsmith, Janyn Perrers. This would have given Alice connections to court circles and would also explain her familiarity with the affairs of the city and litigation, as well as explaining her well-known fondness for jewellery.[74] Nothing is known of Alice's early life. As a member of the merchant class, and the daughter of a successful goldsmith, she was certainly educated and could read, as she owned several books, written in English.[75] She was married by June 1360, when she and Perrers purchased 6 yards of cloth from a tailor in order to make a cloak for Janyn.[76] Perrers died sometime between May 1361 and May 1362; by December 1362, Alice was a young widow, acting on her own behalf as a *femme sole.* Although they had no children, Alice would not have been left destitute, as she would have been entitled to a dower, possibly a portion of Janyn's business income, to sustain her.

It is not known how Alice first came to the attention of the king. She may have been a female attendant in the household of Queen Philippa of Hainault; most of the queen's attendants were from baronial or landed families, but a handful came from the merchant class. Alice was in a very privileged position for a woman of her background. How she attained such a post has remained a mystery. It is unclear whether this was before or after her relationship with Edward III had started. The liaison with Edward appears to have begun in 1364 as in that year a merchant and courtier, Richard Lyons, was ordered not to interfere with Alice's movements when she was on the king's business or her own.[77] Alice's relationship with the king remained a closely guarded secret during the queen's lifetime and only became public after Philippa's death in 1369. We know Alice had been installed as a maid of the queen's bedchamber by October 1366. Indeed, it was probably in 1365 or 1366 that Alice's first son by the king, John de Southeray (or Surrey), was born, as by 1377 he was old enough to be married and in 1381–2 he accompanied the Earl of Cambridge on his Portuguese campaign.[78] Alice had a further two children by the king, daughters named Jane and Joan. In January 1377, Alice's son by the king, Sir John de Southeray, married Mary Percy, a half-sister of Henry, Lord Percy, the future Earl of Northumberland. On 17 June of the same year, just four days before his father's death, the king granted him a satin coat of arms.

Alice Perrers was a divisive figure at court. The king appears to have relied heavily on Alice during his grieving for his queen and it was from this period onwards that she was given numerous and varied gifts, from wardships to lands and jewels. In 1371, she was permitted to purchase the valuable royal manor of Wendover for just £500.[79] In 1373, she was said to have been given a selection of Queen Philippa's jewels, although the jewels were in fact items that had been given, by the queen, to Euphemia, wife of Walter Hasleworth, rather than the queen's own jewellery. The gifts were recorded in the patent rolls, suggesting they were made on Edward's personal orders, rather than as an avaricious acquisition by Alice. Alice was to make many enemies and in the Good Parliament of 1376, things came to a head when the Speaker of the Commons, Peter de la Mare, openly accused Alice of 'relieving the exchequer of *l*2,000 or *l*3,000 a year without profit to the realm'.[80] The chronicler Thomas Walsingham reported:

> ... the Parliamentary knights complained bitterly about one Alice Perrers, a wanton woman who was all too familiar with Edward III. They accused her of numerous misdeeds, performed by her and her friends in the realm. She far overstepped the bounds of feminine conduct: forgetful of her sex and her weakness, now besieging the king's justices, now stationing herself among the doctors in the ecclesiastical courts, she did not fear to plead in defence of her cause and even to make illegal demands. As a result of the scandal and great shame which this brought on King Edward, not only in this kingdom but also in foreign lands, the knights sought her banishment from his side.[81]

It emerged during the proceedings of the Good Parliament that, despite her relationship with the king, Alice was, in fact, married to Sir William Windsor, a knight from the county of Westmorland. The outcome of the parliament saw Alice banished from court and ordered to refrain from instigating legal proceedings, or to face forfeiture of her goods and property and exile from England. In the end, Alice was allowed to stay in England without further prosecution, on condition that she stayed away from the king. Should she break the restrictions placed on her, the punishment would be perpetual exile. Alice's marriage had meant the king had been committing adultery and he is said to have sworn an oath by the Virgin Mary that he did not know she was married. King Edward was devastated on hearing about the marriage, but even more so by the banishment of his mistress. Bereft of his wife, with the death of his eldest son and heir, Edward the Black Prince, on 8 June 1376, and with the rest of his family spread far and wide, the king probably saw Alice as the comfort and companion of his old age.

However, if the banishment was implemented at all it was of short duration and Alice was back at the king's side within months. John of Gaunt had returned from his duties as the king's lieutenant on the Continent and was practically ruling the kingdom, allowing the return of those banished by the Good Parliament. Edward 'recalled his mistress, Alice Perrers, to his company; she had been legally banished from his presence, on account of the scandal and shame which came from her wantonness. This was against the oath by which Alice had bound herself and which the king himself had ratified; namely that she would not come near the king in any way. She stayed with him until his death'.[82] On 22 October 1376, Alice was pardoned by the king and remained at his side from that moment until his death in the following year. Even if she had wanted to slip into obscurity after the king's death, Alice was not allowed just to drift away. The Lords and Commons, who had resented her power and influence over the king, wasted no time in exacting their revenge and Alice was charged on two counts. The first was that in November 1376 she persuaded the king to countermand the council's order to send Sir Nicholas Dagworth to Ireland to investigate the corruption charges against William Windsor, Alice's husband, on the grounds that Windsor and Dagworth were enemies. The second charge was that in May 1377 she persuaded Edward III to grant a full pardon and a gift of 100 marks to Richard Lyons, a friend of Alice's who had been, like her, denounced in the Good Parliament.

Although Alice vehemently maintained her innocence on both charges, she was convicted and sentenced to banishment from England and forfeiture of all her goods and lands. Unusually, the forfeiture included all lands which she had enfeoffed others to her use. Such lands were normally exempt from confiscation and a clause in the sentence specifically stated that it should not be used as a precedent in other cases but was imposed only 'for such an odious thing in this special case'.[83] On 3 December 1377, the orders to seize Alice's lands were issued. The inventory from the resulting inquisitions included properties in at least fifteen counties. It was also claimed that she had hidden £20,000 worth of jewels with Windsor, to prevent their seizure; this may be an exaggeration but at least £3000 was recovered from Alice following her arrest.[84] Alice would spend the remainder of her life in almost endless litigation, in repeated attempts to recover her goods and property. Windsor helped in the early years following the king's death; in October 1378, Alice had still not left England when Windsor petitioned parliament to reverse the judgement against her, for which he was given leave to pursue his suit. A further petition saw the sentence of banishment revoked on 14 December 1379; at the same time, she was pardoned for having not left England and Windsor was pardoned for harbouring her. The recovery of lands was a slow, drawn-out process, and not without setbacks.

Although Windsor was granted some of those lands confiscated from Alice in March 1380, in return for military service to the Crown, his death on 15 September 1384 caused new problems. Not only had he died in debt to the Crown, but the lands that had once belonged to Alice had been enfeoffed to a group of trustees who were to dispose of them according to Windsor's final wishes. Even though Alice claimed that Windsor had intended to leave the lands to her, the trustees insisted he had nominated his nephew, John Windsor, as beneficiary. Alice spent the remaining years of her life in the struggle to recover her lands from John Windsor. In 1393/94, 'Joan daughter of Alice Wyndesor' petitioned the king for the recovery from John de Windsor of money that was due to her from the sale of the marriage of John de Mowbray, Earl of Nottingham which had been granted to her by King Edward III.[85]

Numerous petitions to parliament resulted in John Windsor being imprisoned in Newgate gaol for a very brief time and the recovery of only a small number of properties, including Alice's manor at Gaines in Upminster, where she lived in her final years. Alice's will, dated 15 August 1400, shows that her bitterness lasted to the very end; it bequeathed all the lands, which John Windsor had 'usurped', to her daughters, Jane and Joan, 'for that I say, on pain of my soul, he hath no right to these, nor never had'.[86] She died sometime over the winter of 1400/1401, as her will was proved in February 1401.[87] Alice asked to be buried in Upminster Church, Essex, and left her manor at Gaines to her daughter Jane, who may have moved in with her mother to care for her in her last days; a record from 1402 notes that Jane had been living at Gaines since December 1399.[88] The remainder of Alice's property was to be divided equally between the two daughters. The fate of her son John is far from clear. His marriage to Mary Percy was annulled in 1380 after Mary claimed she had never consented to the union. John fought in the Portuguese campaigns of 1381–2, but nothing is heard of him afterwards and given that he is not mentioned in his mother's will he probably died shortly after the campaign's end.

It is unfortunate for Jane and Joan that they were still children when their father died. They not only lost the king's protection, but also the prospect of prestigious marriages. Edward III had been a doting, benevolent father to his legitimate daughters and there is no reason to doubt that he would have been just as generous with Jane and Joan. Indeed, the advantages he had given to their older brother are evidence that he both acknowledged and intended to provide for his children by Alice. But it was not to be. And maybe the two girls were happy enough in the marriages their mother arranged for them. Joan would be married to Robert Skerne, a lawyer from Kingston-upon-Thames, Surrey. He owned the manor of Downhall in Kingston. His family and profession afforded him connections in Surrey, and he was wealthy enough to provide Joan with the comfortable lifestyle she was used to as Alice's daughter. Jane would marry Richard Northland, a career soldier. He was a knight who had distinguished himself in the Portuguese campaign of 1373, where he had commanded his own men. He served in Ireland with William Windsor in 1374, so would have been known to Alice and her family, possibly even a friend. In 1377–8, Northland led a contingent of 100 men-at-arms in the defence of the Isle of Wight. Prior to that, he was mentioned in a petition of 1377 as the captain of Bourg in France.[89] He had been rewarded for his military service by Edward III, with land on the Welsh Marches, including 30 acres at Minsterworth, Gloucestershire.[90] Given his service during her father's lifetime, Richard must have been some years older than Jane, but was a man of good standing with a proven reputation, personal wealth and landed estates.

Although the daughters were in possession of Gaines at the time of their mother's death, and Alice had left it to them in her will, it was granted elsewhere not long after Alice died and legal wranglings ensued. In 1406, one of the daughters, it is unclear which, reached a settlement whereby she relinquished her interest in the manor in return for a payment of 40 marks a year.[91] Jane does not appear much in the historical record after her mother's death. It may well be that she herself died only a few years after her mother. The similarity in their names also causes some confusion. There is a grant by the king in 1404, requested by Jane's husband, 'to Thomas his son of the custody of all manors, lands, rents and services which the said Richard had as of the right of Joan [Jane] his wife in the city of London and in Compton Moredok'.[92] The wording is ambiguous but could suggest that Jane had died and that Richard was passing her lands to his son as his inheritance. It is unclear, however, whether Thomas is the son of both Jane and Richard, or solely the son of Richard from a previous marriage. Historical records can be so frustrating! In her will, Alice had specified that Compton Moredok be sold to pay for her bequests, even forbidding Joan from receiving her share of Alice's London properties if she failed to comply. The above grant, however, suggests that Jane and Joan found a way around their mother's wishes. It may be that Alice changed her mind at the last minute as in January 1401 the manor had been granted to Jane and Richard, jointly with the Bishop of Salisbury and a few others.[93]

Joan and Jane, with the help of their husbands, continued to pursue the claims to their mother's lands in the years after Alice's death. In July 1401, Robert Skerne helped his sister-in-law, Jane, to recover the manor of Philiberts in East Hanney, Berkshire, a manor Alice had owned prior to her marriage. An inquisition of tenements from 1404, which William Wykeham was renting out in All Hallows the Less, London, is the only indication we have that Jane may still have been alive. The inquisition mentions a 'tenement formerly of John Weston and now of Richard Northlode, knight, and Joan [Jane] his wife, daughter and heir of Alice Perers'.[94] The arrangement over the manor of Gaines from 1406 is the last mention we see of either of Alice's daughters in the records. Jane's date of death is unknown, but Joan appears to have lived until sometime in 1430, as in 1431 Robert Skerne arranged for prayers to be said in his wife's memory after he was admitted into the fraternity of Osney Abbey.[95] Robert would later be buried beside his wife in All Saints' Church, Kingston-upon-Thames, where he commissioned a monumental brass, which still survives, to mark their tomb. The memorial depicts Joan in a sumptuous headdress and veil, wearing a necklace and pendant. She has 'a close-fitting dress with tight sleeves, and a fur-lined mantle is held in place over her shoulders with two large brooches in the same style as her necklace. In the four corners of the monumental brass are spaces for coats of arms, which could have depicted Alice's heraldry, passed on to Joan, but these have not survived'.[96]

Joan and Robert had no children that survived them, and it is unclear if Richard's son, Thomas, was also Jane's son. It may well be that the legacy of Alice and Edward III did not survive beyond their daughters, Joan and Jane. Given the death of their father when they were still children, the two girls at least survived and flourished, inheriting their mother's determination and strength, and fighting for what was theirs. Not the lives of almost-princesses that they might have expected, had their father been able to arrange their marriages, but the lives of wealthy, connected women who obviously had the support of their husbands. And they lived longer and more fulfilling lives than fate gave to four of their five legitimate half-sisters.

Of the daughters of Edward III and Philippa of Hainault who survived infancy, Isabella, Joan, Mary and Margaret, only Isabella survived passed her teenage years. It is no surprise that, given such sad losses, the king was indulgent of his one surviving daughter. That she found happiness in her marriage, with a man of her own choice, is rather remarkable for a princess. That she and Enguerrand were torn apart by the continuing Hundred Years' War is a sad legacy of her father's foreign policy. Plague, war and politics had shaped the lives and marriages of all of Edward III's daughters, legitimate or not.

Chapter Five

The Lancaster Sisters

As a rule, princesses are born, not made – they are the daughters of a king. Except in rare instances of a change of dynasty, such as the Norman Conquest and the usurpation of King Stephen. And the accession of Henry IV.

After the numerous daughters of Edward III, we have an apparent dearth of royal daughters, with no princess born to a reigning king after Margaret in 1346 until the birth of Elizabeth of York, daughter of Edward IV, in 1466. Edward III's successor, Richard II, having succeeded his grandfather at the age of 10 in 1377, died childless in 1400, despite having been married twice. He had married his first wife, Anne of Bohemia, on 10 January 1382, when they were both 15 years old. They were married for twelve years, until Queen Anne's death from plague in 1394, at her favourite palace of Sheen. She was just 28 years old. Richard was so distraught at her death that he ordered Sheen be razed to the ground.[1] Anne was famed for her good works as a mediator, and for interceding for those accused or convicted of crimes in England, so much so that she became known as 'Good Queen Anne'.[2] She is often seen as being a calming factor on the excesses of her husband, pulling him back from the despotism that lingered below the surface. Her death is seen as the tipping point in Richard II's reign that would see his rule descend into tyranny and see him eventually deposed and murdered. Anne may well have held him back; or maybe it was Richard's grief at losing her that sent him over the edge?

Either way, on Anne's death, Richard was a king without a queen and, more importantly, a king without a son. A new wife was essential for Richard to continue the dynasty and for England; a country without an obvious heir was invariably unsettled and subject to in-fighting by noble factions. Even a teenage queen may have been an asset to King Richard. However, in order to achieve peace with France, Richard agreed to marry Isabella de Valois, 7 years old and the daughter of King Charles VI and Isabeau of Bavaria. It may well be that the king was giving himself time to grieve the loss of Queen Anne. After all, it would be another seven years before he had to fulfil the duties of a husband once again. The match was unpopular in England. The lack of a direct heir to the throne caused serious concerns. One scholar, Philip of Mézières, did point out the advantages of a child-queen, saying 'would it not be better that the lady he chooses as helpmeet and wife, from her childhood, before reaching the age of discretion and before acquiring harmful habits of mind, should be well instructed under the prudence and wise guidance of the royal majesty'.[3]

Before negotiations were concluded, Richard's ambassadors visited Isabella so that they could report to the king on her appearance and conduct. The French agreed, though cautioned that:

> they must be content how so ever they found her, for they said she was but a young child of eight years of age, wherefore they said, there couldn't be in her no great wisdom nor prudence; howbeit, she was trained well enough, and that the lords found well when they saw her. The earl Marshall, being on his knees, said to her: Fair lady, by the grace of God you shall be our lady and queen of England. Then answered the young lady well advisedly, without counsel of any other person: Sir, quoth she, and it please God and my lord my father that I shall be queen of England, I shall be glad thereof, for it is showed me that I shall be then a great lady.[4]

There were advantages to the king taking a bride who had not long left the cradle and that was that it guaranteed the legitimacy of any future children. A queen raised in a sheltered environment, within the household of her future husband, would have no dubious sexual past or reputation. Given the scandal of Richard's own mother's marital history, this may have been a great concern for the king. Joan of Kent had secretly married Thomas Holland before he departed on Crusade to eastern Europe, only to be forced into a marriage with William Montagu, the future Earl of Salisbury, before Holland returned. Holland had had to take his case to the Church courts in Avignon to prove that Joan was his wife and reclaim her from Salisbury.

We can only wonder if Isabella de Valois would have lived up to her own promise of being a great lady. Richard and Isabella were married in Calais on 1 November 1396, ahead of Isabella's coronation in Westminster Abbey on 7 January the following year. Due to her youth, the little queen would play no political role in the remainder of her husband's reign. She was sent to Windsor with her own household, where she was expected to continue her education and to grow up. In the meantime, Richard II's troubled reign was heading towards disaster and calamity. The man who would eventually depose and replace him was his first cousin, Henry of Bolingbroke, Earl of Derby, the oldest son and heir of Richard's uncle, John of Gaunt, Duke of Lancaster.

The third surviving son of Edward III and Philippa of Hainault, John of Gaunt was born in 1340 at the Abbey of St Bavon, in Ghent in modern-day Belgium. At the height of his career, he was the most powerful man in the kingdom after the king. He was virtually regent for his father, Edward III, in his old age, thus getting the blame for military failures and government corruption. His reputation was further damaged when he blocked the reforms of the Good Parliament of 1376, which had tried to curb corruption and limit the influence of the king's grasping mistress, Alice Perrers. John of Gaunt's wealth meant he could form the largest baronial retinue of knights and esquires in the country. He alone provided a quarter of the army raised for Richard II's Scottish campaign in 1385. A stalwart supporter of his nephew, he was the target for the rebels during the Peasants' Revolt in 1381; his London residence, the Savoy Palace, was burned to the ground. Luckily for John, he was absent in the north, otherwise he may have been one of the casualties of the insurrection, alongside Simon Sudbury, Archbishop of Canterbury. Gaunt was a soldier and statesman whose career spanned six decades and several countries, including England, Belgium, France, Scotland and Castile.

John of Gaunt's first marriage, at the age of 19, was designed to give him prestige, property and income and was arranged as part of his father's plans to provide for the futures of several of his children. John and 14-year-old Blanche of Lancaster, youngest daughter of Henry of Grosmont, Duke of Lancaster, were married on 19 May 1359 in the Queen's Chapel at Reading. Blanche of Lancaster was described as 'jone et jolie' – young and pretty – by the chronicler Froissart, and also 'bothe fair and bright' and Nature's 'cheef patron of beautee' by Geoffrey Chaucer.[5] She brought John of Gaunt the earldom of Lancaster following her father's death from plague in 1361, and those of Leicester and Lincoln when her older sister, Matilda, died of the same disease in 1362, making him the largest landowner in the country, after the king. The marriage proved very successful, with seven children being born in just eight years, three of whom survived infancy – daughters Philippa and Elizabeth and a son, Henry of Bolingbroke.

It has always been believed that Blanche died in 1369, when John of Gaunt was away fighting in France. Having moved her young family to Bolingbroke Castle in Lincolnshire, to escape a fresh outbreak of the Black Death, she was thought to have succumbed to the dreadful disease while there. However, recent research has demonstrated that Blanche died at Tutbury on 12 September 1368, more likely from the complications of childbirth than from the plague, following the birth of her daughter, Isabella, who died young. Her husband was by her side when she died and arranged to have prayers said for the soul of his lost duchess.[6] At her death, Blanche's surviving children, Philippa, Elizabeth and Henry were aged 8 years, 4 years and eighteen months, respectively. John of Gaunt was a widower with a young family, though not for long. He would marry a second time in September 1371. This was another dynastic marriage and, with it, brought a claim to the crown of Castile. Constance of Castile was the daughter of Pedro I 'the Cruel' and his 'hand-fast' wife, Maria de Padilla; the same Pedro of Castile who had been the intended groom for John's sister Joan, who had died on the way to her wedding.

Born in 1354 at Castro Kerez, Castile, Constance succeeded her father as 'de jure' Queen of Castile on 13 March 1369, but John was never able to wrest control of the kingdom from the rival claimant, Pedro's illegitimate half-brother Enrique of Trastamara, who reigned as Henry II. He would eventually come to an agreement with Enrique's son that would unite the two rival claims to the throne.

John of Gaunt's eldest son and heir, Henry of Bolingbroke was expected to succeed his father as Duke of Lancaster and pursued a similar career of royal service to that of his sire. Henry and Richard II had been born in the same year, 1367, with Richard just four months older than his cousin. However, Richard was the second son of the heir to the throne, Edward of Woodstock, the Black Prince, whereas Henry was the son of the Black Prince's younger brother. After the death of Richard's older brother, Edward, in 1371, Richard had been destined for the throne. He was raised to be king.

Henry, on the other hand, was destined to be the leading – and richest – noble in the land. Having lost his mother when an infant, he was raised in the household of his stepmother, Constance of Castile, with Katherine Swynford as his governess. When he turned 7, Henry was appointed a governor, Thomas Burton.[7] Burton had served in the household of Henry's maternal grandfather Henry of Grosmont, Duke of Lancaster, and would have been able to teach the boy about the history of the duchy he was set to inherit. Henry was taught languages, including Latin, French and English, by his chaplain, Hugh Herle, who also taught him to read and write in French and English. In 1376, the Gascon, Sir William Montendre, was appointed to teach Henry martial arts. Henry was an adept student when it came to riding and hunting, which would lead to his later reputation as an accomplished jouster. The following year, a week after his tenth birthday, Henry was knighted alongside his cousin Richard, at Windsor, on 23 April and both boys were admitted into the Order of the Garter, which had been founded by their grandfather in 1348. Just two months later Edward III died, and Richard became King Richard II of England, with young Henry carrying Curtana, the blunt sword symbolising mercy, at the boy-king's coronation ceremony on 16 July. He now started using the honorary title of Earl of Derby, once held by his maternal grandfather. From 1380 onwards, Henry is seen more in the company of his father and witnessing state events.

Although his father was in Scotland, Henry was in London at the time of the Peasants' Revolt in June 1381. He was besieged in the Tower of London, alongside King Richard and faced danger when Richard left the Tower for Mile End, to negotiate with the rebels. Some of the rebels gained access to the Tower, and several of those sheltering there, including Simon Sudbury, Archbishop of Canterbury, were dragged out and murdered. Henry's life was saved 'in a wonderful and miraculous manner' by one John Ferrour of Southwark.[8] Henry obviously remembered Ferrour's service, as this statement appeared in a pardon issued in 1400, following Ferrour's involvement in the Epiphany Rising that year.

By the time of the Peasants' Revolt, 13-year-old Henry was already a married man – or, rather, boy. John of Gaunt had purchased the wardship of Mary de Bohun in July 1380. With her older sister, Eleanor, Mary was the coheiress of her father Humphrey de Bohun, Earl of Hereford, who had died in 1373. Eleanor was married to Henry's uncle, Thomas of Woodstock. The chronicler Froissart suggests that Thomas had encouraged Mary to become a nun and join the order of the Poor Clares, so that he could control the entire Bohun inheritance of which he already had the larger share. In buying Mary's wardship for £5000, John of Gaunt thwarted his brother's plans, though the dispute over the Bohun estates would go on into the reign of Henry V, who would force a settlement in his favour on Thomas's only child, Anne of Gloucester. Froissart suggests that the marriage was arranged after Mary was lured from Pleshey Castle whilst her brother-in-law was away, on the pretext of visiting her aunt, who was also Henry's distant cousin, Mary FitzAlan, at Arundel Castle. On or shortly after 5 February 1381, when she was still only 10 years old, Mary and Henry were married, most likely at Mary's home of Rochford Hall in Essex.[9] John of Gaunt gave his new daughter-in-law a number of wedding gifts, including a ring set with a ruby, a diamond ring and a diamond set in a clasp.[10] The king and Edmund of Langley, John's younger brother, both sent minstrels for the occasion. As Mary was still underage, the marriage would not be consummated for at least two more years. The young couple had known each other since they were infants, and appear to have got on well together, if the number of children they would have in a short period of time is anything to go by.

After the wedding ceremony and feast, Mary was returned to her mother's care, to allow her to mature before she had to take on the duties of a wife. John of Gaunt is recorded as paying Mary's mother £26 13s 4d at Easter and Michaelmas in 1382, as part of the 100 marks annuity the duke had allotted his daughter-in-law.[11] Mary de Bohun had a pretty impressive pedigree. With Norman origins, the Bohun family had come over with William the Conqueror in 1066 and settled in Wiltshire, serving both Henry I and King Stephen (I will refrain from saying 'boo!'). Through marriages to heiresses, they acquired the earldoms of Hereford and Essex, and the family residence of Pleshey Castle was inherited by Mary's father from a childless uncle. Through her father, Mary was a great granddaughter of Elizabeth of Rhuddlan and through her mother, Joan FitzAlan, the daughter of Richard FitzAlan and Eleanor of Lancaster, Mary was a descendant of Henry III. Mary would have grown up in an atmosphere of privilege and culture; her father was one of the foremost patrons and collector of books in the fourteenth century, eleven of which were created at Pleshey for the Bohun family.[12] Two psalters, one for Mary and one for Henry, were commissioned to celebrate the couple's wedding.[13] Four manuscripts, including illustrations, were made for Mary herself, incorporating heraldic images joining her coat of arms with those of Henry. Other pictures featured the Virgin Mary and two women kneeling in prayer, perhaps depicting Mary and her mother.[14]

Despite her new status as a wife, Mary's life would have changed little as she grew to adulthood. She would have continued with her education, learning how to manage a household, including the ordering and storing of provisions, supervising servants, arranging menus and the completion of household chores. She would have also taken religious instruction, learned to read, though not necessarily to write, and to play music. A love of music was something she shared with Henry and Mary appears to have arranged choirs, enjoyed singing and played the cither or harp.[15] Playing games, such as dice and chess, and hunting with birds would have also been on the curriculum. A young noblewoman was expected to do more than simply birth children. She was to play hostess to her husband's friends and allies and needed to be confident in making small talk and cultivating relationships which could help the family in the future. Though she was not expected to take on the full duties of a wife, Mary may have accompanied her husband to important court occasions. Perhaps she was with Henry at Westminster Abbey for the coronation of Richard II's new queen, Anne of Bohemia, in January 1382, and watching from the stands as Henry participated in the jousting that followed at Smithfield. Mary may also have watched Henry as he took part in the May Day jousts at Hereford in the same year. Such occasions would have been an opportunity for the couple to meet and spend time together, getting to know each other before they truly became husband and wife. However, it may also be that Mary remained secreted at Pleshey, attending to her lessons and sharing the company of her mother and sister. Eleanor gave birth to her first child, Humphrey, at Pleshey in April 1382, with two daughters, Anne and Joan, arriving in 1383 and 1384 respectively.

Henry, in the meantime, remained in his father's household, accompanying John of Gaunt to France in December 1383 to negotiate a peace treaty with King Charles VI. It was about this time, also, that relations between John of Gaunt and Richard II were beginning to strain, with Richard believing court gossip that Gaunt was plotting against him. While Gaunt and his brother Thomas – and probably Henry – were repelling Scottish invaders in the north in 1384, Richard was ordering Gaunt's execution; Gaunt returned south to protest his innocence. John of Gaunt again drew the king's enmity at the end of 1384 when he told Richard that war with France was unavoidable; Gaunt walked out of the council at Richard's extreme response and by February 1385, Richard was again looking for Gaunt's execution. The king backed down when Gaunt refused to attend on him and would only appear when dressed in his armour.[16] They were formally reconciled a month later, but the damage had been done, the trust between the Crown and the House of Lancaster was irretrievably broken.

Amidst this national turmoil, Mary reached the age of consent, her age proven before the escheator of Essex on 22 December 1384, with Henry then inheriting Mary's portion of the Hereford estates and titles, officially taking them into his custody on 10 March 1386.[17] It was likely around this time that Mary and Henry started living together as husband and wife, and sharing a bed. Though Henry was not always by his wife's side. His career was beginning to take off – he joined the king's campaign against the Scots in the summer of 1385 and was summoned to his first parliament in October of the same year. It was a rather fractious parliament at which a commission was set up to reform the royal household, whose spending was out of control, and to tackle the apparent disregard of England's military obligations overseas and the defence of the realm at home.[18] Christmas 1385 was then spent at Leicester, where Henry's household joined that of John of Gaunt's for the festive season.[19] By the spring of 1386, Henry and Mary would have known that she was pregnant, as would John of Gaunt before he departed for Spain that July. Gaunt and his second wife, Constance (Constanza) of Castile, would spend the next three years in the Iberian Peninsula, attempting to claim the crown of Castile from the son of the man who had replaced and murdered her father, Pedro the Cruel. Enrique of Trastamara (Henry II) had died in 1379 and was succeeded by his son, John I. As Constance's husband, Gaunt had been using the title of King of Castile and Leon since 1372. His attempts to claim the crown had amounted to nothing until 1386, when John I of Castile set his sights on the Portuguese throne. John of Avis, King of Portugal, turned to John of Gaunt for help. John saw this as his opportunity.

Bidding his son farewell at Plymouth, John of Gaunt sailed to claim his crown. Having landed in Galicia, however, Gaunt was unable to bring the Castilians to battle and his army succumbed to sickness. The opposing forces eventually agreed the 1388 Treaty of Bayonne, where in return for a substantial sum, John of Gaunt abandoned his claim to Castile. The treaty also saw a marriage alliance, between John of Castile's son, Henry and Constance and John's daughter, Catherine, which would see Catherine crowned as Queen of Castile and Leon in 1390. John of Gaunt would not return to England until November 1389. His three-year absence meant he missed a number of significant events in his son's life – the first being the birth of a son and heir.

After seeing his father off on his Spanish expedition, Henry had taken his young wife and their household to Monmouth Castle, on the Welsh borders, to await the birth of their first child. Thomas Swynford, the son of his father's mistress, Katherine, was with Henry; the young men were a similar age and had grown up together in Gaunt's household. Henry was also accompanied by his chaplain, Hugh Herle, chamberlain, Hugh Waterton, and treasurer, Simon Bache.[20] They spent the summer hunting in the Forest of Dean, playing dice, entertaining and awaiting Mary's lying-in. Henry would not have been in Mary's chamber when she gave birth, but would have been pacing anxiously nearby, no doubt. Mary would have been attended in the birthing chamber by experienced women. It is highly likely that Katherine Swynford and her teenage daughter by John of Gaunt, Joan, were with Mary. Gaunt had been forced to publicly renounce Katherine at the time of the Peasants' Revolt, but she remained close to the family and even lent Gaunt money for his Spanish expedition. Since Gaunt's departure, Katherine shared her time between her own estate and Mary's household. Her experience as a mother would have been invaluable to the young countess during her first labour. Katherine was certainly with Mary at Christmas 1386, when the wardrobe accounts record that two lengths of silk brocade and a number of miniver furs were provided for Katherine and her daughter, Joan.[21]

On 16 September 1386, 15-year-old Mary gave birth to her first child, a boy named Henry, for his father. Known as Henry of Monmouth, he would one day be recognised as one of England's most victorious kings, Henry V. But that was far in the future; in 1386 little Henry was merely the great-grandson of one king, Edward III, and the first cousin once removed of another, Richard II. Although he was born into a rich and powerful family, a crown was not in his foreseeable future. Mary had employed a wet nurse for her new son, Joan Wauryn, who was paid an annual salary of 40s, as well as her board and lodgings.[22] Mary would have spent the first month of Henry's life in her chambers, recovering from the birth and getting to know her baby. She was not expected to appear in public until after her churching, which usually took place thirty to forty days after the baby's birth. Henry may have wished to attend his wife's churching, which would have been a splendid occasion, with days of feasting and jousting, but the king had called a parliament for 1 October. And so, when he left his new family on 24 September, in order to attend to his duties to the king at Westminster, it must have been with great reluctance.

Although he had faced down the Peasants Revolt at the age of 13, the early years of Richard's reign had encountered no effective opposition from within the nobility. That was about to change. And Henry would earn the lasting enmity of the king as a consequence. In August, King Richard had announced his intention to invade France and asked parliament to grant him taxation of £155,000 to pursue his claim to the French throne. They refused, rebuking the king for his failure to reform his finances since the establishment of a commission in 1385, and claiming that he was being poorly advised. The opposition emerged under the leadership of the king's uncle, Thomas, Duke of Gloucester; he and his adherents would become known as the Lords Appellant. They called for the dismissal of Richard's chancellor and treasurer. Richard vehemently refused and stormed out of the chamber, effectively closing parliament.[23] Forced back into parliament with reminders of the fate of his great-grandfather, Edward II, who was deposed and possibly murdered, Richard capitulated. His unpopular chancellor was replaced with Thomas Arundel, Bishop of Ely, while John Gilbert, Bishop of Hereford, was appointed as treasurer. Fourteen lords were established at Westminster, a commission to oversee Richard's government. However, Richard had one final card to play and that was to declare Roger Mortimer, the 12-year-old Earl of March, as his successor, effectively ending the claim of John of Gaunt as Richard's heir, as had been stipulated by Edward III, who had dismissed the Mortimer claim as it passed through a woman, Philippa of Clarence, the daughter of Lionel of Antwerp.

Having not been appointed to the new council, Henry returned to Mary and his baby son in time for Christmas. Within a few weeks of his homecoming, Mary was once again pregnant. The year 1387 was mainly spent away from court, though Henry did attend the Garter ceremony and feast at Windsor on St George's Day.[24] The young family spent the summer at the grandiose Lancastrian stronghold of Kenilworth Castle, which was in the last stages of being transformed into a palace by John of Gaunt's renovations, begun in 1371.[25] The atmosphere at court would have made spending time with his family attractive to Henry, but Henry may also have avoided court as he suffered a 'pox' in this year. The term 'pox' can cover a variety of illnesses, from smallpox to measles to syphilis; the latter seems unlikely given it is a sexually transmitted disease and there is no evidence of Henry consorting with prostitutes or taking mistresses. The illness, whatever it was, was so serious the king's physician, John Middleton, was called upon to attend Henry.[26]

As Henry was recovering from illness and spending time with his family, Richard II was manoeuvring to seize back personal control. He summoned the Duke of Gloucester and Earl of Arundel to his presence and, when they refused, sent out secret orders to have Arundel arrested and, if possible, killed.[27] Gloucester and Arundel assembled a force to the north of London, at Waltham Cross. They accused five of Richard's closest advisers of treason: Alexander Neville (Archbishop of York), Robert de Vere (Earl of Oxford and Duke of Ireland), Michael de la Pole, Justice Robert Tresilian and Sir Nicholas Brembre of London. On 17 November the lords rode to Westminster to meet with the king, accompanied by 300 men-at-arms. They challenged those they had accused to trial by combat, which was ignored. But Richard could not ignore the accusations against his friends and was forced to agree to the charges being heard in parliament on 3 February 1388.[28] Faced with the prospect of a trial, the accused mostly ran away. Only Brembre stayed with the king. De Vere made his way to Chester from where he raised an army of over 4000 men.

Henry had not been with the Lords Appellant when they met the king at Westminster, perhaps not yet ready to commit himself and the House of Lancaster to the Appellants' cause. It may be that he was waiting for direction from his father in Castile before taking sides. He was in London, at his house in Bishopsgate, with Mary. At some point in the late summer or early autumn, Mary had given birth to their second son, Thomas; Henry rewarded the midwife who had helped to deliver the baby while they were in London that November.[29] And it was from London, on 25 November, that Henry sent Mary and their two sons, newborn Thomas and Henry, now fifteen months old, to Kenilworth for safety. Only then did Henry join the Lords Appellant, attending a war council with the other lords at Huntingdon on 12 December, where they resolved to face Robert de Vere, Earl of Oxford, in the field. It was thanks to Mary herself that Henry and the Lords Appellant were able to move to face de Vere and confront him before he reached London. From Kenilworth, Mary wrote to Henry at Northampton, Daventry and elsewhere, apprising him of de Vere's movements and the route his army was taking through the Midlands. Splitting their army, Henry's allies were able to maintain a parallel march to de Vere's forces while Henry headed for the Thames, to guard the bridges against de Vere and cut him off. Thinking the Appellants' force was behind him, de Vere was surprised to find Henry's men blocking the approach to Radcot Bridge. De Vere decided to fight but, as the rest of the Appellant forces arrived, his Cheshire army laid down their arms. De Vere fled on horseback along the riverbank, stripped off his armour and swam his horse across the Thames. Once on the other side of the river, he made his way to Kent from where he fled to the Continent. His armour, horse and other possessions were later recovered. The Battle of Radcot Bridge was barely a battle – it was over swiftly with only a handful of casualties, the most notable of which was Thomas Molyneux, the constable of Chester Castle, who was killed by Thomas Mortimer, despite his pleas for mercy, after being caught trying to cross the River Thames.[30]

After Radcot Bridge, Henry and his allies marched on the Capital. They met with King Richard at the Tower of London on 27 December 1387, where Richard's deposition was proposed and the possible candidates to replace him discussed. As the only one of Richard's uncles present, with John of Gaunt in Castile and Edmund of Langley, Duke of York having taken no part in the hostilities, the Duke of Gloucester was the leading candidate. Such a move would have been against Henry's best interests, and those of his father, so it was eventually decided that the status quo would be maintained, with Richard remaining as king but with the five Lords Appellant in control. And when parliament met on 3 February 1388, a number of the king's friends were condemned by 'appeal', rather than trial, for 'living in vice' and misleading the king; this is where the name Lords Appellant arises. The Merciless Parliament was to sit until June, overseeing the condemnation of the king's friends and then widening the net to include Richard's household chaplains and clerks and the judges who had met with the king at Nottingham and been forced to approve his tyranny. Edmund, Duke of York, vainly defended the king's old tutor, Simon Burley, leading to a breach with his brother the Duke of Gloucester. In the end, eight of Richard's friends were executed, with two more, De Vere and de la Pole, sentenced in absentia. A further seven had their goods declared forfeit and were exiled.[31]

As parliament closed, an uneasy truce was reached between king and lords, though with the flimsiest of sticking plasters. Henry left court, perhaps intending to join the campaign against Scotland which resulted in the Battle of Otterburn, in which the English, under the command of the Earl of Northumberland, were defeated. Henry made it no further north than Nottingham when he appears to have diverted to Kenilworth, possibly having received news that Mary was ill. John of Gaunt's physician, a priest and scholar from Oxford named Geoffrey Melton, had been sent for, to attend the countess. The reason for Melton's attendance is unknown. It may be that Mary was suffering a difficult pregnancy, complications after the birth of her last son, Thomas, in 1387, or an issue entirely unrelated to childbirth. Whatever the ailment, Mary appears to have recovered quickly and was pregnant again by September, just before Henry departed for a parliament at Cambridge which lasted until mid-October. He returned to spend Christmas with his family at Kenilworth. Having attended a council meeting in London in the spring of 1389, Henry was back home again in time for the birth of his third son, John, on 20 June.

John was no doubt named for his grandfather, who returned home in November 1389. The whole family were together for Christmas at Hertford Castle, during which time Mary became pregnant once again, just seven months after John's birth. It cannot have escaped Mary and Henry's notice that while their nursery was rapidly filling up, King Richard and his wife, Anne of Bohemia, remained childless. And it cannot have escaped Richard's notice, either. And while Henry attended to his duties at court, or went jousting in France, Mary was occupied in overseeing the care of her children, with trusted women such as Joan Wauryn and their governess Mary Hervy.[32] She was six months pregnant when she and Henry travelled north to arrange the provisions and fitting out of a ship for Henry, in preparation for his Crusade to Lithuania. Saying his goodbyes to Mary and their three small sons at Lincoln on 19 or 20 July 1390, Henry boarded his ship at Boston and departed for Eastern Europe. It must have been a frightening time for the young countess. Still only 20 years old, her husband was going off to fight in distant lands, and she was facing the birthing chamber for the fourth time. As any medieval woman would tell you, each pregnancy was a fresh danger to a mother's life.

Having said her farewells to her husband, Mary and the children returned to Kenilworth to await the birth of the baby. Her wardrobe accounts for the time record the purchase of 'three dozen and four knots' of strings for musical instruments.[33] On the 3 October a fourth son, named Humphrey after her father, was born. The letter announcing the birth, possibly written by Mary herself, reached Henry on 1 November via a sailor from Könisberg.[34] Having campaigned hard against the pagans in Lithuania, Henry had set up his winter quarters in Könisberg, not quite ready to return home, though travelling by sea in winter would have been a perilous undertaking. He moved on to Danzig in mid-February and at the end of March departed for England. The sea journey taking four weeks to complete, he and Mary would have been reunited at the end of April, or early May, when he would have met his youngest son, already seven months old, for the first time.

Once home, apart from attending a tournament at Kennington in July, Henry spent his time with his wife and family. At Peterborough, payments were made to foreign minstrels who had entertained the couple by playing the lute and fiddle.[35] And, of course, Mary was pregnant again. She was midway through her fifth pregnancy when Henry had to leave for the opening of parliament at the beginning of November. He sent his wife a present of 100 apples and 150 pears from London.[36] During the proceedings, an uneasy peace was maintained between the king, Henry and his father but no sooner was parliament over than Henry left London. The Lancaster family gathered at Hertford for the Christmas season with Henry giving his wife, as a New Year's gift, a jewel of a golden hind with a white enamelled body and wearing a golden collar, costing £9.[37] Henry then attended a council meeting at Westminster in early February, where it was determined that John of Gaunt would lead an embassy to France to negotiate peace. Leaving London on 25 February, Henry and his father, and the other emissaries, were met at Calais by four French dukes, who escorted the 200-man contingent to Amiens and the waiting King Charles. Negotiations went on for fifteen days, but no permanent agreement could be reached, so the truce was merely extended for one more year. It was a disappointing outcome.

Henry may have been home by mid-April or early May, by which time Mary had probably already given birth to her fifth child, a girl who was named Blanche after Henry's mother. Henry's account book records payment, in May, for clothing for little Blanche's nurse.[38] Her two oldest brothers, Henry and Thomas, at the ages of 5 and 4 respectively, wore their new silver-gilt collars of linked Ss, the livery of the House of Lancaster, at the christening.[39] There seems to be some confusion over Blanche's place of birth. Victorian historian James Hamilton Wylie stated that the baby was born at Walmsford, now known as Wansford, which is a village to the west of Peterborough, on the River Nene. Others suggest Blanche was born at Peterborough Castle, which does seem more likely. There is a possibility, of course, that Blanche was premature, and that Mary was on her way to Peterborough Castle, for her lying in, when she went into labour and was forced to stop *en route*. It is a small detail, and irrelevant to most, I suppose. Little Blanche was born as a member of the nobility, rather than the daughter of a king, so details such as these get lost, as did her actual birth date. At the time of her birth, no one was to know that she would be a princess one day.

No sooner had Henry met his baby daughter than he was on his travels again. He left England in July 1392, ostensibly to rejoin the Crusade in Lithuania, but when he arrived at Danzig, it was to discover the war was over and peace had been established.[40] Instead of returning home to England having achieved nothing, Henry decided to make a pilgrimage to Jerusalem. And Mary was again left to wait at home, now with five young children. One consolation was that Mary was not pregnant when Henry left England, which would give her body extended time to recover from the almost-constant pregnancies she had endured since she was 15. However much she was going to miss Henry, she would be the healthier for his absence.

Unfortunately, there is no record of Mary's movements whilst Henry was away on his pilgrimage. Her eldest boys, Henry and Thomas, were turning 6 and 5, respectively, that year, and would have been placed under the supervision of a tutor, learning all they needed as members of the nobility, both as administrators of the vast Lancaster lands and as soldiers. In the meantime, Henry reached Jerusalem in late January 1393 and visited the Holy sites before making the return journey. He had travelled in style; he had visited some of Europe's greatest cities and met with kings including Wenceslas of Bohemia and Sigismund of Hungary. He had been welcomed and fêted at every stop along the way. He landed at Dover on 30 June 1393, after almost exactly a year away. There is no record of his reunion with his wife and children. Henry and Mary would have exchanged letters during his absence, but the frequency would have been sporadic and unpredictable given the distances involved. It may be that Mary had travelled to Dover to greet Henry as he disembarked from his ship from France, or she and the children awaited his return in London, which he reached by 5 July.[41]

No sooner was he home than Henry was off again, joining his father in a campaign against rebels in Lancashire and Cheshire, who were targeting Henry, his father and the Duke of Gloucester, blaming these lords for the unpopular peace that had been negotiated, whereby Richard had agreed to relinquish his claim to sovereignty over France. The rebels were quickly dealt with, and Henry was home with Mary at Peterborough by late August. Within weeks Mary was pregnant for the sixth time. Mary and Henry were to spend the rest of the summer and autumn together, before joining John of Gaunt at Hertford for their habitual family Christmas. Entertainments included the King of France's own jester and the traditional Christmas joust, in which Henry took part alongside his half-brother, Thomas Beaufort; Henry paid for a new suit of armour for Thomas especially for the occasion.[42] As usual, there was a long list of gifts, both sent and received, for New Year, including presents from the king and queen. Henry left it as late as possible to depart for parliament. As he had done previously, he sent his wife a gift in his absence, this time it was oysters, mussels and sprats; perhaps she was craving seafood during this pregnancy?[43]

The parliamentary session was to sit from 27 January until 6 March 1394. It was a fractious session, with the succession still unresolved and a growing rift between Gaunt and the Earl of Arundel over the northern rebellion and Gaunt's growing influence over the king. Although Richard II defended Gaunt against Arundel, both Gaunt and Henry, father and son, rode away from parliament disappointed. John of Gaunt's hard work in negotiating the treaty in France had come to nothing as parliament rejected it. And Henry had been ignored, given no offices and no recognition as the king's heir. John of Gaunt and the Duke of Gloucester were then tasked with taking the news of the treaty's rejection to the French ambassadors. Henry's movements are unknown for spring 1394; he may have returned to Mary at

Hertford or Peterborough, which had been chosen for Mary's lying in. Or he may have accompanied his father, confident that Mary had successfully navigated five pregnancies and that the sixth would be no different. Just a few days after his father's departure, he would have received news of the death of his stepmother, Constance of Castile, on 24 March. Gaunt made the arrangements for his duchess's funeral at Leicester, which was not to take place until his return, so that he could be present.

Duchess Constance had been a part of Henry's life since he was a toddler, but her loss was to be nothing compared to the news that followed just a few months later. On 4 June 1394, Mary was delivered of her sixth and last child – another baby girl, named Philippa after Henry's grandmother, Queen Philippa of Hainault. However Mary, at just 24 years of age, did not recover from the birth, dying during or shortly after little Philippa's arrival. Whether Henry was with his wife, or in France with his father, we do not know. According to Helen Castor, he was in the north, mopping up the last disturbances from the recent rebellion.[44] Wherever he received the news of his wife's death, it must have been devastating. He and Mary had been married for more than half of their lives and now had six children together. It must also have been a reminder to Henry – and especially John of Gaunt – of the loss of his own mother when he was just a baby. Father and son would have been united in their grief at the funerals in Leicester, a day apart. Constance was laid to rest on 5 July in the church of St Mary de Castro and Mary was interred in the Lady Chapel of the same church on 6 July. The church had been hung with black cloth for both ceremonies and John and Henry had joined in the funeral processions, alongside other family members and retainers of the House of Lancaster. Devastated at this unexpected loss, Henry went into mourning for a whole year.[45]

Mary's death was a tragedy for Henry but a devastating loss for his children. As their father grieved, the children were taken under the wing of their grandmother, Joan FitzAlan, Countess of Hereford, who took them, along with their familiar nurses and attendants, to live with her at Bytham Castle in Lincolnshire. It cannot have been easy for the dowager countess of Hereford, grieving the loss of her youngest daughter and now tasked with raising the motherless children. Little Philippa was a newborn, and Blanche was only two years old. The older boys continued their education there for a short while but would soon be set up in their own establishment.[46]

One more death in a year of tragedy had occurred almost simultaneously with that of poor Mary de Bohun. On 7 June at Sheen Palace, Queen Anne had succumbed to plague. King Richard was so devastated that he ordered the palace destroyed and demanded that the funeral, held at Westminster Abbey on 3 August, would be the most lavish ever held. Anne's death also marked a shift in Richard's behaviour towards Henry, who was increasingly isolated. Although he came to court on occasion, attending parliaments and great councils, and witnessing fourteen of the forty-two royal charters granted between 1393 and 1398, Henry remained excluded from Richard II's inner circle, and was denied duties, such as diplomatic missions, which he might have expected to be given as a cousin of the king. On a personal note, John of Gaunt had married his long-time mistress, Katherine Swynford, in Lincoln Cathedral in February 1396, and had successfully petitioned the Pope to declare his four children by Katherine, three sons and a daughter, legitimate, supported in his request by the king. In November 1396, John and Katherine, the new Duchess of Lancaster, along with Henry and his oldest son, 10-year-old Henry of Monmouth, joined the host of nobles gathered in Calais to witness the wedding of King Richard and Isabella de Valois, who would turn 7 five days later. Ironically, Isabella's younger sister, Katherine, who would be born in 1401, would be the bride of Henry of Monmouth, by then Henry V, in 1420.

For Henry, spring 1397 had meant spending Easter with his father and Duchess Katherine at Tutbury Castle in Staffordshire, followed by a visit to his daughters, 5-year-old Blanche and Philippa, now 2, at the Herefordshire home of Henry's chamberlain, Hugh Waterton, in whose care they had been placed.[47] Matters at court were rapidly coming to a head when, in July 1397, the three leading Lords Appellant were arrested and charged with treason. The Earl of Arundel was executed, the Duke of Gloucester was murdered while imprisoned at Calais and the Earl of Warwick was imprisoned. On 29 September, Henry was created Duke of Hereford, and on the same day received a pardon for his actions with the Lords Appellant ten years earlier. Henry was still wary of the king and sought to please Richard by coming to court more often and giving him a great feast and entertainment during the September parliament. But in December of the same year, Henry encountered Thomas Mowbray, now Duke of Norfolk. Mowbray had initially been a close friend of Richard II but had alienated the king by marrying the daughter of the Earl of Arundel without Richard's permission. He had joined the Lords Appellant at the same time as Henry but, most recently, had reconciled with the king and been responsible for the Duke of Gloucester's murder. Now he intercepted Henry on the road between Brentford and London, with a warning. According to Henry, Mowbray told him 'We are on the point of being undone', in revenge for 'what was done at Radcot Bridge' in 1387.[48] Mowbray then went further, saying 'it is a false world indeed, for I know well that, had several of us not taken action, you and your father would have been murdered on the way to Windsor after the parliament. But Edward, duke of Aumale [York], John Holland, duke of Exeter, Thomas Percy, earl of Worcester and I all swore that we would never agree to destroy a lord without a just and reasonable cause…'[49] Mowbray also informed Henry that there was a plot to reverse the pardon of Earl Thomas of Lancaster, Edward II's arch nemesis, which would see all the Lancaster heirs, including Henry and his father, disinherited.

Henry reported the conversation to his father, who then told Richard. And on 30 January, Henry himself related the conversation in parliament. In further meetings with the king, Henry accused Mowbray as 'a traitor, false and recreant towards you and your royal majesty, to your crown, to the nobles and all the people of your realm'.[50] In his turn, Mowbray declared that Henry 'has lied in what he has said and wishes to insinuate against me, like a false traitor and disloyal subject that he is'.[51] The bitter arguments between the two lords, continued, with Henry accusing Mowbray of embezzlement and the murder of Gloucester. The dispute was to be decided in a trial by combat at Coventry in the autumn. It was set to be a hard fight. Mowbray was just as proficient a jouster as Henry; the combatants were well matched. But the contest never happened. As the two dukes took to the lists to fight, Richard intervened and sent both combatants into exile: Henry for ten years, Norfolk for life. They were given one month to leave England.

It was a devastating blow for Henry. With the death of Roger Mortimer, Earl of March, in Ireland in July 1398, Henry was now the obvious heir to Richard II, Mortimer's sons both being under 10 years of age. But if anything happened to Richard whilst Henry was in exile, he would not be in a position to pursue his claim to the throne. On a more personal level, Henry's father was in his late fifties and in failing health. And there were the children. They had already lost their mother. The older boys were now nearing their teens and in need of a father's guidance as they approached adulthood. Philippa, the youngest, was only 4 years old, her sister Blanche was 6. Henry may have been caught up in national events, but he had kept his daughters in his thoughts throughout the year and had bought them two ABC grammar books, an obvious sign that he wanted his daughters to be as well educated as their mother.[52] During their father's exile, the girls were to remain in the custody and care of Henry's friend and chamberlain, Hugh Waterton. The eldest boy, Henry, now 12, was to remain with King Richard, whether as his ward or a hostage is unclear. Henry would take his second son, 10-year-old Thomas, with him into exile, perhaps thinking it not wise to leave both of his oldest boys in Richard's custody. John, at 9 years old, was to stay in London with a tutor while 7-year-old Humphrey would remain with his sisters.[53]

Henry left London for exile on 13 October 1398. He was welcomed to Paris by King Charles VI and was given the use of a house, the Hôtel de Clisson, and financial support. Despite the warm welcome, Froissart noted that Henry:

> Was at times very melancholy, and not without reason, on thus being separated from his family. He was impatient to return, and much vexed that for such a frivolous cause he should be banished from England, and from his four promising sons and two daughters. [He] frequently dined with the king, the duke of Orléans and other great lords, who did everything they could to make his time pass agreeably.[54]

Whilst in France, Henry contemplated remarrying, with Mary of Berry, the daughter of the Duke of Berry, the youngest son of King John II. When King Richard heard of the plan, he sent the Earl of Salisbury to King Charles to persuade him to break off the engagement, accusing Henry of treason. The affair soured Henry's stay in France, and he decided to move on, writing to his father for permission to travel to Hungary. John replied with the suggestion that Henry visit his sister Philippa in Portugal, or his half-sister Catherine in Castile. With Gaunt's letters, the messenger also brought the news that the old duke's health was failing. Having been visited by the king in early January, John of Gaunt died on 3 February 1399 and was buried beside his first wife, Blanche of Lancaster, in St Paul's Cathedral, London, on 15 March. Blanche, Philippa and their brothers were all bought mourning robes of black to wear at the funeral. The little girls, aged 6 and 4, were dressed from head-to-toe in black, including their shoes.[55] Gaunt may have hoped that Richard would relent and allow Henry to return to England for his father's funeral, but it was not to be. Still in Paris, Henry attended a Mass for his father's soul with the French royal family, but they were in an awkward position. They may have felt sympathy for Henry and the situation in which he found himself, but the French king's daughter was Richard's wife. And Richard now showed his implacable hatred for Henry when on 18 March 1399, he revoked all of Henry's pardons and confiscated the vast Lancastrian inheritance. Henry's banishment was extended from ten years to life.

Richard must have felt he had triumphed. Henry was banished and penniless. But not quite friendless. When, on 1 June 1399, Richard II was landing his army in Ireland, Henry was putting the final touches to his own plans of invasion, with Thomas Arundel, the exiled Archbishop of Canterbury, and Thomas FitzAlan, the son and heir of the executed Earl of Arundel. With no more than 15 knights and a total force not exceeding 300, Henry sailed for England. He landed at Ravenspur on the Yorkshire coast on 4 July. Edmund, Duke of York, had been appointed keeper of the realm during the king's absence but although he was aware that Henry was likely to invade, he had no idea where his nephew would land. Making landfall at Ravenspur meant that Henry was three days' hard ride from London, but close to his Lancastrian heartlands. After visiting Bridlington Priory, he made his way to Pickering Castle, which opened its gates to him. Knaresborough Castle resisted but was quickly subdued and Henry left his own garrison there before leaving for the Lancastrian's northern power base, Pontefract Castle, which he reached on 13 or 14 July. His army had been gradually growing as he travelled through Yorkshire but by Pontefract, men were flocking to his banner. He then made his way to Doncaster, where he is said to have sworn an oath that he would not take the throne by force.[56]

Henry advanced south, via Derby, Leicester, Coventry and Warwick, meeting his uncle, the Duke of York, at Berkeley Castle, where Edmund agreed that Henry's attempt to reclaim his inheritance was just and right. He was not prepared to go to war to defend his other nephew, the tyrannical king. At the end of July, Richard landed with his army at Milford Haven but abandoned them soon after, fleeing north with only two dozen men. The decision not to stand and fight put the final nail in the coffin of his kingship.

The Earl of Northumberland was sent to Richard to persuade him to surrender, perhaps with promises that his life would be spared and that Henry had only come to claim his rightful inheritance. The assurances given were enough to persuade Richard to ride out of Conwy, when he was promptly surrounded by the armed force Northumberland had hidden outside the castle walls. The captive king was taken to Flint Castle, where the two cousins finally came face to face. Richard and his captor then rode to London. Parliament was summoned for 30 September and Richard was placed in the Tower while Henry and his allies decided on their course of action. It was not so cut and dried that Henry could just depose Richard and have himself crowned. Richard had named his uncle Edmund, Duke of York as his heir. After much legal discussion and further pressure, King Richard II abdicated the throne on 29 September 1399. Parliament met the next day, with the throne laying vacant, draped in cloth of gold. As Duke of Lancaster, Henry took the seat formerly occupied by his father. The assembly was then informed of the charges laid against Richard and of the king's abdication, with the Bishop of St Asaph declaring that the throne of England was now vacant. Henry then stood, made the sign of the cross on his forehead and breast and spoke to the gathering:

> In the name of the Father, Son and Holy Ghost, I, Henry of Lancaster claim this realm of England, and the Crown with all its members and appurtenances, as I am descended by right line of the blood coming from the good lord King Henry the Third, and through that right, God of his grace has sent me, with the help of my kin and my friends, to recover it; the which realm was at the point of ruin for the default of governance and the undoing of good laws.[57]

The lords, both spiritual and temporal, were then asked to affirm that they would accept Henry as their king. Henry was then led to the throne and took his seat. He was King Henry IV, his sons were now princes and his young daughters, Blanche and Philippa, were princesses. They are the only two princesses in England not born to that estate since the birth of Matilda of Boulogne, oldest daughter of King Stephen, in the early 1130s. To this point, the two little girls had barely made an impression on the historical record. And it would remain that way, to a great extent, as they grew up. There is no mention of them attending their father's coronation on 13 October 1399, though their brothers were present and the three younger boys – Thomas, John and Humphrey – had been knighted and created knights of the Order of the Bath on the eve of the coronation. It may be that the girls were thought too young to attend the hours-long ceremony and grand celebrations that followed. There being no queen, the roles for women in the coronation would have been limited or non-existent. Or, perhaps, they got to watch their father being crowned from a secluded viewpoint.

As Henry consolidated his position, the two girls were established in London, though away from court. With no queen, the royal court was a mostly male environment, unsuitable for young girls. They were sheltered from the effects of the Epiphany Rising of January 1400, when the plan was to assassinate Henry and his sons and place Richard, held prisoner at Pontefract Castle, back on the throne. With the plot, the former king's fate was sealed, and he died under mysterious circumstances the following month, on 14 February, starved to death, though it is unclear whether this was deliberately done by his gaolers, or by Richard himself refusing to eat. Later in the year, Henry IV was visited by the emperor of Byzantium, Manuel II, who was hoping to persuade Henry to send an army to defend Constantinople. The king entertained the emperor at Eltham Palace, with tournaments, hunts and plays. Blanche, although just 8 years old, in the absence of a queen was now the first lady of the court and presided over the entertainments and jousting, which took place on 1 January 1401, with blunt lances.[58] What an experience it must have been for the little princess! The participants took names from chivalric literature, such as Ardent Desirous, Lancelot, Ferombras and Lost Wisdom, while the ladies presented by their challengers were romantically named Venus, Virtue, Nature, Penelope and Cleopatra.[59] Ornately written letters of recommendation were presented to the child as 'the most excellent and most noble princess, lady Blanche, daughter to the most puissant prince, King of Albion'.[60] King Henry was the very embodiment of chivalric courtesy, though he could not give the emperor what he asked for, an army. He could not afford to leave England with his throne still insecure, and the royal finances were in a perilous state. All he could do was entertain the emperor and send him on his way with £2000 as a contribution towards his fight against the Turks.

Henry's reign was never going to be easy. Having usurped his cousin, there were always questions as to his legitimacy, and factions keen to exploit any weakness. On top of this, the rising price of corn, due to two years of bad harvests, was causing increasing lawlessness. His financial woes were then exacerbated by a substantial drop in wool revenues, which had once been £47,000 annually under Richard II but stood at £39,000 a year in 1401.[61] Against this backdrop of fiscal difficulties, Henry was thinking of marriage, not only for his daughters, but for himself. Just two months after her appearance at the New Year joust, Blanche's future was sealed with the signing of her marriage contract on 7 March. The princess was to marry Louis, or Ludwig, Count Palatine and future Elector Palatine. He was the son of Rupert III, or Ruprecht, Elector Palatine and King of the Romans, having recently deposed Richard II's hapless brother-in-law, Wenzel of Bohemia. In January 1401, Ruprecht had written to Henry proposing the dynastic alliance. The union would give Henry an ally on the French flank. The king had to raise a dowry of £13,333 6*s*. 8*d*., which he only achieved by reviving the old feudal responsibility, enshrined in clause 15 of Magna Carta, of paying a 'reasonable aid' from the knight's fee for the marriage of the king's eldest daughter.[62] It was not a popular tax, but the only way Henry could raise the money for Blanche's marriage. The next year, at the age of 10, Blanche left England for her new life. She was married at Cologne Cathedral on 6 July 1402. Her new husband was 24. Blanche was the same age as her mother had been on her wedding day but was to continue her education with her husband's family, rather than be sent back to her own family, as had happened with Mary de Bohun twenty years earlier. The princess was sent to her wedding with a trousseau which included a crown, known as the Crown of Princess Blanche, that may have once belonged to Queen Anne of Bohemia. Also known as the Palatine Crown, or the Crown of Bohemia, it was made of gold with diamonds, rubies, emeralds, sapphires, enamel and pearls. Blanche wore it on her wedding day, and it has been in the possession of the Wittelsbach family ever since. With grace and composure beyond her years, Blanche delighted the Imperial court, and her new husband wrote to Henry shortly after the wedding, saying, 'Most serene prince, I know not how to thank you fully for so rich and rare a gift'.[63] Ludwig served his father as Imperial vicar during Germany's military campaign in Italy. Highly educated and interested in the arts, he may well have been the ideal match for Blanche, given that it is likely she inherited her parents' love of literature and music.

It cannot have been an easy time for Princess Blanche. After years of upheaval, her mother's death, her father's exile, her grandfather's death and then the coup that removed Richard II from the throne and made her a princess, she was now being sent far away from home, and from everything and everyone she knew. And she was only just 10 years old. Her sister, Philippa, now taking Blanche's place as the first lady of the court, would have felt the separation just as keenly. Their youngest brother, Humphrey, may also have felt Blanche's departure deeply. He had spent longer in the nursery with his sisters than their older brothers, Henry, Thomas and John, and had lived with them at Eaton Tregoz during their father's exile.[64] And now Blanche was living in a country she would have known little about, where she did not even know the language, knowing she would never see her family again. What a daunting prospect for a child.

Although she married in 1402, the consummation of the union would not happen until Blanche was a little older. Her first child, Rupert, was born on 22 June 1406 at Heidelberg; sadly, he would never succeed his father as Elector Palatine, dying just a month before his twentieth birthday, on 20 May 1426.[65] Blanche must have delighted in sending her father the news. Despite the distance, Blanche would retain close contacts with her family in England, especially with King Henry IV. In 1408, her father honoured Blanche by appointing her a Lady of the Garter and in the following year Blanche was able to announce that she was, once again, pregnant. Sadly, sometime around her seventeenth birthday, the princess fell ill with a fever and died, at Neustadt in Alsace, on 22 May 1409, the baby dying with her.[66] She was buried in the Church of St Aegidius in Neustadt. Blanche's father-in-law, King Ruprecht, wrote to King Henry with the dreadful news, announcing, 'It weighs heavily with us, the tearful case of your illustrious daughter, our late daughter-in-law…'[67] Blanche's husband, Ludwig, sent his own letter to Henry, speaking of his grief at losing his 'most loved and sweetest wife', saying 'Now that she is gone, the delight and joy of my life are gone too'.[68] Ludwig's letter is far from formulaic and suggests a genuine fondness, and even love, for Blanche. In the midst of his grief, Henry wrote back to Ruprecht, his letter, though formal, tinged with sadness. The king wrote, 'Excellent prince, very dear brother, having read your letters our mind is filled with sorrow, for in the beginning of those accounts as well as at the end, one senses her extraordinary beauty and a bitter sadness mixed with consolation'.[69] The consolation of which Henry spoke may well have been the continuing survival of his grandson, Rupert, who was thriving, and the knowledge that Blanche had received the holy sacrament before her death. It must have been a hard blow for the king to take, however, having now lost his mother, his first wife and his oldest daughter in childbirth.

As Henry had been saying 'goodbye' to Blanche in 1402, he was making arrangements for his own marriage, to Joan of Navarre, the widowed Duchess of Brittany. Although the marriage had a political dimension, and was hampered by the likelihood of war between England and France, Henry and Joan's relationship appears to have been a love match – they chose each other. They were married by proxy on 3 April 1402 and then in person, in Winchester Cathedral, on 7 February 1403.[70] Already in Germany by the time Joan arrived in England, Blanche would never meet her new stepmother. Philippa, on the other hand, had time to get to know Joan and was at her father's wedding in Winchester. In that same year, the 9-year-old princess made a pilgrimage to Canterbury and the shrine of St Thomas Becket. Her future was already in the process of being arranged. Even as he was arranging Blanche's marriage in 1401, Henry IV approached Margarethe I of Denmark, Norway and Sweden with the idea of a double wedding. Philippa would marry Margarethe's great-nephew, Eric of Pomerania, while her big brother Henry would marry Eric's sister, Catherine. Born in Poland in 1381 and named Boguslaw at birth, Eric had been brought to Denmark in 1389 to be raised by Margarethe, who recognised him as her heir. He was crowned as King of Norway in 1389 and King of Denmark and Sweden in 1396, with his great-aunt acting as regent. In 1406, during negotiations for the marriage, English envoys wrote a report on the succession practices of all three Scandinavian kingdoms for the English government:

> The kingdom of Denmark is transmitted by free election, but nevertheless those there are accustomed always to elect those who are nearest to the royal blood, and if there are several children they are accustomed at all events to elect the one of them who seems to the electors most suitable and capable … the kingdom of Sweden is transmitted by election and not by succession and yet they are

> accustomed to elect the nearest of the royal blood or one of the children, just as was said of the kingdom of Denmark, but the kingdom of Norway is transmitted by succession not election.[71]

Although the idea of Henry and Catherine marrying fell by the wayside, arrangements for Philippa and Eric to marry continued apace. Before the end of 1402 agreement had been reached and Philippa and Eric were betrothed, although it was agreed that the 8-year-old princess would remain with her father until she was closer to marriageable age. Towards the end of 1405, Henry IV spent a month with his family at Kenilworth Castle before going on to London and the palace of Westminster, where 11-year-old Philippa was married by proxy to King Eric, now 24-years old, with the Swedish nobleman Ture Bengtsson Bielke standing in for the groom. She was meant to be in Denmark by early May, but the king suffered an illness which affected his leg so badly that he could not travel. It was only in June 1406 that Henry was well enough to accompany Philippa to King's Lynn from where the little queen of Denmark was to depart for her new life.[72] Also accompanied to Lynn by three of her brothers, Henry, Thomas and Humphrey, it may have been a particularly hard farewell with her youngest brother, Humphrey. He was closest in age to Philippa and had spent the most amount of time with her when growing up. Henry and Thomas had left the nursery just as Philippa was born, but Humphrey had stayed with his sisters throughout their father's exile and into the early years of his reign.

The preparations, celebrations and provisions for Philippa's departure to Denmark cost her father £4000.[73] Queen Philippa departed Lynn in the flagship of a small fleet of ships, her cabin hung with fine red worsted and cloth of gold. Her entourage, dressed in scarlet and green livery, included many with whom she was familiar, the most senior of which was her cousin, Richard of Conisbrough, the youngest son of the Duke of York. Hugh Waterton's wife, Katherine, who had been Philippa's governess throughout her childhood, was also in her retinue. As was Sir Henry FitzHugh, a Yorkshireman who had served Henry IV loyally for years, and who would later be chamberlain to Philippa's brother, Henry V.[74] They would, however, return to England within a few weeks of Philippa landing at Helsingborg, leaving the young queen to familiarise herself with her new surroundings and responsibilities.[75] It must have been a daunting time for Philippa, having left behind everything with which she was familiar and now having to wave goodbye to the people who were her last remaining links to her homeland. On 26 October 1406, in Lund Cathedral, Philippa and Eric were married. Philippa wore white; it is the first recorded time in history that a princess wore white on her wedding day. Her white tunic was accompanied by a cloak in white silk, bordered with grey squirrel and ermine. Her coronation ceremony followed immediately after the wedding.

Following the festivities, Philippa appears to have established herself in Sweden, where all of her dower lands were situated. She and Eric lived together in Kalmar Castle for the first three years of their marriage.[76] Philippa had her own court, supervised by her chief lady-in-waiting, Lady Katarina Knutsdotter. Through her mother, who was herself a lady-in-waiting to Queen Margarethe, Lady Katarina was a granddaughter of Saint Bridget of Sweden. We have very little information regarding Philippa's relationship with Eric. The period was a particularly turbulent time for the Scandinavian countries, with Eric at loggerheads with the Hanseatic League and the Teutonic knights. At home he faced opposition to his attempts to consolidate the government of his three kingdoms in one place. Eric is described as close to 190 cm tall (over 6 ft), handsome with an impressive physique and a keen intelligence.[77] As for Philippa, Eric obviously had great trust in her. She acted as regent during the king's periods of absence abroad and in Sweden she was, to a great extent, its *de facto* ruler.[78] Both contemporary and modern writers give a favourable account of her rule. She also fulfilled a queen's traditional role as protector and benefactor of religious institutions, especially the Brigittine monastery at Vadstena. Philippa is mentioned ten times in the *Diarium Vadstenense* in regard to matters relating to the monastery. However, the main evidence for her involvement in matters concerning Vadstena consists of letters, either written by her or where she is mentioned. Philippa's own letters give the impression of great concern and contain some personal arguments. The most important subjects of these are the difficulties of obtaining the confirmation of the Rule by the Pope. The correspondence includes letters between Eric and Philippa and the Pope, and Emperor Sigismund, as well as cardinals and members of the English Royal family.[79] Indeed, as the fulfilment of a penance imposed on their father by Pope Gregory XII, for his deposition of Richard II and execution of Richard Scrope, Archbishop of York, in 1405, Henry V founded a dual house for men and women at Syon, to be seeded with the Brigittine sisters, so popular with Queen Philippa.[80] The queen was also very generous to the order and the church at Vadstena in particular, testifying to her commitment to the Brigittines. It is, perhaps, no surprise then that it was at the convent at Vadstena that Philippa chose to be buried.[81]

Philippa was queen of Denmark, Norway and Sweden for 24 years. She and Eric had a great degree of trust, but do not appear to have been very close. They were apart for long periods of time during the marriage, with Eric travelling throughout his three kingdoms and beyond, while Philippa largely remained in Sweden. Indeed, in the spring of 1426, Eric sent Philippa to Sweden, to summon the Swedish council and secure their support, and funds, for the Dano-Hanseatic War (1426–35).[82] When the war was going against Eric the following year, Philippa again summoned the Swedish Council, to Nyköping, to secure further support from the Swedes, after which she returned to Denmark, where she established herself for the next three years. Philippa is particularly revered in Copenhagen for her resolve during a full-scale assault by the Hanseatic League in 1428. King Eric was absent, but the queen was in residence and rallied the Danes, demonstrating her 'royal heart and royal courage' as she encouraged the defenders to fight the Hanseatic fleet in Copenhagen Harbour.[83] Once the attack was repulsed, the queen then went among the survivors, tending to the sick and wounded with her own hands.

Unlike her mother, Philippa was never to have a nursery full of babies. As the years went by, the lack of children, and of an heir, would have added a greater strain to the marriage. In 1416 in the Pomeranian Act of Succession, Eric named his cousin, Boguslaw IX of Pomerania, as heir to the three kingdoms, should he and Philippa remain childless. In 1420 the Act was amended, appointing Queen Philippa as regent until the coronation of Boguslaw, or until he attained his majority if he was still a minor when Eric died.[84] When she finally did fall pregnant, Philippa was 35 years old. She was old for a first-time mother and her pregnancy and health caused a great deal of concern. Towards the end of 1429, the queen had once again travelled to Sweden to ensure its continuing support for the war, staying at Vadstena Abbey.[85] It was at the abbey that she welcomed a delegation of the Swedish riksråd (privy council). Not long after, however, Queen Philippa fell ill, with a recurring illness she had been suffering from for the last five years. The baby was, sadly, stillborn and Philippa's health continued to deteriorate. Philippa herself died on 5 January 1430.[86]

Neither Blanche nor Philippa had been born to be princesses, but rather to be members of the higher nobility of England, great-granddaughters of a king. Their father's seizure of the throne in 1399 not only changed their status in England, but also their marriage prospects. As the daughters of the Duke of Lancaster, they would have expected to be married to noblemen within the English realm. As daughters of the king, they were married to form and strengthen international alliances. Whether they were content in their new lives, whether they missed England, their father and their brothers, we know not. That they fulfilled their duties as wives, albeit in different ways, is beyond doubt. Blanche gave her husband a son and heir before dying at a tragically young age, whereas Philippa acted as a partner to Eric, aiding him in the rule of his three disparate kingdoms, acting as regent and leader in his absence. That she never experienced the joys of motherhood is a personal tragedy for her and a dynastic sorrow for Denmark, Sweden and Norway.

Blanche and Philippa were the only two princesses of the royal House of Lancaster. Their brother, Henry V, and nephew, Henry VI, would each only produce one child, a son. In Henry V's case it was, of course, Henry VI. In Henry VI's case, it was Edward of Westminster, the Prince of Wales who would be killed at the Battle of Tewkesbury by Yorkist forces in 1471. Following Philippa's death in 1430, England would have no princess until the birth of Elizabeth of York, daughter of Edward IV and Elizabeth Woodville, in 1466. She would be the oldest of six princesses of the royal House of York.

Chapter Six

Royal Daughters of the House of York

Many, many books have been written about the period 1455 to 1485, known as the Wars of the Roses. So, I will be brief. Sometimes referred to as the Cousins' War, it was an epic dynastic struggle between the royal Houses of Lancaster and York, who were both descended from Edward III. Richard, Duke of York's struggle against Henry VI's rule was not, initially, a challenge for the throne. Rather it was born out of York's frustration with Henry VI's ineffective rule and York's increasing isolation and exclusion from the centre of government. It was a complex and bloody struggle, marked by political manoeuvrings, vicious battles and the frequent, arbitrary execution of nobles on both sides. Animosity ran long and deep. The year 1460 had ended badly for the Yorkist cause, with defeat at the Battle of Wakefield, fought on 30 December, in which Richard of York was killed, along with his second son, 17-year-old Edmund, Earl of Rutland. York's stalwart supporter and brother-in-law, Richard Neville, Earl of Salisbury, was executed at Pontefract the following day by the victorious Lancastrians.

York's oldest son and heir, Edward, took up the leadership of the Yorkist cause. Although only 18, he was already an experienced warrior and general. He won the Battle of Mortimer's Cross on 2 February 1461, just over a month after the deaths of his father and brother. And despite the defeat of his cousin and ally, Richard Neville, Earl of Warwick, at the Second Battle of St Albans on 17 February, Edward was proclaimed King Edward IV in London on 4 March. Edward's subsequent victory at Towton, in Yorkshire, on Palm Sunday, 29 March, fought in a snowstorm, confirmed his position. It was one of the bloodiest battles ever to take place on English soil. Three months later, on 28 June, Edward of York was crowned as King Edward IV in Westminster Abbey. Henry VI was still alive, and still at large. He would be captured the following year and imprisoned in the Tower of London. His wife and son, Margaret of Anjou and Edward of Westminster, would continue the struggle, first seeking shelter in Scotland before making their way to France. They would return, but more on that later.

Edward was tall, handsome and young, and a king! His marriage was a great concern to the country and his cousin, Richard, Earl of Warwick sought to make a political match that would be advantageous to England. He was negotiating with France for a bride, either Anne of France or Bona of Savoy, the daughter and sister-in-law of Louis XI, respectively. Edward had other ideas and rather rashly, as most observers thought, married Elizabeth Woodville (or Wydeville), thwarting Warwick's plans. Elizabeth and Edward were married in a clandestine ceremony. Kings were not expected to marry for love but for the good of their realm, a diplomatic marriage that would bring peace and trade agreements to the country at large. Edward's marriage for love, to Elizabeth Woodville, deprived England of the opportunity of a profitable foreign alliance. Moreover, Elizabeth was a lowly widow of a minor Lancastrian knight, Sir John Grey, and her father was also a mere knight, Sir Richard Woodville. Elizabeth's mother, Jacquetta, was of more exalted blood, descending from the royal House of Luxembourg, and her first marriage had been to John, Duke of Bedford, the third surviving son of Henry IV, king of England. Far from being the innocent virgin that most kings married, Elizabeth was already the mother of two sons, Thomas and Richard, and was about five years older than the king.

Dominic Mancini, an Italian visitor to England, gave a wonderful description of King Edward. He described him as:

> 'by nature mellow and of aspect genial: yet should he adopt a wrathful countenance he could be very terrible to behold. He was easy of access to his friends and to others, including those of least consequence … He would show himself to those who wished to view him, seizing any available opportunity to display more openly and at length how impressive he was to onlookers. He was so affable in his greeting that if he espied a newcomer taken aback by his appearance and royal splendour, he would encourage him to speak by means of a kindly hand placed on his shoulder.'[1]

Edward was also known as a womaniser. As Mancini goes on to say: 'In carnal lust he indulged to an extreme, while his behaviour was also said to have been most insulting to many women after he had possessed them; for as soon as his lust was sated he passed them on, much against their will, to other members of his court. Married or single, high-born or lowly, it made no difference. However, he ravished none by force: all were prevailed upon by means of money or promises, and having prevailed, he dropped them'.[2]

Edward's reputation for womanising would have dire consequences for his children after his death. And his clandestine marriage would add fuel to the fire, leading many to conclude that it was not the only time that Edward had agreed to marriage in return for a woman's caresses. It was assumed that Elizabeth Woodville was more astute that any others, insisting that the marriage was valid and that she was Edward's wife. With the distance of 500 years and the absence of private letters, it is impossible to know. The waters have been rendered murkier by claim and counterclaim of whether Edward had conducted a secret marriage, before that with Elizabeth Woodville, with a lady called Eleanor Butler, thus making himself a bigamist and his children illegitimate.

But we are getting ahead of ourselves. In 1464, possibly in May but certainly before October when the marriage was made public, Elizabeth and Edward were married. The marriage was unpopular among the nobility, who rarely liked to see one of their own raised above all others, especially when she had twelve siblings who would need to be given suitable appointments and spouses. However, the deed was done, the marriage consummated and Elizabeth, at least, looked every part the queen. She was beautiful and had a strength of character and personality that would rise to the challenge of queenship.[3] She was also, to put it bluntly, fertile. She already had two sons and, being only in her mid-twenties, she was still young enough to bear more. The union could also be seen as an act of reconciliation. Elizabeth was from a Lancastrian family; her husband had died fighting for Henry VI at the second Battle of St Albans in February 1461. She was crowned queen at Westminster Abbey on 26 May 1465, amidst great splendour and pageantry, with the coronation feast afterwards hosting 3000 invited guests.

Less than a year later, the Crowland chronicler recorded 'I now come to the sixth year of the reign of the said king, when Elizabeth, the eldest daughter by his marriage already mentioned, was born. This took place in the month of February, it being the year of our Lord, according to the computation of the English church, 1465, but according to that of the church of Rome, 1466'.[4] Edward and Elizabeth's first child, Elizabeth of York was born at Westminster on 11 February 1466 and baptised in the magnificent Westminster Abbey. Her godparents were her grandmothers Cecily Neville, Duchess of York and Jacquetta of Luxembourg, Duchess of Bedford, along with Richard Neville, Earl of Warwick, famously known as the Kingmaker.[5] The king gave his wife a jewelled ornament, costing £125 'against the time of the birth of our most dear daughter'.[6] The younger Elizabeth would be the eldest of seven daughters and three sons born to Edward and Elizabeth; eight of whom would survive infancy. At the time of her birth, England was enjoying a few years of peace and prosperity, following a decade of conflict and political upheaval. The baby girl was set up in her own household under the supervision of Margaret, Lady Berners, at the palace of Placentia in Greenwich.[7] The household would have included rockers, nurses, maids, pages, cooks and clerks. Sixteen months later, Elizabeth was joined in the nursery by a sister, Mary, who was born on 11 August 1467. Another sister, Cecily, joined them in March 1469. Queen Elizabeth was granted 400*l.* a year for the provision of her daughters' household.[8]

In the early summer of 1469, the king undertook a progress to East Anglia. He had faced down two rebellions in the north the year before and knew that the Earl of Warwick was dissatisfied with his own position within the king's administration, and with seeing members of the Woodville family promoted. He thought he should have more. Leaving baby Cecily in the care of her nurses, the queen and their two eldest daughters, Elizabeth and Mary, joined Edward at the family seat of Fotheringhay, in Northamptonshire, for a week. As the king departed to try to stabilise the kingdom, Elizabeth and her daughters continued on to Norwich, arriving on 18 July.[9] They were welcomed to the city by Mayor John Aubrey and entertained with a series of pageants, which must have delighted the two little princesses. They were then escorted to their lodgings at the convent of the Friars Preachers. It would have been while she was still in Norwich with her daughters that the queen received news that Edward had been, essentially, arrested by George Neville, Archbishop of York and brother of the Earl of Warwick. With Edward in his custody, Warwick was England's ruler in all but name and set about ridding himself of those he perceived as enemies. The queen was still in Norwich when news reached her of the deaths of her father, Sir Richard Woodville, and her brother John, who were executed on 12 August 1469 after being apprehended by Warwick's forces. No doubt grieving and fearing for her husband's life, the queen left Norwich and returned to London where she heard that her mother, so recently widowed, was being accused of using witchcraft to bring about the marriage of Edward and Elizabeth. The accusations were only dropped as Warwick's regime crumbled.

Warwick's attempts to rule through Edward while keeping the king in custody ultimately failed; the barons were happy for Warwick to have a place in the government of England but not for him to usurp royal authority. An uprising in favour of Henry VI, still a prisoner in the Tower, did not help matters. Warwick was forced to release Edward and work with him to defeat the Lancastrians. Edward then attempted to reconcile with Warwick. John Neville, Warwick's younger brother, lost his earldom of Northumberland, as it was restored to the Percy heir, but was made Marquess of Montague in compensation and given lands in Devon. Warwick lost some of the offices he had granted to himself when he had Edward in custody but otherwise escaped punishment. Warwick was the most powerful landowner in the kingdom and needed to be placated.

From the moment of her birth and until the birth of her baby brother Edward in November 1470, Elizabeth was her father's heir. With female rule still frowned upon, Elizabeth's husband would be *de facto* ruler of England should the princess succeed her father. Which meant her marriage was a primary concern not just for her parents, but for the whole of the country. She was the most valuable gift the king could bestow. A month before her fourth birthday, on 5 January 1470, little Princess Elizabeth was betrothed to her cousin George, the son of John Neville, Marquess of Montague, in an attempt by the king to build bridges; the boy was also made Duke of Bedford. The arrangement was short-lived, however, as the Neville brothers rose in rebellion again just two months later. Having been told by Edward to submit or be declared a traitor, Warwick took ship for Calais, taking the king's brother George, Duke of Clarence with him. George had defied his brother and married Warwick's oldest daughter, Isabel, with hopes of Warwick putting him on the throne in Edward's place. But Warwick changed his plans. After being refused entry to Calais, the exiles made their way to France, where Louis XI orchestrated a reconciliation between Warwick and Henry VI's queen, Margaret of Anjou. Not an easy task, given Margaret saw Warwick as the cause of all her woes. As part of the agreement, Margaret's son, Edward of Westminster, Prince of Wales, was to marry Warwick's younger daughter, Anne Neville. This alliance, moreover, facilitated the temporary re-adeption of Henry VI, with Warwick now leading a Lancastrian army in an invasion of England.

As Warwick seized control of the kingdom and took Henry VI from the Tower and placed the crown on his head, Edward IV fled to Burgundy with his youngest brother, Richard, and his closest friends. Elizabeth Woodville, who was awaiting the birth of her next child, fled her lodgings in the Tower of London just days before Warwick arrived in London. Although heavily pregnant, she went by boat with her three daughters and sought sanctuary at Westminster Abbey, her mother Jacquetta of Luxembourg with her. It must have been a desperate time for the queen, and a scary one for the three little girls, fleeing the Tower in the dark. While Cecily was still only eighteen months old, Mary was now 3 and Elizabeth $4^1/2$. Both would have been able to pick up on the tensions experienced by the adults around them. The desperate women and the children were lodged in sanctuary at Westminster Abbey, perhaps in the abbot's own rooms. Henry VI's government paid Elizabeth, Lady Scrope, £10 to attend the erstwhile queen, and she was sent weekly supplies of beef and mutton.[10] Her midwife, Margery Cobbe, was also allowed to attend her and on 2 November, Elizabeth Woodville gave birth to a son, Edward, the heir to the fallen Yorkist dynasty.[11] All the queen could do was sit and wait for events to play out, and hope for better days, safe in her sanctuary, though in straitened circumstances.

By the spring of 1471, Edward had secured aide from his ally, Charles of Burgundy and landed on the Yorkshire coast, claiming he had come to reclaim his family inheritance, just as Henry IV had done in 1399. Warwick was still waiting for Margaret of Anjou to arrive from France, basing himself in Coventry as Edward made his way to London. On 11 April, Edward was reunited with his queen and his three daughters, and met his son for the first time. The relief and joy must have been palpable. After months of confinement and uncertainty the family were together again, though there were still battles to be fought. Three days later, Warwick and his brother Montague were defeated and killed at the Battle of Barnet. The war was almost over, but not quite. Margaret of Anjou had finally set sail for England and landed at Weymouth on the same day that Warwick had been defeated. On 4 May, Edward met the Lancastrian queen's army at Tewkesbury. Edward of Westminster, the son and heir of Henry VI, was killed. It was all over bar the shouting. Almost. There was one more skirmish when the Bastard of Fauconberg, an illegitimate cousin of Warwick, demanded entry into London. His forces attacked the Capital on 12 May and for three days the citizens resisted, mounting a stout defence. The queen, her children and her brother, Anthony Woodville, were secured behind the walls of the Tower of London. Fauconberg's forces were forced to retreat on hearing news of the advance of Edward's army; Fauconberg was captured and executed. On 21 May, King Edward IV entered his Capital once again and that very night Henry VI died in the Tower of London, officially from melancholy on hearing of the death of his son but that he was quietly put to death seems more likely.

With the last vestiges of opposition removed, life could return to normal for the royal family. Although, it must be noted that Princess Elizabeth's position had been diminished by the arrival of her baby brother. She was no longer her father's heir, with a kingdom as her dowry. She was, however, still the king's eldest daughter and her marriage was still a matter of politics and diplomacy. In 1475, as he was preparing for war against France, Edward IV drew up a will in which he set aside 10,000 marks for Elizabeth's marriage, even though no suitable candidate was on the horizon. Peace with France changed that and, as part of the Treaty of Picquigny, it was agreed that Elizabeth would marry the French dauphin (heir) Charles, with a jointure of £60,000 to be provided by Charles's father, King Louis XI. Were Elizabeth to die before the marriage could be solemnised, her younger sister, Mary, would take her place.[12] From that moment on, Elizabeth was referred to as 'My Lady the Dauphine' or 'Madame La Dauphine'.[13] In the event, neither Elizabeth nor Mary would marry the French dauphin as alliances shifted. By the time of her father's death, on 9 April 1483, Elizabeth of York was 17 and still unmarried.

Despite her father's exile from England and her own time in sanctuary with her mother, grandmother and sisters in 1470 and 1471, when Henry VI was briefly returned to the throne, Elizabeth's childhood was happy and secure.[14] As the future dauphine of France, she was taught to speak and write both French and Spanish.[15] Elizabeth and her siblings grew up, at the palace of Placentia in Greenwich, away from the hustle and bustle of court. She did attend court on special occasions and was there in 1472 for the visit of Louis de Gruuthuse, the man who had sheltered and supported Edward IV during his exile in Burgundy. Elizabeth was seated at the high table, with her parents, for the feast, and danced with the king, her father.[16] After dinner 'my lady Elizabeth, the Kinges oldest daughter, daunsed with the Duke of Bokingham'.[17] In 1476, Elizabeth, Mary and Cecily accompanied the court to Fotheringhay, where they attended the reburials of their grandfather and uncle, Richard, Duke of York and Edmund, Earl of Rutland.[18] Elizabeth was made a Lady of the Garter in 1477, with Mary and Cecily being given the same honour in 1480. The nursery's occupants were added to at regular intervals. After the short life of Margaret, who was born at Winchester on

10 April 1472 and died eight months later, Queen Elizabeth gave birth to another son, Richard, on 7 August 1473, at Shrewsbury. A month later, Prince Edward, as the king's heir, was given his own establishment at Ludlow, in the Welsh Marches, with a set of ordinances drawn up to regulate every aspect of his daily routine and education. As the younger son, Richard was to remain in his mother's custody and with his sisters. On 2 October 1475 another daughter, Anne, was born, and she was followed by a son, George, in March 1477. The little prince was given the title Duke of Bedford but died about the time of his second birthday in 1479. Two more daughters, Catherine and Bridget, were born at Eltham in August 1479 and November 1480, respectively.

As the children grew and applied themselves to their studies, arrangements were being made for their futures. Negotiations were opened for a possible marriage between Mary and Hans of Denmark, Norway and Sweden, though nothing came of them and Hans married elsewhere in 1478. At the age of 5, Cecily was betrothed to the son of James III of Scotland, the future James IV, to whom 'king Edward had long paid a yearly sum of one thousand marks by way of dowry for Cecily, one of his daughters, who had been promised in marriage by a formal embassy to the eldest son of the king of the Scots'.[19] After which she was referred to as 'Princess of Scotland'. In 1482, however, the groom was substituted with the Duke of Albany, brother and rival of James III, by the Treaty of Fotheringhay, but the marriage never materialised. Prince Edward was betrothed at the age of 10 to 3-year-old Anne of Brittany. Anne would eventually become queen of France, twice, firstly as the wife of Charles VIII, Princess Elizabeth's erstwhile betrothed, and then as the wife of Louis XII. Richard of Shrewsbury had been betrothed at the age of 4 to 5-year-old Anne de Mowbray, only daughter and heiress of the Duke of Norfolk. Anne of York was betrothed at the age of 4 to Philip the Handsome, son of Maximilian of Austria. When she was just two weeks old, Catherine was promised as the future bride of John of Asturias, son and heir of Ferdinand and Isabella, the rulers of Spain.

The youngest daughter, Bridget, was never considered for the royal marriage market. This may be because her father died before he could find a suitable spouse, or because Bridget was always destined for the convent. Bridget, named for Saint Bridget of Sweden, was christened in the chapel at Eltham Palace on the day after her birth by the Bishop of Chichester. Her godmothers were her paternal grandmother Cecily, Duchess of York, and her oldest sister, Elizabeth of York, who was approaching her fifteenth birthday. Lady Maltravers, a younger sister of Elizabeth Woodville, would act as godmother at Bridget's confirmation. The Bishop of Winchester, William Waynefleet, was godfather and Margaret Beaufort carried the newborn to the baptismal font.[20] She was assisted by Bridget's oldest half-brother Thomas Grey, Marquess of Dorset. A hundred torches borne by knights preceded the procession of nobles who were to assist in the baptism: Lord Maltravers bearing the basin, the Earl of Northumberland carrying the unlit taper and the Earl of Lincoln bearing the salt. The baby princess was presented with 'great gifts' which were carried before her when she was returned to her mother's chamber.[21] A description of Bridget's christening has survived and was reprinted, in *The Gentleman's Magazine* in January 1831 and again in *The Ricardian*, by Pauline E. Routh, in 1975:

> . . . the twentieth year of the reign of King Edward IV on St. Martin's Eve was born the Lady Bridget, and christened on the morning of St. Martin's Day in the Chapel of Eltham, by the Bishop of Chichester in order as ensueth:
>
> First a hundred torches borne by knights, esquires, and other honest persons.
>
> The Lord Maltravers, bearing the basin, having a towel about his neck.
>
> The Earl of Northumberland bearing a taper not lit.
>
> The Earl of Lincoln the salt.
>
> The canopy borne by three knights and a baron.
>
> My lady Maltravers did bear a rich crysom pinned over her left breast.
>
> The Countess of Richmond did bear the princess.
>
> My lord Marquess Dorset assisted her.
>
> My lady the king's mother, and my lady Elizabeth, were godmothers at the font.
>
> The Bishop of Winchester godfather.
>
> And in the time of the christening, the officers of arms cast on their coats.
>
> And then were lit all the foresaid torches.
>
> Present, these noble men ensuing:
>
> The Duke of York.
>
> The Lord Hastings, the king's chamberlain.
>
> The Lord Stanley, Stewards of the King's house.
>
> The Lord Dacre, the queen's chamberlain, and many other estates.
>
> And when the said princess was christened, a squire held the basins to the gossips [the godmothers], and even by the font my Lady Maltravers was godmother to the confirmation.

> And from thence she was borne before the high altar, and that solemnity done she was borne eftsoons into her parclose, accompanied with the estates aforesaid.
>
> And the lord of Saint Joans [possibly John St. John] brought thither a spice plate.
>
> And at the said parclose the godfather and the godmother gave great gifts to the said princess.
>
> Which gifts were borne by knights and esquires before the said princess turning to the queen's chamber again, well accompanied as appertaineth, and after the custom of this realm.[22]

The year 1482 must have been difficult for the family with the death, at the age of 14, of Mary, while the family were at the palace of Placentia, Greenwich. The princess appears very little in the historical record, beyond a proposed husband from Denmark, her presence at the re-internment of her grandfather and uncle at Fotheringhay, and her attendance at the wedding of her younger brother, Richard, Duke of York, and Lady Anne de Mowbray, the heiress to the Duke of Norfolk; the bride and groom were 6 and 5, respectively. According to Mary Anne Everett Green, the body of the princess was not embalmed 'but tightly enveloped in multitudinous folds of cere cloth, and placed in a leaden coffin which was rudely ornamented with the moulding of a human head'.[23] On the Monday following her death, Mary's body was conveyed to a church in Greenwich, where four wax tapers were kept constantly burning around it. A funeral dirge was recited by the Bishop of Norwich. The same bishop performed a second service the following day, this time in the presence of the Bishop of Chichester, the Dean of Windsor and several gentlemen of the court, including Lords Dacre, Dudley and Beauchamp. Among the female mourners were Lady Grey of Ruthin, the queen's sister Lady Katherine Grey, Lady Strange and Lady Dacre, who may have been the princess's governess.[24] Later that day 'a mourning chariot, adorned with the arms of the royal maiden in lozenges, and drawn by horses trapped with sable, conveyed her remains to the burial place of her royal race in St. George's chapel, Windsor'.[25] The funeral procession stopped at Kingston-upon-Thames overnight before continuing the journey to Windsor the next day. The hearse, underneath a canopy borne by four gentlemen, was now accompanied by up to thirty poor men, carrying lighted torches. On arrival at Windsor, Mary's brother, 11-year-old Edward, Prince of Wales, met the coffin and acted as chief mourner as the princess was laid to rest in the south-east end of the chapel. Mary was buried beside her baby brother, George.[26]

Although we have no written account of the grief of her parents, the care taken over the funeral arrangements certainly suggests Mary was no neglected daughter. Elizabeth of York may have felt the loss keenest, being closest to Mary in age and having been each other's almost-constant companions for the whole of Mary's short life. Christmas 1482 was a magnificent celebration, grander even than previous years, perhaps to ward off the residual grief of Mary's passing. The king appeared in a variety of costly garments, presenting a 'distinguished air to beholders, he being a person of most elegant appearance, and remarkable beyond all others for the attractions of his person'.[27] All the family were present at the celebrations, with the Crowland (or Croyland) chronicler commenting 'You might have seen, in those days, the royal court presenting no other appearance than such as fully befits a most mighty kingdom, filled with riches and with people of almost all nations, and (a point in which it excelled all others) boasting of those most sweet and beautiful children, the issue of his marriage, which has been previously mentioned, with queen Elizabeth'.[28] The chronicler goes on to give a succinct summary of the marital, or lack of, arrangements for the princesses at the time of the Christmas court:

> Their five daughters, most beauteous maidens, were called, naming them in the order of their respective ages, the first, Elizabeth, the second, Cecily, the third, Anne, the fourth, Catherine, and the fifth, Dorothy [Bridget]. Although solemn embassies had been despatched, and promises made, on the faith and words of princes, respecting the marriage of each of these daughters, and the same had been, in former years, agreed upon under letters of covenant concluded in the most approved form, still, it was not believed at this time that any one of the alliances above-mentioned would take place; to such mutability was everything subject, in consequence of the vacillating conduct of France, Scotland, Burgundy, and Spain, in regard to England.[29]

The Crowland chronicler clearly blames the machinations of Louis XI of France, known to many as the Universal Spider. He writes of King Edward:

> this spirited prince now saw, and most anxiously regretted, that he was thus at last deluded by king Louis; who had not only withdrawn the promised tribute, but had declined the alliance which had been solemnly agreed upon between the Dauphin and the king's eldest daughter; encouraged the Scots to break the truce, and to show contempt for the match with our princess Cecily; and, taking part with the burghers of Ghent, used his utmost endeavours to molest the party of the duke of Austria, the king's ally; as well as, with his singular craftiness, carried into execution every possible kind of maliciousness, both by sea and by land, in order that he might annihilate the power of this kingdom.[30]

It may be that the king was already ill at Christmas 1482, and that the celebrations were grander in order to take his mind off his worries. His health certainly was in decline in the early part of 1483, and he took to his bed at the end of March, dying on 9 April. His funeral was held at Westminster Abbey on 17 April, and he was laid to rest in St George's Chapel, Windsor, two days later. With the death of their father, the fortunes of Edward IV's children would take a dramatic turn. His 12-year-old son Edward was now King Edward V, though he was soon deposed by his uncle Richard, Duke of Gloucester. When news reached London that Gloucester had taken possession of the young king as he had travelled towards London, 'queen Elizabeth betook herself, with all her children, to the sanctuary at Westminster'.[31] Elizabeth Woodville was then persuaded to relinquish custody of her younger son, who was housed in the Tower of London alongside his brother, the king. Plans for the coronation of Edward V were abandoned when Richard Duke of Gloucester took the throne for himself on 26 June 1483. As Richard III, the new king justified his actions by claiming that Edward IV's marriage to Elizabeth Woodville had been bigamous, due to the king already having been married to another woman, and therefore Edward V, Elizabeth of York and their brother and sisters were all illegitimate and not entitled to inherit the crown.

Edward IV had been a notorious womaniser, his most famous mistress being Jane Shore and he is known to have had at least two illegitimate daughters, Elizabeth and Grace, although the identity of their mother – or mothers – is unknown. Elizabeth appears to have been born sometime between 1461 and 1464, before Edward's marriage, and married Thomas Lumley. A manuscript dated to 1500, which mentions the marriage, names her as 'the bastard daughter of King Edward'.[32] We do not have even a general date for the birth of Grace but it is possible that she was raised in the household of Elizabeth Woodville as she was on the boat which conveyed the late queen's body to Windsor Castle for burial alongside Edward IV on 10 June 1492.[33]

As events unfolded, and the two princes were gradually seen less and less within the Tower precincts, until they were no longer seen at all, Elizabeth of York and her sisters remained in sanctuary with their mother, a focus for political disaffection and an embarrassment to the new regime that Richard III could not allow to continue.[34] The precarious situation was made worse at Christmas 1483 when Henry Tudor, the Lancastrian claimant to the throne, despite the failure of a rebellion in his name, swore an oath at the cathedral in Rennes that he would marry Elizabeth of York if he succeeded in claiming the English throne. Tudor writers saw this oath as the fruits of negotiations between Elizabeth Woodville and Henry's mother, Margaret Beaufort. It was a shrewd move on the part of Henry Tudor, a political unknown who had spent his adulthood in exile on the Continent and whose claim to the throne was shaky at best: marrying Elizabeth of York would give him credibility and a strong association with the royal blood of Edward IV. It would also gain him allies among the Yorkists alienated by Richard III's actions. Rumours abounded that 'some of the king's daughters should leave Westminster, and go in disguise to the parts beyond sea; in order that, if any fatal mishap should befall the said male children of the late king in the Tower, the kingdom might still, in consequence of the safety of the daughters, some day fall again into the hands of the right heirs'.[35] The guards around the abbey were increased to protect against this eventuality.

The situation could not continue as it was. As a consequence, Richard decided to open negotiations with Elizabeth Woodville to persuade her to allow her daughters to leave sanctuary. Agreement was reached in March 1484, whereby Elizabeth of York and her sisters would be treated as befitted the king's kinswomen; as the eldest of the sisters, Elizabeth was placed in the household of Richard's queen, Anne Neville.[36] The king promised:

> That I , Richard, by the grace of God, King of England, and of France, and Lord of Ireland, in the presence of you, my lords spiritual and temporal, and of you, mayor and aldermen, of my city of London, promise and swear, on the word of a king, upon these holy evangelists of God, by me personally touched, that if the daughters of Dame Elizabeth Gray, late calling herself Queen of England that is to wit, Elizabeth, Cecily, Anne, Catharine, and Bridget – will come unto me out of the sanctuary of Westminster, and be guided, ruled, and demeaned after me, then I shall see that they shall be in surety of their lives, and also not suffer any manner of hurt, by any manner of person or persons, to them or any of them, or their bodies and persons; nor them or any of them imprisoned within the Tower of London, or other prison; but that I shall put them in honest places of good name and fame, and them honestly and courteously shall see to be found and entreated, and to have all things requisite and necessary for their exhibition and findings, as my kinswomen; and that I shall marry such of them as now be marriageable to gentlemen born, and every one of them give in marriage – lands and tenements, to the yearly value of cc. [200] marks, for the term of their lives; and, in likewise to the other daughters, when they come to lawful age of marriage, if they live. And such gentlemen as shall happen to marry with them, I shall straightly charge, from time to time, lovingly to love and entreat them, as their wives and my kinswomen, as they will avoid and eschew my displeasure.[37]

After almost a year within the confines of Westminster Abbey, the daughters of Edward IV emerged from their sanctuary and were given lodgings at court. It is hard to imagine the emotions of these five girls, aged between 4 and 18, returning to court after a year of turmoil and upheaval, in which they had lost their father, and their brothers had been taken from them, possibly murdered. They had also lost the prospect of dazzling futures as queens and duchesses, their status now tinged with the taint of illegitimacy. Richard's actions in taking custody of his brother's daughters ostensibly put Elizabeth of York out of the reach of Henry Tudor. It has been suggested that Richard himself was planning to marry Elizabeth following the death of his wife, Anne Neville, in March 1485. Richard and Anne's only son and heir, Edward of Middleham, Prince of Wales, had died in April 1484. Richard was desperately in need of an heir and so went in search of another wife. Many potential brides were proposed, and it may be that Elizabeth of York's name was thrown into the hat. It is possible, moreover, that Elizabeth herself contemplated marrying Richard. There is suggestion of a letter, now lost, from Elizabeth of York to the Duke of Norfolk, asking if he would mediate on her behalf to bring the marriage about. Apparently, the princess also said that she feared that Anne Neville would never die.[38] The letter is no longer extant but shows a side of Elizabeth's character that we are unfamiliar with, if she ever wrote it. Elizabeth's wishes mattered for nought, however. Such a suggestion, of the king marrying his own niece, made Richard's own supporters anxious about the political ramifications. The resulting hostility meant that Richard was forced to make a public denial that he had ever contemplated such a match.

Neither did the king find Elizabeth a husband, however, probably fearing that marriage would transfer Elizabeth's claim to the throne, albeit tainted by the declaration of illegitimacy, to her new husband, thus making him a threat to Richard. In the event, Cecily, the next eldest sister to Elizabeth after the death of Mary in 1482, was the only one to be married during Richard's reign. She was married to Ralph, the younger brother of Thomas Lord Scrope of Upsall, Richard III's ally. It was a disparaging marriage for the daughter of a king, to marry the younger son of a mere lord. It would have been seen as a mark of favour for Scrope whilst at the same time highlighting Cecily's new, reduced status as the illegitimate daughter of Edward IV.

The sisters' fortunes were to take another dramatic turn on 22 August 1485 when Richard III was killed at the Battle of Bosworth and succeeded by the battle's victor, Henry Tudor, who became King Henry VII. Although he was now king, Henry did not rush to fulfil his promise to Elizabeth. He was keen first to establish his own authority as monarch and emphasise that he did not need an association with Elizabeth's royal blood in order to do that. Henry was crowned on 30 October 1485. The new king's first parliament, on 7 November, not only asserted the legitimacy of Henry's title to the throne but also repealed the Act of Titulus Regius, the instrument by which Elizabeth and her siblings had been declared illegitimate. On 10 December, the House of Commons urged Henry to fulfil his promise to marry 'that illustrious lady Elizabeth, daughter of King Edward IV'.[39] Which he did on 18 January 1486, an event that was received with great joy throughout England. One chronicler wrote:

> By reason of whiche marriage, peace was thought to discende oute of heuen [heaven] into England, considering that the lynes of Lancastre and Yorke, being both noble families equivalent in ryches, fame and honour, were now brought into one knot and connexed together, of whose two bodyes one heyre might succeed, whiche after their tyme should peaceably rule and enjoye the whole monarchy and realme of England.[40]

The papal bull, issued in 1486 and read out in churches the length and breadth of the country on Trinity Sunday, emphasised the marriage's importance as the union of the two warring Houses of York and Lancaster:

> Understanding of the long and grievous variance, contentions and debates that have been in this Realm of England between the House of the Duchy of Lancaster on the one party and the House of the Duchy of York on the other party. Willing all such divisions following to be put apart by the council and consent of his college of Cardinals approves, confirms and establishes the matrimony and conjunction made between our sovereign lord King Henry the Seventh of the House of Lancaster of that one party and the noble Princess Elizabeth of the House of York of that other with all their issue born between the same.'[41]

Elizabeth of York fulfilled her primary duty as queen within eight months of saying her wedding vows, when a son, Arthur, was born on 20 September 1486, at Winchester. The baby prince united the royal houses of York and Lancaster in one precious body and his name harked back to the greatest legendary king of the Britons. The little prince was christened in Winchester Cathedral in a lavish ceremony in which his grandmother, Elizabeth Woodville, stood as godmother. He was carried to the font by his aunt, Cecily, while another of his aunts, Anne, carried the chrisom.[42] It was not until a year after Arthur's birth, in September 1487, that Elizabeth was finally accorded a coronation – over two years after Henry had taken the throne and just three months after he had put down the most serious danger to his throne to date. The threat came from the emergence of a pretender, Lambert Simnel, who claimed to be 12-year-old Edward, Earl of Warwick, the son of Elizabeth's uncle George, Duke of Clarence. Supported by Elizabeth's cousin, John de la Pole, Earl of Lincoln, and aunt, Margaret, Duchess of Burgundy, the rebellion was only crushed on 6 June 1487, with a battle at Stoke Field in Nottinghamshire. Lincoln was killed in the fighting and young Simnel taken prisoner; he would be put to work in the royal kitchens and eventually became one of the king's falconers. The pageantry surrounding the queen's coronation played down her personal claim to the throne; there was a notable absence of Yorkist badges and Elizabeth was attended by Margaret Beaufort, the king's mother, rather than her royal relatives.[43] Her sister, Cecily and aunt, the Duchess of Bedford, were also part of the coronation procession, with Cecily acting as the queen's train bearer.[44] Henry was not present at the coronation, watching from behind a screen, although he had welcomed Elizabeth to London ahead of the ceremony, as though she were a foreign bride, rather than one who had been born in Westminster Palace itself.

It was only after her coronation that Elizabeth was given a formal land settlement to maintain her household, and this was made out of the provision that had originally been settled on Elizabeth Woodville as dower in March 1486.[45] In February 1487, Elizabeth Woodville had been deprived of this dower and all her possessions. According to Vergil, 'This was done because she had made her peace with King Richard, had placed her daughters at his disposal and had, by leaving sanctuary, broken her promise to those … who had, at her own most urgent entreaty, forsaken their own English property and fled to Henry in Brittany'.[46] The official line was that Elizabeth Woodville had voluntarily surrendered her lands and chosen to retire to a secluded life at Bermondsey, in the tradition of widowed queens. Other theories suggested that the dowager queen had become involved in the Lambert Simnel plot, actively working to remove her son-in-law from the throne in order to replace him with the impostor. It seems highly unlikely that Elizabeth Woodville would work to overthrow her daughter's husband, and therefore her daughter, to place an impostor on the throne, or even to support the cause of her husband's nephew, the Earl of Warwick, when her own grandson was now the heir. The most plausible theory behind Elizabeth Woodville's retirement comes from Lisa Hilton, who suggests that the dowager queen was too wealthy and that Henry wanted her lands, so pressured her into giving them up, probably emphasising that his wife needed them more, and leaving her with no option but to retire from public life as she did not have the financial means to do otherwise.[47]

Elizabeth of York's dower settlement included six Duchy of Lancaster manors in Essex, with additional land and revenues, though it was a smaller provision than had been allotted to her immediate predecessors, Anne Neville and her own mother, Elizabeth Woodville.[48] Further lands were settled on Elizabeth of York in February 1492, with the reversion of some of the Duchy of York's lands that had been held by her grandmother, Cecily Neville, including Wareham, Weymouth and Portland. Duchess Cecily died on 31 May 1495 and the parliament of October that year confirmed Elizabeth's possession of her grandmother's estates.[49] Elizabeth and her sisters, Cecily, Anne, Catherine and Bridget, were also the co-heiresses to the

Mortimer-Clare inheritance, but they did not see any of it. Henry quietly absorbed the lands into his own estates, not even using the revenues to provide his wife's sisters with dowries.

This explains the relatively humble marriages of the queen's sisters – the daughters of Edward IV. With no dowries, they could not make diplomatic foreign matches, though the queen provided each of her sisters with allowances of £50 a year and £120 annuities for their husbands from her privy purse. Cecily's marriage to Ralph Scrope had been annulled in 1486. Cecily played a prominent role in the court ceremonial of the new Tudor monarchy, carrying Prince Arthur to the font during his christening and bearing the train of her sister at Elizabeth's coronation. It was not long before a new marriage was arranged, with John, Viscount Welles, half-brother of the king's mother, Margaret Beaufort, towards the end of 1487. John had actively supported his half-nephew against Richard III, fleeing to Brittany after taking part in Buckingham's failed rebellion of 1483. The family had lost their lands when John's brother, Richard, had joined Warwick's rebellion in 1470, and was executed as a result. On Henry VII's accession, the Welles lands were restored to John, and he was promoted from his father's rank of baron to that of a viscount. With this marriage, Cecily was sister-in-law to both the king and the king's mother. The couple appear to have spent their first Christmas at court, with note being taken of them attending a banquet whereby 'the viscount had a place at a table on the right side of the hall, whilst his lady took the head of the table at the left'.[50] There is little record of Cecily after this date, which may suggest that she left court to live a quiet family life. Welles and Cecily had two daughters, Elizabeth and Anne. A marriage had been made for Elizabeth in 1498, to George Stanley, Lord Strange, but she died that same year and was buried in the church of the Austin Friars in London.

It is unclear whether Anne died before or shortly after her father. Either way, the deaths of all her family in such a short space of time must have been devastating for Cecily, especially given how close she and Welles appear to have grown, despite a twenty-year age gap. When Welles died of pleurisy in February 1499, he left Cecily a life interest in his lands, referring to her in his will as 'my dere beloved lady and wife Cecille' and saying it was she of 'whome I trust above all oder'.[51] King Henry confiscated these lands, however, when Cecily made a secret marriage with Thomas Kyme of Friskney, an obscure Lincolnshire esquire whose origins are difficult to discern. They married in 1502, sometime after the death of Prince Arthur and whilst her sister, Queen Elizabeth was pregnant and ill. Cecily had returned to court after Welles' death and acted as train bearer for Catherine of Aragon at her wedding to Prince Arthur. It was only the intervention of the king's mother, who sheltered Cecily and her new husband, that persuaded Henry to show mercy. Henry VII came to an agreement whereby Cecily would surrender some of the lands in return for a life interest in the remainder; she was allowed to keep the revenues she had already received from the estates.[52] Cecily and Thomas may have had two children, Richard and Margaret, though this is uncertain. Cecily died on 24 August 1507, at Hatfield in Hertfordshire where she had been staying for the last three weeks. Her cause of death is unrecorded, and she was buried at 'the friars' though the actual religious house this refers to remains unidentified.[53] Unlike many medieval princesses, however, we do have surviving samples of her handwriting, in a handful of books that she owned, where she had written variations of the phrase 'Thys booke ys myn Cecyl Welles sister to ye queen'.[54]

The next to marry was Anne of York, the fifth daughter of Edward IV and Elizabeth Woodville. She was 7 years old when her father died and 10 when her sister became queen of England. She had first been betrothed at the age of 5, to Philip the Handsome, the future Duke of Burgundy but the marriage treaty was repudiated after Edward IV's death. During the reign of her uncle, Richard III, Anne was betrothed to Thomas Howard, the oldest grandson of John Howard, Duke of Norfolk, but when Henry VII took the crown, the marriage appears to have been set aside or delayed. Anne attended court, serving as lady-in-waiting to her sister and becoming the queen's chief attendant following Cecily's marriage in 1487. She carried the chrisom at the baptisms of her nephew and niece, Arthur and Margaret, respectively. On a more sombre occasion, Anne acted as chief mourner at the funeral of her mother, Elizabeth Woodville, in 1492 as the queen was eight months pregnant and unable to attend. Howard continued to press his claim to the princess, and they were eventually married at Greenwich on 4 February 1495. They had four children together, three of whom appear to have died in infancy. Their longest surviving child, Thomas, died aged about 12 in 1508.[55]

The royal York sisters had been co-heirs of their great-grandmother Anne Mortimer, Countess of Cambridge, and in 1510 the new king Henry VIII, Anne's nephew, granted his aunt and the heirs of her body a number of properties in compensation for the Mortimer-Clare lands claimed in right of Countess Anne, including the castle and manor of Wingfield. In the event, Anne's children all predeceased her. Anne died on 23 November 1511 and was buried at Thetford Priory, the mausoleum for the Bigod and Howard families. Following the dissolution of the monasteries, her body was moved to the Church of St Michael the Archangel at Framlingham. During their marriage, Thomas Howard held no titles but would later succeed his father as third Duke of Norfolk.[56] After Anne's death, Thomas married, successively, Elizabeth Stafford and then Eleanor Percy.

Anne was not the only York sister to marry in 1495. Catherine had been considered for a marriage with James, Marquess of Ormond, the second son of King James III of Scotland, in 1487 but nothing came of it. In 1495 she was married to the son of a staunch supporter of Henry VII, Sir William Courtenay, heir of Edward Courtenay, Earl of Devon. They would have three children together, including two sons, Edward who died in 1502 and Henry, who would succeed his father as earl. A daughter, Margaret, married Henry Somerset, Baron Herbert, the son and heir of Charles Somerset, first Earl of Worcester. High in the king's favour, Catherine and William settled at court once they were married. However, in 1502 William was suspected of being involved with a conspiracy led by the Yorkist claimant Edmund de la Pole. He was attainted and imprisoned for the remainder of Henry VII's reign. Poor Catherine was dependant on the assistance of her sister, the queen, who looked after her and her children until her death in February 1503. Catherine would be chief mourner at her sister's funeral.[57]

William Courtenay was released after the accession of Henry VIII and his father died at about the same time. He was restored to his lands and titles as Earl of Devon on condition that Catherine renounce her claims on the Mortimer-Clare inheritance, including the lands of the earldom of March. Catherine was widowed before the negotiations were completed. William was created Earl of Devon on 10 May 1511, but had little time to enjoy it as he died of pleurisy on 9 June.[58] A month later, on 6 July, the newly-widowed Countess of Devon transferred all her rights in the earldom of March to the Crown and took a vow of chastity, thus guaranteeing her freedom and independence. The following February she received the lands of the earldom of Devon, in her own right, for the remainder of her lifetime. And on 4 November the same year, her 10-year-old son, Henry was created Earl of Devon. Catherine made only infrequent visits to her nephew's court, although she acted as godmother to Princess Mary in 1516. From 1511, she was the last surviving of the ten children of Edward IV and Elizabeth Woodville.

Primarily residing at Tiverton Castle, Catherine maintained a large household, supported by an annual income of £2750 from the Devon estates. Surviving records show that Catherine lived in some luxury, with regular purchases of spices, French and Rhenish wines and fine cloths, such as velvet and satin. Her chapel was supplied with sacred vessels, books and images of saints. She enjoyed a good relationship with the Church, receiving gifts from the bishop of Exeter and from the abbots of the nearby abbeys, including Ford, Buckland and Newenham.[59] Her vow of chastity was not an indication of her seclusion from the world, however, and she enjoyed hunting and the entertainment of minstrels and visiting troupes, including the Exeter Waits. She even employed three fools, named Dick, Mug and Kit.[60]

Catherine's last year may have been marred by failing health. She made her will on 2 May 1527, setting aside £21 a year, to pay for three priests at St Peter's Church Tiverton, to pray for her soul three times daily, in perpetuity, in the presence of three poor men who would receive 8*d* a week. She died six months later, on 15 November, at Tiverton Castle, and was buried at St Peter's on 3 December, having directed that all her servants and officers should receive black gowns for the occasion, in addition to a year's wages. A further 8000 poor people were to be paid 2*d.* each to offer prayers for Catherine's soul.[61] Although she had become a countess by marriage, Catherine had lived and died as a princess, styling herself 'the excellent Princess Katherine, Countess of Devon, daughter, sister and aunt of kings'.[62]

Catherine was the last surviving of the royal York sisters. The youngest sister, Bridget, would never marry. She was only 2 years old when her father died and not yet 5 when Henry VII defeated Richard III at Bosworth. She appears in Richard III's Wardrobe Accounts for 1483/4 when she was ill and order was given 'To the Lady Brygitt, one of the daughters of K. Edward IIIIth, being sick in the said Wardrobe for to have for her use at that time two long pillows of fustian, stuffed with down, and two pillow beres of Holland cloth unto them'.[63] Bridget is also included in the invitation issued by Richard III, in March 1484, for her and her sisters to come out of sanctuary 'to be guided, ruled and demeaned after me, then I shall see that they be in surety of their lives. . . and to have all things requisite and necessary for their exhibitions and findings as my kinswomen'.[64]

We have no record of where Bridget was living in the early years of Henry VII's reign. It may be that she joined the household of her sister, Queen Elizabeth, or remained with her mother, who retired from court to live at Bermondsey Abbey in 1487. Bridget entered Dartford Priory in 1490, then under the rule of Elizabeth Cressner, its prioress from 1489 until 1536. At 10 years old, she was still too young to take her vows as a nun, so may have lived there as a border, continuing her education, until she was old enough to take the veil, probably in her teenage years. Given how old Bridget was at the time she entered the Church, it seems possible that the young princess had chosen her vocation, rather than being forced into it. Henry VII had found husbands for her sisters and would likely have been able to do the same for her, even without the provision of a dowry. Dartford was a Dominican house sixteen miles from London and is said to have been one of the ten largest and richest religious houses in the country. The only house for Dominican nuns in England, it followed the rule of St Augustine, defined by poverty, chastity, communal charity and obedience.

Although she was cloistered, Bridget was not forgotten, nor isolated from her family. In 1492, she was able to attend her mother's funeral. In 1495 she was remembered in the will of her grandmother Cecily Neville, Duchess of York, who left her three books, the *Legenda Aurea*, a life of St Katherine of Sienna and 'the boke of St Mathilde'.[65] Elizabeth of York's wardrobe accounts from 1502 to 1503 indicate that the queen sent money to her sister at Dartford. Accounts from the previous years are lost, so we do not know if this was a one-off payment; I suspect it was a regular arrangement. On 6 July 1502, 66*s.* 8*d.* was delivered to the prioress at Dartford by a servant of the queen: the same amount was paid to Bridget in March 1503. And in September another servant was paid travel expenses for a visit to Bridget.[66] It was fortunate for Bridget, perhaps, that she did not live to see the dissolution of the monasteries, wrought by her nephew Henry VIII. There is, however, some confusion as to the date of her death. John Weever, writing in the seventeenth century, recorded: 'This Lady Bridget here interred, was the fourth daughter of Edward the fourth, by his wife Queene Elizabeth, she was borne at Eltham, here by, the tenth of November, 1480. She tooke the habite of Religion when she was young, and so spent her life in contemplation unto the day of her death: which happened about the year 1517. the eight of King Henry the eight'.[67] Green suggests that Bridget was dead by 1513, when Thomas More notes that her sister Catherine was yet living, but makes no mention of any other sister being still alive.[68] However, an entry in Henry VII's Chamber Accounts clearly indicates that Bridget was dead by 19 December 1507, which would suggest that she died shortly after turning 27. It was on that date in December that an order was made 'for a Marbulstone bought to ley upon my lady Brygett [Bridget] within the quere of Dertford xlvj s viij d'.[69] The wording of the order suggests that Bridget was buried beneath the earth, rather than in a tomb. The princess was laid to rest in the choir of the priory church, which was also occupied by the priory's four founding nuns, including its first two prioresses. A place of honour befitting a royal princess.

Throughout her marriage and reign as queen consort, Elizabeth fulfilled her primary duty as a wife in filling the royal nursery with a succession of infants, though not all survived to adulthood. After Arthur, Margaret was born in 1489. Another son, Henry – the future King Henry VIII – was born in 1491 and a daughter, Elizabeth, in 1492. An unnamed son, probably born prematurely, was born and died in 1497. Mary, the future queen of France and duchess of Suffolk, was born in 1498 and another son, Edmund, arrived in 1499. Elizabeth and Henry's last child, Catherine, was born in 1503.[70] Of the seven children, little Elizabeth died at the age of three in 1495, Edmund died the year after his birth and baby Catherine lived only a few days. Elizabeth of York is said to have been particularly fond of her second son, Henry, who resembled her father in looks. As the heir to the throne, Arthur had been given his own household as an infant, but Henry was allowed to stay with his mother.

Elizabeth's political role during Henry VII's reign has always been played down or portrayed as non-existent. Her influence is often overshadowed by that of her mother-in-law, Margaret Beaufort, who is portrayed as overbearing. One Spanish observer reported that Elizabeth was 'kept in subjection by the mother of the king'.[71] However, it seems that the queen's traditional public role as intercessor may have been shared by Elizabeth and Margaret, rather than that Margaret replaced the queen in that role. It was to Elizabeth that a Welsh tenant appealed over an injustice involving the king's uncle, Jasper Tudor. And it was Elizabeth who responded by writing a firm letter to Jasper. Rosemary Horrox argues that Elizabeth of York's activities as an intercessor were non-controversial rather than non-existent, suggesting that Elizabeth's actions went unremarked because they did not overstep the boundaries of the traditional role of a queen. This is supported by the queen's private accounts, which record several gifts from eminent personalities who obviously thought it necessary to court favour with Elizabeth.[72] The queen's presence is also found in the distribution of patronage. Elizabeth and Margaret Beaufort jointly sponsored William Caxton's printing of *The Fifteen Oes* in 1491, and Elizabeth patronised a number of composers, including William Cornish and Robert Fayrfax, from whom she commissioned a Christmas carol and an anthem of Our Lady and St Elizabeth, respectively.[73]

Elizabeth's patronage also helped those of her household to obtain favours and livings, such as her chaplains. In one such instance, Elizabeth wrote to the prior of Christ Church, Canterbury, requesting that he honour a promise to allow her the right to present one of her chaplains to the next vacancy in the living of All Saints, Lombard Street. Christ Church Cathedral at Canterbury held the advowson and therefore the final decision on who to appoint to the living. Although she does not appear to have yet decided which of her chaplains would have the honour. I do like that her practical mind instructs that the name should be left blank:

> To our Right Trusty and well beloved in God the prior of the monastery of Christ's Church at Canterbury.
>
> Right trusty and well beloved in God, we greet you well, and as we recently in other letters desired you to grant unto us the living of the parish church of All Saints in Lombard Street in my lord's city of London, whenever it should fall vacant through the death of Sir Marques Husy, the late incumbent; whereupon it pleased you, out of your loving and kindly heart, to grant us freedom of the said benefice in writing, to nominate it for whichever of our chaplains we should choose at its next vacancy, for which we heartily thank you; we have been informed that it is now the case, the said Sir Marques being recently departed out of this transitory life into the mercy of God, so that the said benefice is now vacant.
>
> We therefore request and require you, that in honouring the said promise, you shall send us under your usual seal the giving of the said benefice, with a blank space on it, with the intention that we shall enter the name of whichever of our chaplains we shall think able and suitable to have charge of the curacy there. We sincerely trust that you will effect this desire of ours, whereby you will greatly deserve our special thanks, to be recalled in connection with any reasonable desires of your own concerning your well-being or that of your office in time to come. Given under our signet at my lord's city of London the sixth day of June.'[74]

Elizabeth of York's surviving privy purse accounts from 1502–1503 show her income of £3585 19s. 10 ½d. slightly exceeds her expenditure of £3411 5s. 9 ¼d., though the queen's revenue had not always proved sufficient to cover her costs. Elizabeth ran her household economically, the average salary she paid to her ladies being £3 6s. 8d. compared to the £40 her mother had paid. From her privy purse, the queen also paid for, among other things, repairs to her barge and litters, gifts, servants' wages, cloth for her own and her ladies' use, jewellery and religious offerings. Elizabeth also paid the expenses of the children of her sister, Catherine, following the imprisonment and attainder of Catherine's husband.[75]

One area in which Elizabeth and her mother-in-law were in complete agreement and worked together was in the futures of the royal children, especially Princess Margaret. After having been married and become pregnant at the age of 12 herself and then enduring a traumatic labour when just 13 years old, Margaret Beaufort was determined to ensure her granddaughters did not go through similar experiences. Princess Margaret was betrothed to King James IV of Scotland in 1498, when she was just 9 years old. Both the queen and Margaret Beaufort urged that Margaret should not be sent to Scotland to her husband until she was physically mature enough to be his wife. Henry himself reported that, 'the Queen and my mother are very much against this marriage. They say if the marriage were concluded we should be obliged to send the Princess directly to Scotland, in which case they fear the King of Scots would not wait, but injure her and endanger her health'.[76] Henry heeded their caution and it was not until January 1503, when Margaret was 13 years old, that James and Margaret were married by proxy before the princess set out for Scotland, crossing the border into her new country on 1 August, 1503, just over three months shy of her fourteenth birthday.

The continuation of the fledgling Tudor dynasty was dependent on the marriages of the children, and particularly of Prince Arthur. In 1489, by the Treaty of Medina del Campo, an alliance with the Spanish kingdoms of Castile and Aragon, united by the marriage of Isabella of Castile and Ferdinand of Aragon, it was agreed that 4-year-old Prince Arthur would marry Catalina (Catherine of Aragon), the Spanish monarchs' youngest daughter. Such a prestigious royal marriage was not only a diplomatic coup for Henry but also a validation of his kingship. The marriage was jeopardised, however, by the most serious threat to Henry's throne, the rebellion of Perkin Warbeck, who claimed to be Richard, Duke of York, the younger of the Princes in the Tower. The rebellion failed and Warbeck was captured in 1497. Shortly afterwards, Catherine and Arthur were formally betrothed, and Elizabeth of York sent a most eloquent letter to Catherine's mother:

> 'To the most serene and potent princess, the Lady Elizabeth [Isabella], by God's grace queen of Castile, Leon, Aragon, Sicily, Granada, etc, our cousin and dearest relation, Elizabeth by the same grace, Queen of England and France, and lady of Ireland, wishes health and the most prosperous increases of her desires. Although

> we before entertained singular love and regard to your highness above all other queens in the world, as well for the consanguinity and necessary intercourse which mutually take place between us, as also for the eminent dignity and virtue by which your majesty so shines and excels that your most celebrated name is noised abroad and diffused everywhere; yet much more has this love increased and accumulated by the accession of the most affable affinity which has recently been celebrated between the most illustrious princess the Lady Catherine, the infanta, your daughter. Hence it is that, amongst our other cares and cogitations, first and foremost we wish and desire from our heart that we may often and speedily hear of the health and safety of your serenity, and of the health and safety of the aforesaid most illustrious Lady Catherine, whom we think of and esteem as our own daughter, than which nothing can be more grateful and acceptable to us. Therefore we request your serenity to certify of your estate, and that of the aforesaid most illustrious Lady Catherine our common daughter. And if there be anything in our power which would be grateful or pleasant to your majesty, use us and ours as freely as you would your own; for, with most willing mind, we offer all that we have to you, and wish to have all in common with you. We should have written you the news of our state, and of that of this kingdom, but the most serene lord the king, our husband, will have written at length of these things to your majesties. For the rest may your majesty fare most happily according to your wishes. From our palace of Westminster, 3rd day of December 1497.[77]

Despite the betrothal and Warbeck's imprisonment in the Tower of London, the Spanish monarchs were still reluctant to send Catherine to England. Following his capture, Warbeck had initially been kept at court, close at hand so that Henry could watch him. There is no record of him having met Elizabeth of York, nor of her showing any inclination to meet the man who had claimed to be her long-lost brother. On 9 June 1498, Warbeck escaped the king's custody, possibly through a window from his chamber in Westminster Palace.[78] Warbeck did not get far – less than 7 miles in fact – before he sought help at the Carthusian priory at Sheen. It may be that he regretted his rash escape, as the prior travelled personally to Westminster to see the king and speak on Warbeck's behalf. The pretender was taken into custody once more but spared his life. His public punishment was to spend hours in the stocks at Westminster on 15 June, under the scorching summer sun, enduring the scorn of the public, and again at Cheapside a few days later. He was then incarcerated in the Tower of London, 'secured in such a manner, and in such a prison, that, with the help of God, he will never be able to play such a trick again'.[79]

The following year, on 19 May, with Warbeck safely lodged in the Tower, Arthur Prince of Wales was married by proxy to Catherine of Aragon, at Tickenhall Manor in Worcestershire. The Spanish ambassador, de Puebla, stood proxy for the Spanish Infanta.[80] However, Ferdinand and Isabella were still reluctant to send Catherine to England; they were concerned that all potential threats to the Tudor crown should be eliminated before despatching their daughter to England's shores. They were thinking, of course, of Perkin Warbeck – but also of Edward, Earl of Warwick. Edward was the son of Edward IV's brother George, Duke of Clarence, and had been held in the Tower since the defeat of Richard III at Bosworth in 1485, when he was only 10 years old. He was now a man of 24 and, as a prince of royal blood, was a possible focus for Yorkist discontent.

In the summer of 1499, Warbeck and Warwick joined forces in a conspiracy to escape the Tower and seize the throne. The plot was discovered, however, and the conspirators arrested. Warbeck was tried at the White Hall in Westminster on 16 November. Found guilty, he was sentenced to be hanged, drawn and quartered. On 21 November 1499, Edward, Earl of Warwick, was tried in Westminster's Great Hall in front of a jury of his peers, presided over by John de Vere, 13th Earl of Oxford. Warwick freely confessed his guilt and submitted to the king's grace with a plea for mercy. He, too, was condemned to the same fate. Warbeck was executed on the morning of 23 November, with the king commuting the sentence from the full traitor's death to that of hanging; he was posthumously beheaded, the head later displayed on a spike on London Bridge. Edward, Earl of Warwick, with deference to his royal blood, was beheaded on Tower Hill on the afternoon of 28 November 1499.[81] Poor Warwick had never had much of a life.

With Warbeck and the Earl of Warwick out of the way, the last serious challengers to Henry's rule were definitively dealt with and there was nothing more preventing the arrival of Catherine of Aragon and her wedding to Prince Arthur. The Spanish Infanta arrived in England in October 1501 and was placed in the care of Elizabeth of York until her marriage. The young couple were married at St Paul's Cathedral in London on 14 November; the ceremony was followed by a week of pageants and tournaments in celebration.[82] Arthur was the only one of her four surviving children that Elizabeth would see married. After the celebrations, Catherine and Arthur, still only in their mid-teens, were established at Ludlow and given the government of Wales. On 2 April 1502, Arthur died of an unknown illness, possibly sweating sickness or a form of influenza. Catherine also contracted the illness, but she recovered. A messenger rode through the night to reach the king at Greenwich and give him the dreadful tidings. Henry himself broke the news to his queen, and Elizabeth comforted her grieving husband with the words: 'God has left us yet a fair prince and two fair princesses … and we are both young enough'.[83] Elizabeth then returned to her own chamber, where she collapsed to the floor sobbing, and it was Henry's turn to offer succour to his wife. Once recovered from her illness, a grieving Catherine returned from Ludlow and joined the queen's household.

True to her word, Elizabeth of York conceived again, hoping to provide the king with another prince to guarantee the succession, which now rested heavily on the shoulders of 10-year-old Henry, Duke of York – the future King Henry VIII. In January 1503, she arrived at the Tower of London by barge, where she was to have her final confinement. On 2 February 1503, Elizabeth of York gave birth to a daughter, Catherine, who died a few days later. The queen fell ill from a post-partum infection and on 11 February, her thirty-seventh birthday, Elizabeth of York died. The king was devastated and 'privily departed to a solitary place and would no man should resort unto him'.[84] The king gave Elizabeth a splendid funeral and she was laid to rest in the newly built Henry VII Lady Chapel, in Westminster Abbey in a tomb in which Henry would join her when he died in 1509. Of her surviving children, Margaret was 13 years old, Henry 11 and Mary just two months shy of her seventh birthday. One cannot help but wonder how their lives may have turned out, especially Henry's, if Elizabeth had survived another ten or twenty years to guide and advise them.

Elizabeth of York had been the consummate queen to her husband Henry VII. She had fulfilled her primary duty in filling the nursery with sons to guarantee the succession and daughters who would aid in arranging alliances, Margaret with Scotland and Mary with France. In her own quiet and unassuming way, she had supported her husband throughout his reign, acted as patron of the arts and to those who needed the queen's intercession. She and her sisters had lived through the drama of the Wars of the Roses, the tragedy of their father's early death, the upheaval of Richard III's seizure of the throne, the disappearance of their brothers, and the fall of the House of York with the death of Richard III. When they were children, as the daughters of a king, the Yorkist princesses had dazzling futures ahead of them, perhaps as queens and duchesses of foreign lands. But the wheel of fortune turned against them with the early death of their father and only one, Elizabeth of York, achieved the glittering future that had been predicted, queen of England as the wife of Henry VII. In a story that is unique for England's medieval princesses, not one of the five surviving royal daughters of the House of York married outside of England.

Chapter Seven

The Last White Rose

If history was neat and tidy, this book would end with the glamorous procession of Edward IV's daughters and their riches-to-not-quite rags story. But history never comes wrapped in a pretty bow. Edward IV was not the last medieval king of England when he died in 1483. He was not the last Plantagenet, or even Yorkist, king. He was succeeded all-too briefly by his 13-year-old son Edward V and then a little less briefly, albeit a still-short reign of some twenty-six months, by his own brother, Richard III. Richard's seizure of the throne from his young nephew has garnered millions of words in his defence and condemnation, almost in equal measure. So, I am not going into the validity of his usurpation (cough!). It happened and certainly contributed to the downfall of the House of York at Bosworth Field on 22 August 1485.

Richard was the youngest son of Richard, Duke of York and his wife, Cecily Neville. By all accounts, he was loyal to his brother, Edward IV, and was given the administration of the north of England, protecting the northern border against the Scots. He had married, in about 1472, Anne Neville, the younger daughter of Richard Neville, Earl of Warwick – the Kingmaker – and widow of Edward, Prince of Wales, the son of Henry VI and Margaret of Anjou. Anne had died in March 1485, just eleven months after the death of their only child, Edward of Middleham, Prince of Wales, who was not yet 10 years old. The king was effectively childless, as far as the Crown of England was concerned. But he did have at least two illegitimate children and one of those was a daughter, Katherine. She would not be a princess, but as the daughter of a king, and the last medieval king in England at that, she deserves her place in the pages of this book. Unfortunately, the information on Katherine Plantagenet is scant. Her date and year of birth are unknown. Given Richard's reputation for piety and loyalty, it is assumed that she was born before Richard's marriage to Anne, which took place sometime in 1472; the exact date is unknown but a dispensation for the marriage was issued from Rome on 22 April 1472.[1] This theory is also supported by the fact that Richard had arranged Katherine's marriage before his death at Bosworth, though that is no cast-iron guarantee that Katherine was of marriageable age.

It is estimated that Richard's illegitimate son, John of Pontefract, who had still to attain his majority in 1485, was born around 1471. He was appointed Captain of Calais by his father in 1485, and was referred to as the Lord Bastard, though he was not a lord. This, perhaps, is to afford him honour as the son of the king, albeit an illegitimate son. An entry from March 1485 refers to money paid for 'leavened bread allowed for the Lord Bastard riding to 12d. and paid for a pike given to Master Brackenbury Constable of the Tower who at that time returned from Calais from the Lord Bastard 3s 4d.'[2] John appears to have returned to England during the first year of Henry VII's reign. The new king granted him an annuity of £20 from Kingston Lacy, Dorset, a manor which had once belonged to his father.[3] John appears to have died in the Tower of London in November 1499 when it's recorded that 'there was a base son of King Richard III made away, having beene kept long before in prison' after 'the attempt of certaine Irishmen in the west and south parts, who would have got him into their power and made him their cheife'.[4] This was about the time that Perkin Warbeck and Edward, Earl of Warwick, were arrested and condemned for conspiring against the Crown, so it may be that John was also involved or that the conspiracy was a convenient smoke screen in which to despatch John of Pontefract as well.

The identities of the mothers of both John and Katherine are unknown. It has been speculated that John's was an Alice Burgh as Richard granted her an annuity of £20 on 1 March 1474 when he was staying at Pontefract.[5] The grant was made, rather ambiguously, for 'certain special causes and considerations'.[6] A grant of £5 was made to Katherine Haute in 1477, from Richard's estates in East Anglia, which has led to the suggestion that she was the mother of Katherine Plantagenet. It is possible that Katherine Haute may have been the wife of John Haute, a kinsman of Elizabeth Woodville, but we simply do not know. There is, of course, the possibility that John and Katherine shared a mother, either Katherine or Alice, or a third woman who has gone unnoticed. It is all conjecture. We do know that Richard acknowledged both children as his own. It is thought that Katherine was born before Richard's marriage as she herself was married in 1484. The minimum age for girls to marry was 12, but most parents waited until their daughters were 14 or 15, at least, before finding them husbands. There were instances of children under 12 being married, the most recent example being that of Richard III's nephew Richard, Duke of York and Anne de Mowbray, when they were still only 5 and 6, respectively. But this was uncommon and usually only done to protect the inheritance of estates. Katherine had no estates to protect, but her father would have been eager to see her married in order to guarantee her a stable future. She grew up in obscurity, with nothing known of how or where she spent her childhood. However, her father's accession to the throne in 1483 not only changed her circumstances, but it also changed her marriage prospects. In 1484, Richard would have been looking for allies and marrying the king's daughter, albeit an illegitimate one, was a great honour for most nobles of the land.

Richard chose his friend William Herbert, Earl of Huntingdon, as his daughter's husband. Born in 1455, William Herbet had been married to Mary Woodville, sister of Queen Elizabeth Woodville, but she had died in 1481, leaving him with a daughter, Elizabeth, Herbert's sole heir. Herbert had been Earl of Pembroke until 1479, when he had resigned that earldom at the instigation of Edward IV and been created Earl of Huntingdon instead. This had severely diminished Herbert's revenues and as an incentive for the marriage, Richard gave him an annuity of 1000 marks, practically doubling the earl's annual income.[7] Dated to 29 February 1484, the agreement reads:

> This indenture made at London the last day of February in the first year of the reign of our sovereign lord King Richard the Third, between our said sovereign lord King Richard the Third on the one party, and the right noble lord William, earl of Huntingdon, on the other party, witnesseth that the said earl promiseth and granteth to and with our said sovereign lord the king that, before the feast of St. Michael next coming [September 29, 1484], by God's grace he shall take to wife Dame Katherine Plantagenet, daughter to our said sovereign lord; and before their marriage to make or cause to be made to her behalf a sure, sufficient, and lawful estate of certain his manors, lordships, lands and tenements in England to the yearly value of two hundred pounds over all charges, to have and to hold to him and to the said Dame Katherine and the heirs of their two bodies lawfully begotten in manner and form following: [that] is to wit, remainder to the right heirs of the said earl. For the which our said sovereign lord the king granteth to the said earl and to the said Dame Katherine to make or cause to be made before the said day of marriage a sure, sufficient, and lawful estate of manors, lordship, lands, and tenements in possession to the yearly value of one thousand marks over all reprise, to have to them and to their heirs males of their two bodies lawfully begotten: that is to say, lordships, manors, lands, and tenements in possession at that day to the yearly value of six hundred marks, and manors, lordships, lands, and tenements in reversion after the death of Thomas Stanley, knight, Lord Stanley, to the yearly value of four hundred marks. And in the mean our said sovereign lord granteth to the said earl and Dame Katherine an annuity of four hundred marks yearly to be had and perceived to them from Michaelmas last, during the life of the said Lord Stanley, of the revenues of the lordships of Newport, Brecknock, and Hay in Wales by the hands of the receivers of them for the time being. And over this our said sovereign lord granteth to make and bear the cost of the said marriage at the day of the solemnization thereof. In witness whereof our said sovereign lord to that one part of these

> indentures remaining with the said earl hath set his signet, and to that other part remaining with our said sovereign lord the said earl hath set his seal the day and year abovesaid.[8]

Herbert agreed to provide Katherine with a jointure worth £200 a year.[9] For his part, the king agreed to bear the costs of the marriage and to endow that couple with lands and lordships that they could pass on to their male heirs.[10] The king granted the annuity on 3 March and Katherine and Herbert were married sometime between then and May, when 'William Erle of Huntingdon and Kateryn his wif' received a grant of the proceeds of a number of manors in Devon, Cornwall and Somerset.[11] The following year, a further grant was made of £152 10s.[12] We know nothing of Katherine and Herbert's relationship beyond the financial arrangements. William Herbert was not involved, on either side, in the Bosworth campaign of August 1485, but did not receive a pardon from King Henry VII until 22 September 1486. We have no more mention of Katherine, living or dead, in the records. Herbert, as Earl of Huntingdon, is recorded as having attended the coronation of Elizabeth of York in November 1487, but 'at that time the substance of all the earls of the realm were widowers or bachelors', perhaps meaning that Katherine had died by this point.[13] Rosemary Horrox, does suggest that Herbert might have repudiated Katherine after Richard's death at Bosworth, which would mean he is recorded as a widower of his first wife, Mary Woodville.[14]

The recent discovery of Katherine's grave, at the church of St James Garlickhithe by Dr Christian Steer, confirms that Katherine was not set aside by her husband and therefore must have died before the queen's coronation, as she is recorded amongst records of Church monuments as Lady Herbert, Countess of Huntingdon.[15] The Herbert's London residence, Worcester House, was in the parish of St James Garlickhithe, which may explain why she was buried there, rather than at Tintern Abbey, where her husband's first wife was buried in a double tomb and where Herbert himself would be laid to rest beside her in 1491. Whether Katherine died as a result of the sweating sickness that plagued London after Bosworth, or in childbirth, accident or some other ailment, we do not know. There are no surviving children recorded from the marriage and Herbert's eventual heir was his daughter by his first wife.

Katherine Plantagenet fared better than some illegitimate children of kings in that she made a good marriage and that there is some trace of her beyond her name. We have more on her than we do of either of Edward IV's known illegitimate daughters. And Richard III, who had more than enough problems to distract him, did at least make sure that his daughter was well provided for. It is a sad twist of fate that she did not long survive her father and was not blessed with children.

Maybe one day, we will know more.

Postscript

Plus Ça Change...

What is the saying? *Plus Ça Change, plus c'est la même chose;* the more things change, the more they stay the same. In over 400 years of English royalty, from 1066 to 1484, the fate of the royal princess did not change much. A number of William the Conqueror's daughters became nuns, as did Edward I's daughter Mary and Edward IV's daughter Bridget. Some had that life chosen for them, but others found a vocation, or perhaps a way to avoid the royal marriage market. Just like William's daughter Adelida of Normandy, Edward's eldest daughter, Elizabeth of York, endured a number of broken engagements. Whereas Adelida retired from the world after these disappointments, Elizabeth became the glue that joined together the Houses of Lancaster and York and ushered in the Tudor period.

The experiences of the royal daughters throughout the latter part of the of the medieval era, however, are disparate, not just in their futures but even in their family lives as they were growing up.

Henry III raised a tight-knit family. He and Eleanor of Provence took a keen interest in the lives of all five of their children, even little Katherine. They were distraught when the princess died at the tender age of 3. And even though their other two daughters married foreign princes, they were not sent so far away that they could not visit and be visited. Indeed, it would have been difficult for Henry III to find a foreign prince closer to home than Alexander III of Scots and John of Brittany. Father and mother kept a watchful eye on their offspring and the frequent visits, and joint enterprises undertaken by not just parents and children, but also siblings, shows how close and loving the family continued to be. Margaret, as queen of Scotland, enjoyed visits from both of her brothers and Beatrice's husband even joined her brothers, Edward and Edmund, on the Ninth Crusade.

Edward I continued the model of a close-knit family unit, though he was often absent from it himself, as was his wife Eleanor of Castile. On several occasions, they spent long periods of time separated from children – years, even, when they took part in the Crusade and, later, spending three years on the Continent in the late 1280s. Their children were not always present in their lives, but they were never far from their thoughts, with care taken over their guardianship and education and a steady stream of gifts during long absences. Edward and Eleanor lost a large number of children in the first ten years of their lives and it has often been suggested that the distance was a guard against the constant grief. We will never know. What we do know is that the children were raised in comfort and well educated. Every care was taken to find the girls suitable husbands and Edward, in particular, seems to have been a soft touch where his daughters were concerned.

The marriages of Edward I's daughters were, largely, successful and mostly happy, in stark contrast to the marriages of Edward II's daughters. Eleanor of Woodstock and Joan of the Tower were both to experience difficult, unhappy marriages. One cannot imagine the frustration and humiliation Eleanor must have felt, seeing her husband under the influence of a man who would accuse her of leprosy. And Joan's marriage to David II of Scotland was destined to be miserable given her brother, Edward III, had never countenanced it and was determined to disrupt peace in Scotland from the moment he assumed personal control of England in 1330. It makes one wonder if there is a causal link between the unhappiness and eventual breakup of their parents' marriage and their own relationships. They were the children of a broken home, after all.

The example of his parents' relationship may also explain Edward III's own closeness with his daughters. The father of four daughters to survive infancy, he was indulgent and loving. He and Philippa of Hainault gave their large brood of children a nurturing childhood which also prepared them for the lives they were to lead as royal ambassadors. Perhaps Edward was a little too indulgent in that he appears to have allowed his daughters more leeway than most medieval kings in giving them a say in who they would marry, especially with his eldest daughter, Isabella. But these girls were growing up in a time of great upheaval. The Hundred Years' War was in its opening stages and plague was ravaging Europe, taking rich and poor alike, including Princess Joan as she travelled to Castile for her marriage. Her death cannot have failed to devastate such a close family.

Edward III's large family would mean war and political unrest further down the line, starting with Henry of Bolingbroke's usurpation of his cousin Richard II. Henry IV's two daughters, Blanche and Philippa, had been born as daughters of the high nobility, not princesses. And yet they would grow up to realise the traditional roles as princesses, with Blanche marrying the son of the Elector Palatine, and Philippa enjoying great success as queen of Denmark, Norway and Sweden. Blanche fulfilled her duties by producing a son and heir, though dying young as a consequence. Philippa never realised the joy of motherhood, but ably attended to her duties as queen in other ways, as a protector and patron of her people and a trusted consort and regent for her husband, King Eric.

The fates of Blanche and Philippa, taking on the traditional roles of royal daughters, though they had not been born to it, are a stark contrast to the princesses of York. Edward IV's daughters were born to splendour and comfort. They were educated in languages, diplomacy and all they would need to dazzle at whichever court in Europe they married into. And yet, it was not to be. The ambitions of others saw their glittering futures reduced as their circumstances and legal status as bastards left them with uncertain futures. Whereas the eldest, Elizabeth of York, would leave the lasting legacy of uniting the warring Houses of York and Lancaster, and founding the Tudor dynasty, the royal blood of her sisters meant that Henry VII had to keep them close. Although the *Titulus Regius* was repealed by Henry VII, the king saw to it that the girls' marriages were to loyal, English noblemen. An international dynastic marriage was never going to happen. The fledgeling Tudor dynasty could not risk sending the princesses, with their royal, Yorkist blood, abroad, to a European monarch who could press his wife's claim to the throne. When England was the prize, such a possibility was a risk not worth taking. So, they all stayed in England, married below their station to nobles, lives very different and unspectacular compared to the royal daughters of the past. But, hopefully, they found a little happiness.

Not all princesses were made in the same mould and each one found her own way to deal with her life and the cards that she was dealt. In my research I frequently discovered instances of happy medieval marriages – and even if a marriage was not based on love, it did not mean that it would not be successful. Indeed, in many such cases the young woman concerned found her own way of succeeding, whether it was through her children or the management of estates – or the fact that a lasting peace was achieved between her two countries.

It has long been believed that princesses were sent off to foreign lands and never seen again. As we have seen, there were very few instances; in the 300 years covered in this book, it happened only with the daughters of Henry IV. It was so rarely the case. Nor was it the purpose. Royal daughters were raised to be a personal and diplomatic link to their homeland. They were the means of keeping communications open when all other options failed. It was never in the king's interest to abandon his daughter, or sister, once she was married abroad. Most visited home after they married or were visited by members of their family. It must also be remembered that marriages for these girls were not made on a whim. Care was taken to ensure that they were suited to their bridegrooms, and more than one betrothal was broken because one side changed their minds, or a different daughter was considered more suitable. It was very important that these marriages would be successful, to ensure that the relationship between the two countries involved was as stable as the marriage. Life was not easy for the bride when this diplomacy failed.

It is also worth noting that English kings married French princesses, and Scottish kings married English princesses, but the reverse happened rarely, if ever. Only one Scottish princess, Matilda of Scotland, married an English king, Henry I, in the whole medieval period. And no English princess married a French king or heir to the French throne, no matter how many betrothals were made over the years.

That is not to say English princesses did not marry Frenchmen. It is, perhaps, a clear indication of Anglo-French relations in medieval times that kings of England were far happier to marry their daughters to counts and dukes of the many semi-autonomous regions of France, such as Brittany, Toulouse and Bar, regions that challenged and stalled the expansion of the kingdom of France itself. The marriages of daughters into Germany, the Low Countries and Spain also served the policy of containing England's biggest rival within its borders and preventing expansion into territories that could challenge England's trading routes.

What I hope I have demonstrated here is that these women were not mere pawns, or ornaments on the arm of a king, prince, duke or lord. They were not simply baby-making machines. Yes, in the masculine world they inhabited, a boy was always a prime requirement. A son was needed to continue the family line, to rule and command armies. But daughters were also necessary. They had a purpose – to seal alliances and act as diplomats to protect English interests in the countries into which they married. The one thing we lack, though, is the one thing we most desire: their voices. We do not – and cannot – know about their own emotions. There are letters, appeals and acts of patronage that give us a glimpse of the woman, of who she cared for and where her interests lay. We know, through their actions, such as with Philippa of Lancaster in the defence of Copenhagen and Elizabeth of York in her protection of her children, that these were strong women who could rise to the challenges that life threw at them. I cannot tell you their thoughts and feelings, but I hope that I have shone a light on their stories and given these incredible women another day in the spotlight.

Writing two books on just the medieval English princesses has been a mammoth task. I take my hat off to Mary Ann Everett Green, the nineteenth-century historian who inspired this project. Her epic six-volume work, *Lives of the Princesses of England from the Norman Conquest*, was original and comprehensive. And so respected that there has been no similar work since. Until now. I can only hope that my contributions, *Princesses of the Early Middle Ages* and this book, *Princesses of the Later Middle Ages*, provide a similar, updated insight into the lives of these incredible women, England's original ambassadors.

Notes

Introduction

1. Helen Castor, *The Eagle and the Hart: The Tragedy of Richard II and Henry IV*, London, Penguin, 2024, p. 5.

Chapter One: Cherished Daughters

1. David Crouch and Anthony J. Holden, *History of William Marshal: Text & translation (II. 10032–end),* Anglo-Norman text society from Birkbeck College, 2002, p. 215.
2. Ibid.
3. David Carpenter, *Henry III: The Rise to Power and Personal Rule 1207–1258*, London, Yale University Press, 2021, p. 207.
4. *Holinshed's Chronicles of England, Scotland, and Ireland*, english.nsms.ox.ac.uk/holinshed (1587, Vol. 6, p. 269).
5. Darren Baker, *The Two Eleanors of Henry III: The Lives of Eleanor of Provence and Eleanor de Montfort*, Barnsley, Yorkshire: Pen and Sword Books, 2019, p. 57.
6. Carpenter, *Henry III*, p. 209.
7. *Calendar of Liberate Rolls (CLR)*, *25 Hen III, m. 22* and *CLR seac., 24 Hen. III* quoted in Mary Anne Everett Green, *Lives of the Princesses of England from the Norman Conquest*, London: Longman, Brown, Green, Longman, & Roberts, 1857, Vol. 2, p. 111, and Carpenter, *Henry III*, p. 209.
8. *Close Rolls of the Reign of Henry III preserved in the Public Record Office* (*CR*) quoted in Carpenter, *Henry III*, p. 209.
9. Carpenter, *Henry III*, p. 315.
10. Green, *Lives of the Princesses of England*, Vol. 2, p. 111.
11. Baker, *The Two Eleanors of Henry III*, p. 66.
12. Green, *Lives of the Princesses of England*, Vol. 2, p. 113.
13. Carpenter, *Henry III*, p. 315.
14. Ibid., p. 263.
15. Baker, *The Two Eleanors of Henry III*, p. 66.

16. *CLR, 26 H. III, m. 17* quoted in Green, *Lives of the Princesses of England,* Vol. 2, p. 113.
17. Green, *Lives of the Princesses of England,* Vol. 2, p. 112.
18. Ibid., p. 226.
19. *John of Fordun's Chronicle of the Scottish Nation*, p. 291.
20. Ibid.
21. Ibid.
22. Ibid.
23. Baker, *The Two Eleanors of Henry III*, p. 82.
24. Ibid., p. 83.
25. *Scottish Annals from English Chroniclers A.D. 500 to 1286,* Alan Orr Anderson (ed.), London: Nutt, 1908, p. 366.
26. *CLR, 1251-60, pp. 8, 10* quoted in Baker, *The Two Eleanors of Henry III*, p. 83.
27. Rosalind K. Marshall, *Scottish Queens 1034–1714*, Edinburgh, Birlinn Ltd, 2019, p. 22.
28. *Mediaeval chronicles of Scotland: the chronicles of Melrose and Holyrood,* Joseph Stephenson (trans.), London: Seeleys, 1850, p. 88.
29. Ibid.
30. *John of Fordun's Chronicle of the Scottish Nation*, p. 291.
31. Marshall, *Scottish Queens 1034–1714*, p. 22.
32. Ibid., p. 23.
33. D. Watt, 'The Minority of Alexander III of Scotland', *Transactions of the Royal Historical Society, 21* (1971), pp. 1–23. doi:10.2307/3678917, p. 10.
34. Ibid.
35. Baker, *The Two Eleanors of Henry III*, p. 89.
36. Ibid., p. 92.
37. Martha Carlin and David Crouch (eds. and trans.), *Lost Letters of Medieval Life: English Society, 1200–1250,* Pennsylvania: University of Pennsylvania Press, 2013, p. 199.
38. Baker, *The Two Eleanors of Henry III*, p. 94.
39. *Scottish Annals from English Chroniclers A.D. 500 to 1286*, p. 370.
40. Ibid., p. 371.
41. Baker, *The Two Eleanors of Henry III*, p. 99.
42. *Scottish Annals from English Chroniclers A.D. 500 to 1286*, p. 372.
43. Marshall, *Scottish Queens 1034–1714*, p. 24.
44. *Mediaeval chronicles of Scotland*, p. 90.
45. Watt, *The Minority of Alexander III of Scotland*, pp. 13–15.
46. Marshall, *Scottish Queens 1034–1714*, p. 24.
47. Baker, *The Two Eleanors of Henry III*, p. 102.
48. Norman H. Reid, 'Alexander III (1241–1286)', *Oxford Dictionary of National Biography, online edition,* revised 19 May 2011.

49. Charter Rolls Henry III 1226-1257, p. 444 quoted in fmg.ac/Projects/MedLands/ENGLAND.
50. Baker, *The Two Eleanors of Henry III*, p. 109.
51. Ibid.
52. Ibid.
53. Ibid.
54. Ibid., p. 110.
55. Walter Bower, *Scotichronicon*, Vol. 5, Books 9 and 10, open source, archive.org, 1440, p. 319.
56. *Scottish Annals from English Chroniclers A.D. 500 to 1286*, p. 376.
57. Ibid.
58. *Scottish Annals from English Chroniclers A.D. 500 to 1286*, p. 376.
59. Baker, *The Two Eleanors of Henry III*, p.131.
60. Ibid., pp. 132–133.
61. Marshall, *Scottish Queens 1034–1714*, p. 25.
62. *John of Fordun's Chronicle of the Scottish Nation*, p. 295.
63. Baker, *The Two Eleanors of Henry III*, p. 139.
64. Ibid, p. 147.
65. Ibid.
66. Anne Crawford (ed. and trans.), *Letters of Medieval Women*, Stroud: Sutton Publishing, 2002, p. 36.
67. Ibid., pp. 36–37.
68. Green, *Lives of the Princesses of England*, Vol. 2, p. 229.
69. Ibid., p. 246.
70. Ibid.
71. Ibid., p. 253.
72. *John of Fordun's Chronicle of the Scottish Nation*, p. 295.
73. Reid, 'Alexander III (1241–1286)'.
74. *Mediaeval chronicles of Scotland*, pp. 95–96.
75. Ibid., p. 118.
76. Bower, *Scotichronicon*, Vol. 5, p. 353.
77. Ibid., p. 355.
78. Ibid., p. 371.
79. Ibid., p. 367.
80. Bower, *Scotichronicon*, Vol. 5, p. 371.
81. *The Chronicle of Lanercost*, Sir Herbert Maxwell (ed.), J. Maclehose, Glasgow, 1913, p. 7.
82. Marshall, *Scottish Queens 1034–1714*, p. 25.
83. *The Chronicle of Lanercost*, pp. 7–8.
84. Susan Abernethy, *Margaret of England, Queen of Scots*, thefreelance historywriter.com, 26 October 2012.

85. Bower, *Scotichronicon*, Vol. 5, p. 401.
86. *The Chronicle of Lanercost*, pp. 8–9.
87. Baker, *The Two Eleanors of Henry III*, pp. 182–183.
88. *John of Fordun's Chronicle of the Scottish Nation*, p. 300.
89. *The Chronicle of Lanercost*, p. 9.
90. *John of Fordun's Chronicle of the Scottish Nation*, p. 302.
91. *The Chronicle of Lanercost*, p. 32.
92. Baker, *The Two Eleanors of Henry III*, p. 109
93. *Flores Historiarum* (C.D. Yonge, trans.) quoted in ibid., p. 183.

Chapter Two: Tragedy and Temper Tantrums

1. Marc Morris, *A Great and Terrible King: Edward I and the Forging of Britain*, London, Windmill Books, 2009, p. 20.
2. Kathryn Warner, *Daughters of Edward I*, Yorkshire: Pen and Sword History, 2021, p. 10.
3. 'Chronicles of the Mayors and Sheriffs: 1255–6', in *Chronicles of the Mayors and Sheriffs of London 1188-1274*, H. T. Riley (ed.) (London, 1863), *British History Online*, https://www.british-history.ac.uk/no-series/london-mayors-sheriffs/1188-1274/pp24-25 [accessed 7 April 2025].
4. Ibid.
5. Warner, *Daughters of Edward I*, p. 15.
6. *Calendar of Liberate Rolls*, Vol. V 1260–1267 quoted in fmg.ac/Projects/MedLands/ENGLAND.
7. Ibid.
8. Sara Cockerill, *Eleanor of Castile: The Shadow Queen,* Stroud: Amberley, 2014, ebook, p.171.
9. Original Latin: 'Johanne filie Edwardi primogeniti regis nuper defuncte et in ecclesia Westmonasterii sepulti' Close Rolls, 1264—1268, quoted in fmg.ac/Projects/MedLands/ENGLAND.
10. Warner, *Daughters of Edward I*, p. 19.
11. *Foedera I*, pp. 441, 443, quoted in Baker, *The Two Eleanors of Henry III*, p. 161.
12. Cockerill, *Eleanor of Castile*, ebook, p. 181.
13. Ibid., p. 187.
14. Calendar Patent Rolls, 53 Henry III, p. 349 quoted in fmg.ac/Projects/MedLands/ENGLAND.
15. Warner, *Daughters of Edward I*, p. 23.
16. Ibid.
17. Green, *Lives of the Princesses of England*, Vol. 2, pp. 277–278.

18. TNA E 101/15 quoted in Warner, *Daughters of Edward I*, p. 27.
19. Warner, *Daughters of Edward I*, p. 26.
20. Ibid., p. 27.
21. Warner, *Daughters of Edward I*, p. 28.
22. Kelcey Wilson-Lee, *Daughters of Chivalry: The Forgotten Children of Edward I*, London: Picador, 2019, p. 8.
23. Ibid., p. 14.
24. Warner, *Daughters of Edward I*, p. 31.
25. Ibid., p. 36.
26. Ibid., p. 37.
27. Ibid., p. 39.
28. Cockerill, *Eleanor of Castile*, ebook, p. 337.
29. Rymer, T. (ed.), *Foedera, conventions, literae* (London: Record Commission, 1816–69), p. 550.
30. Warner, *Daughters of Edward I*, p. 42.
31. Cockerill, *Eleanor of Castile*, ebook, p. 377.
32. Ibid., loc. 3206.
33. Warner, *Daughters of Edward I*, p. 46.
34. Ibid., p. 48.
35. Cockerill, *Eleanor of Castile*, ebook, p. 391.
36. Ibid., p. 332.
37. *Calendar of Papal Letters 1198–1304*, quoted in Warner, *Daughters of Edward I*, p. 51.
38. Warner, *Daughters of Edward I*, p. 55.
39. Ibid.
40. Cockerill, *Eleanor of Castile*, ebook, p. 331.
41. *CCR 1288–96*, p. 25, quoted in Warner, *Daughters of Edward I*, p. 56.
42. *The Chronicle of Lanercost*, p. 51.
43. CPR 1281–92. p. 190.
44. Warner, *Daughters of Edward I*, p. 58.
45. Ibid., pp. 58–59.
46. Ibid., p. 64.
47. Wilson-Lee, *Daughters of Chivalry*, pp. 70–71.
48. Ibid., p. 72.
49. Crawford (ed. and trans.), *Letters of Medieval Women*, p. 142.
50. Wilson-Lee, *Daughters of Chivalry*, p. 73.
51. Crawford (ed. and trans.), *Letters of Medieval Women*, p. 194.
52. Wilson-Lee, *Daughters of Chivalry*, p. 77.
53. Ibid., pp. 78–79.
54. Warner, *Daughters of Edward I*, p. 67.
55. Ibid., p. 68.

56. Ibid.
57. Cockerill, *Eleanor of Castile*, ebook, p. 445.
58. *The Chronicle of Lanercost*, p. 58.
59. Cockerill, *Eleanor of Castile*, ebook, p. 445.
60. Ibid., loc. 7261.
61. Nicholas Trivet, *Annales Sex Regum Angliae*, T. Hog (ed.), 1845.p. 310.
62. Warner, *Daughters of Edward I*, p. 83.
63. '1294, membrane 12', in *Calendar of Patent Rolls, Edward I: Volume 3, 1292–1301*, H C Maxwell Lyte (ed.) (London, 1895), *British History Online* https://www.british-history.ac.uk/cal-pat-rolls/edw1/vol3/pp76-107 [accessed 9 April 2025].
64. *The Chronicle of Lanercost*, p. 126.
65. Warner, *Daughters of Edward I*, p. 84.
66. 1291–2, membrane 27, in *Calendar of Patent Rolls, Edward I: Volume 2, 1281–1292*, ed. H C Maxwell Lyte (London, 1895), *British History Online* https://www.british-history.ac.uk/cal-pat-rolls/edw1/vol2/pp461-481 [accessed 9 April 2025].
67. Warner, *Daughters of Edward I*, p. 90.
68. '1293, membrane 19', in *Calendar of Patent Rolls, Edward I: Volume 3, 1292–1301*, H C Maxwell Lyte (ed.) (London, 1895), *British History Online* https://www.british-history.ac.uk/cal-pat-rolls/edw1/vol3/pp51-76 [accessed 9 April 2025].
69. *The Chronicle of Lanercost*, p.70.
70. Warner, *Daughters of Edward I*, p. 92.
71. Ibid.
72. Mary Anne Everett Green suggests 1295 as Joan's date of birth. *Lives of the Princesses of England*, Vol. 2, pp. 310–311.
73. Wilson-Lee, *Daughters of Chivalry*, p. 145.
74. Warner, *Daughters of Edward I*, p. 108.
75. Wilson-Lee, *Daughters of Chivalry*, p. 192.
76. Ibid., p. 208.
77. Ibid., pp. 232–233.
78. Warner, *Daughters of Edward I*, p. 99.
79. Ibid.
80. *SC1/18/125* in the National Archives, quoted in Ibid., p. 107.
81. *CCR 1296–1302*, p. 25, quoted in Warner, *Daughters of Edward I*, p. 101.
82. *SC 1/19/110* quoted in Crawford (ed. and trans.), *Letters of Medieval Women*, p. 38.
83. *Annales Sex Regum Angliae* by Nicholas Trivet, 310.
84. Warner, *Daughters of Edward I*, p. 138.
85. Morris, *A Great and Terrible King,* pp. 375–376.

86. *Rymer, T. (ed.), Foedera, conventions, literae* (London: Record Commission, 1816–69), 1272–1307, p. 1013.
87. Ibid., p. 1016.
88. Cockerill, *Eleanor of Castile*, ebook, p. 478.
89. *PRO SC 1/34/128* quoted in Crawford (ed. and trans.), *Letters of Medieval Women*, pp. 55–56.
90. *Calendar of Papal Registers, Papal Letters* (p. 116) quoted in Fairbank, 'The Last Earl of Warenne and Surrey', p. 246.
91. Ibid., p. 246.
92. Warner, *Daughters of Edward I*, pp. 133–134.

Chapter Three: No Comfort in Marriage

1. Elizabeth Hallam (ed.), *Chronicles of the Age of Chivalry,* Twickenham: Tiger Books, 1995, p. 171d .
2. Stephen Spinks, *Edward II the Man: A Doomed Inheritance*, Stroud: Amberley Publishing, 2017, pp. 94–94.
3. Ibid., p. 103.
4. Hallam, *Chronicles of the Age of Chivalry*, p. 177.
5. Kathryn Warner, *Isabella of France, The Rebel Queen,* Stroud: Amberley, 2016, p. 116.
6. Ibid.
7. Thomas Stapleton, 'A Brief Summary of the Wardrobe Accounts of the tenth, eleventh, and fourteenth years of King Edward the Second', *Archaeologia*, 26 (1836), p. 337, quoted in Warner, *Isabella of France*, p. 117.
8. *Calendar of the Fine rolls preserved in the Public Record Office,* Vol. 2, London: H. M. Stationery Off., 1912, p. 389.
9. Ian Mortimer, *The Perfect King, the Life of Edward III*, Kindle edition, London: Jonathan Cape, 2006, p. 57.
10. *CPR 1307–19* quoted in Warner, *Isabella of France*, p. 117.
11. Spinks, *Edward II the Man*, pp. 148–149.
12. *CPR 1321–4*, 23 quoted in Warner, *Isabella of France,* p. 137.
13. *CPR 1317–1321*, pp. 222–223.
14. Spinks, *Edward II the Man*, p. 198.
15. *CPR 1317–1321, 453*, quoted in Warner, *Isabella of France*, p. 172.
16. Warner, *Isabella of France*, p. 171.
17. *The Chronicle of Lanercost*, p. 249.
18. *CCR 1323–1327*, p. 344.
19. Ibid.
20. *CPR 1324–1327*, pp. 103–104.

21. Warner, *Isabella of France*, p. 167.
22. *The Chronicle of Lanercost*, pp. 249–250.
23. Warner, *Isabella of France*, pp. 207–208.
24. *The Chronicle of Lanercost.*, p. 259.
25. Ibid., pp. 259–260.
26. Ibid., p. 260.
27. Marshall, *Scottish Queens 1034–1714*, p. 36.
28. Ibid.
29. Ibid.
30. *The Chronicle of Lanercost*, p. 260.
31. Bower, *Scotichronicon*, Vol. 7 Bks 13 & 14, p. 39.
32. *The Chronicle of Lanercost.*, p. 257.
33. *John of Fordun's Chronicle of the Scottish Nation*, p. 345.
34. *The Chronicle of Lanercost*, pp. 260–261.
35. Bower, *Scotichronicon*, Vol. 7, p. 43.
36. Bruce Webster, 'Joan [Joan of the Tower]', oxforddnb.com, 23 September 2004.
37. *John of Fordun's Chronicle of the Scottish Nation*, p. 346.
38. Bower, *Scotichronicon*, Vol. 7, p. 73.
39. Ibid., p. 83.
40. Warner, *Isabella of France*, p. 171.
41. Mortimer, *The Perfect King*, pp. 133–134.
42. Kathryn Warner, *Philippa of Hainault: Mother of the English Nation*, Stroud: Amberley Publishing, 2019, p. 97.
43. Ibid., p. 98.
44. Ibid., p. 100 and Mortimer, *The Perfect King*, p. 152.
45. '1331–1332, membranes 18, 17, 16, 15, 14, 13, 12, 11, 10, 9, 8, 7, 6, 5, 4, 3, 2, 1', in *Calendar of Patent Rolls, Edward III: Volume 2, 1330–1334* (London, 1893), *British History Online* https://www.british-history.ac.uk/series/calendar-of-patent-rolls-edward-iii/vol2/pp208-235 [accessed 11 April 2025].
46. Green, *Lives of the Princesses of England,* Vol. 3, p. 73.
47. '1331, membranes 20, 19, 18, 17, 16, 15, 14, 13, 12, 11, 10, 9, 8, 7, 6, 5, 4, 3, 2, 1', in *Calendar of Patent Rolls, Edward III: Volume 2, 1330–1334*(London, 1893), *British History Online* https://www.british-history.ac.uk/series/calendar-of-patent-rolls-edward-iii/vol2/pp169-198 [accessed 11 April 2025].
48. Green, *Lives of the Princesses of England,* Vol. 3, p. 74.
49. Ibid., p. 75.
50. Ibid.
51. Ibid., pp. 75–76.
52. Warner, *Philippa of Hainault*, p. 105–106.

53. Susan Abernethy, *Eleanor of Woodstock, Duchess of Guelders*, thefreelance historywriter.com, 4 March 2022.
54. Ibid.
55. *John of Fordun's Chronicle of the Scottish Nation*, p. 346.
56. Bower, *Scotichronicon*, Vol. 7, p. 151.
57. 'Volume XX: 9 Clement VI', in *Petitions to the Pope 1342–1419*, W. H. Bliss (ed.) (London, 1896), pp. 197–208. *British History Online*, www.british-history.ac.uk/noseries/ petitions-to-pope/1342-1419/pp197-208 [accessed 24 January 2024].
58. Ibid..
59. *John of Fordun's Chronicle of the Scottish Nation*, p. 366.
60. Bower, *Scotichronicon*, Vol. 7, p. 321.
61. Ibid.
62. *RotS*, 1.817, 822 quoted in Webster, 'Joan [Joan of the Tower]'.
63. Bower, *Scotichronicon*, Vol. 7, p. 305.
64. *Calendar of documents relating to Scotland*, Vol. 4, no. 37, p. 10.
65. *Regesta regum Scottorum*, Vol. 6, B. Webster (ed.), 1982, 237, quoted in Webster, 'Joan [Joan of the Tower]'.
66. 'swete, and debonare, Curtas, hamely, plesande, and faire', Wyntoun, *The orygynale cronykil of Scotland*, p. 502.
67. *Calendar of documents relating to Scotland*, Vol. 4, no. 94, p. 22.
68. Ibid.

Chapter Four: Precious Daughters

1. Joyce Marlow, *Kings & Queens of Britain* (sixth edition), London: Artus Publishing, 1979, p. 45.
2. Elizabeth Hallam (ed.), *Chronicles of the Age of Chivalry,* Twickenham: Tiger Books, 1995, p. 231.
3. Ibid.
4. Mortimer, *The Perfect King,* pp. 113–114
5. Mike Ashley, *The Mammoth Book of British Kings & Queens,* London: Robinson, 1998, p. 598.
6. Ibid., p. 600.
7. Green, *Lives of the Princesses of England*, p. 165.
8. Ibid.
9. Ibid., pp. 165–166.
10. Mortimer, *The Perfect King*, pp. 158.
11. Ibid.
12. Green, *Lives of the Princesses of England,* Vol. 3, p. 166.

13. Ibid., pp. 166–167.
14. Mortimer, *The Perfect King*, p.182.
15. Green, *Lives of the Princesses of England,* Vol. 3, pp. 230–231.
16. Warner, *Philippa of Hainault,* p. 98.
17. Mortimer, *The Perfect King*, p.182.
18. Green, *Lives of the Princesses of England*, Vol. 3, p. 168.
19. Mortimer, *The Perfect King*, p. 234.
20. Green, *Lives of the Princesses of England*, Vol. 3, p. 232.
21. Warner, *Philippa of Hainault*, p. 127.
22. Ibid., p. 132.
23. Green, *Lives of the Princesses of England*, Vol. 3, p. 170.
24. Ibid., p. 171–172.
25. Ibid.
26. Ibid.
27. Ibid, p. 172.
28. Ibid.
29. Ibid, pp. 172–173.
30. Membrane 43 '1339–1340, membranes 47, 46, 45, 44, 43, 42, 41, 40, 39, 38, 37, 36, 35, 34, 33, 32, 31, 30, 29, 28, 27, 26, 25', in *Calendar of Patent Rolls, Edward III, Volume 4, 1338–1340* (London, 1898), *British History Online* https://www.british-history.ac.uk/series/calendar-of-patent-rolls-edward-iii/vol4/pp411-446 [accessed 6 March 2025].
31. Green, *Lives of the Princesses of England*, Vol. 3, pp. 174–175.
32. 1341, membranes in *Calendar of Patent Rolls, Edward III, Volume 5, 1340–1343* (London, 1900), *British History Online* https://www.british-history.ac.uk/series/calendar-of-patent-rolls-edward-iii/vol5/pp161-201 [accessed 25 February 2025].
33. Warner, *Philippa of Hainault*, p. 147.
34. Green, *Lives of the Princesses of England*, Vol. 3, p. 176.
35. *CPR 1345–8*, p. 431 quoted in Warner, *Philippa of Hainault*, p. 159.
36. Warner, *Philippa of Hainault*, p. 169.
37. Ibid., p. 175.
38. Ibid., p. 177.
39. *CPR 1345–8*, quoted in ibid., p. 159.
40. Ibid., p. 178.
41. *TNA SC 1/40/5* quoted in ibid., p. 178.
42. Green, *Lives of the Princesses of England*, Vol. 3, p. 181.
43. Ibid., p. 184.
44. Mortimer, *The Perfect King*, p. 387.
45. Warner, *Philippa of Hainault*, p.190.
46. Mortimer, *The Perfect King*, p. 393.
47. Ibid., p. 394.

48. Warner, *Philippa of Hainault*, p.192.
49. Ibid., p. 194.
50. Ibid.
51. Thompson (ed.) *Galfridi le Baker*, p. 97 quoted in Mortimer, *The Perfect King*, p. 395.
52. *Foedera 1344–61*, quoted in Warner, *Philippa of Hainault*, pp. 196–197.
53. *Syllabus (in English) of the documents relating to England and other kingdoms contained in the collection known as 'Rymer's Foedera'*, Sir Thomas Duffus Hardy (ed.), London, Longmans, Green, 1869, p. 363.
54. *CPR 1350–4, p. 114* quoted in Warner, *Philippa of Hainault*, p.203.
55. Amy Licence, *Red Roses: Blanche of Gaunt to Margaret Beaufort*, Stroud, The History Press, 2016, p. 29.
56. Mortimer, *The Perfect King,* p. 534.
57. Warner, *Philippa of Hainault,* p. 208.
58. Mortimer, *The Perfect King*, p. 431.
59. Warner, *Philippa of Hainault*, p. 212.
60. Mortimer, *The Perfect King*, pp. 500–501.
61. Warner, *Philippa of Hainault*, p. 222.
62. Mortimer, *The Perfect King*, p. 505.
63. Ibid., p. 527.
64. Ibid., p. 534.
65. Translation. Letters Patent granting to Isabella, eldest daughter of the King – Hull History Centre Catalogue, https://catalogue.hullhistorycentre.org.uk/, accessed 25/02/25.
66. Paul Johnson, *The Life and Times of Edward III*, London: Wiedenfeld and Nicolson and Book Club Associates, 1984, p. 119.
67. Warner, *Philippa of Hainault*, p. 244.
68. *CPR 1364–7, p. 190,* quoted in Warner, *Philippa of Hainault*, p. 244.
69. Warner, *Philippa of Hainault*, p. 258.
70. Mortimer, *The Perfect King, the Life of Edward III*, p. 582.
71. fmg.ac/Projects/MedLands/ENGLAND.
72. Gemma Hollman, *The Queen and the Mistress: The Women of Edward III*, Cheltenham, The History Press, 2022, pp. 111–112.
73. Paul Johnson, *The Life and Times of Edward III,* London: Wiedenfeld and Nicolson and Book Club Associates, 1984, p. 198.
74. W. M. Ormrod, 'Alice Perrers and John Salisbury', *English Historical Review* December 2015.
75. Hollman, *The Queen and the Mistress*, p. 113.
76. Ibid., p. 115.
77. C. Given-Wilson, 'Perrers, Alice (d. 1400/01)', *Oxford Dictionary of National Biography*, Oxford University Press, online edition, January 2008.

78. Ibid.
79. Ibid.
80. Ibid.
81. Thomas of Walsingham, *Thomae Walsingham Historia Anglicana* (in part one of *Chronica Monasterii Sancti Albani*) H. T. Riley (ed.) in Rolls Series 1863–4, Vol. 1.
82. Ibid.
83. J. Strachey (ed.); *Rotuli parliamentorum ut et petitiones, et placita in parliamento*, 6 vols. (1767–77), p. 14.
84. Given-Wilson, *Perrers, Alice.*
85. Hollman, *The Queen and the Mistress*, p. 202.
86. Given-Wilson, *Perrers, Alice.*
87. Hollman, *The Queen and the Mistress*, p. 206.
88. Ibid., p. 205.
89. Ibid., p. 204.
90. Ibid.
91. Ibid., p. 208.
92. *CPR, Henry IV, vol.2, 421* quoted in ibid., p. 207.
93. Hollman, *The Queen and the Mistress*, p. 207.
94. *CIPM 18, Henry IV, no. 1192* quoted in ibid., p. 207.
95. Hollman, *The Queen and the Mistress*, p. 208.
96. Ibid.

Chapter Five: The Lancaster Sisters

1. Elizabeth Norton, *England's Queens: From Boudica to Elizabeth of York*, Stroud: Amberley Publishing, 2015, p. 187.
2. Ibid., p. 186.
3. Ibid., p. 188.
4. 'they muste be content howe so ever they founde her, for they sayde she was but a Yonge chylde of eighty yere of age, wherefore they sayd, there coulde nat be in her no great wysdome nor prudence; howbeit, she was indoctryned well ynough, and that the lords found well when they sawe her. The erle Marshall, beynge on his knees, sayde to her: Fayre lady, by the grace of God ye shall be our lady and queen of Englande. Than aunswered the yonge lady well advisedly, without counsayle of any other persone: Syr, quod she, and it please God and my lorde my father that I shall be queen of Englande, I shall be glad thereof, for it is shewed me that I shall be then a great lady.' Froissart quoted in ibid., p. 189.
5. Sharon Bennett Connolly, *Heroines of the Medieval World*, Stroud: Amberley Publishing, 2017, p. 30.
6. Licence, *Red Roses*, p.44.
7. Ibid., p. 84.

8. TNA: PRO, E 37/28 quoted in A. L. Brown, and Henry Summerson, 'Henry IV [known as Henry Bolingbroke]' *Oxford Dictionary of National Biography*, Oxford University Press, online edition, 2023.
9. Licence, *Red Roses*, p. 87.
10. Ian Mortimer, *The Fears of Henry IV: The Life of England's Self-Made King*, London: Vintage Books, 2008, p.41.
11. Licence, *Red Roses*, p. 87.
12. Ibid., p. 85.
13. Mortimer, *The Fears of Henry IV*, pp. 40–41.
14. Licence, *Red Roses*, p. 86.
15. Mortimer, *The Fears of Henry IV*, p. 46.
16. Licence, *Red Roses*, p. 86.
17. CCR, Richard II, December1384, quoted in Licence, *Red Roses*, p. 92 and Mortimer, *The Fears of Henry IV*, p. 62.
18. Mortimer, *The Fears of Henry IV*, p. 64.
19. Licence, *Red Roses*, p. 92.
20. Mortimer, *The Fears of Henry IV*, p. 64.
21. Licence, *Red Roses*, p. 94.
22. Ibid., p. 96.
23. Mortimer, *The Fears of Henry IV*, p. 65.
24. Ibid., p. 69.
25. Licence, *Red Roses*, p. 98.
26. Ibid., p. 97.
27. Mortimer, *The Fears of Henry IV*, p. 71.
28. Ibid.
29. Licence, *Red Roses*, p. 98.
30. Mortimer, *The Fears of Henry IV*, pp. 71–74 and Licence, *Red Roses*, pp. 98–100.
31. Mortimer, *The Fears of Henry IV*, p. 78.
32. Licence, *Red Roses*, p.102.
33. Ibid.
34. Ibid.
35. Mortimer, *The Fears of Henry IV*, p. 99.
36. Ibid.
37. Licence, *Red Roses*, p.103.
38. Ibid.
39. Castor, *The Eagle and the Hart*, loc. 3115.
40. Mortimer, *The Fears of Henry IV*, pp. 104–106.
41. Ibid., pp. 110–115.
42. Ibid., p. 117.
43. Licence, *Red Roses*, p.105.
44. Castor, *The Eagle and the Hart*, loc. 3516.

45. Mortimer, *The Fears of Henry IV*, p. 121.
46. Dan Jones, *Henry V: The Astonishing Rise of England's Greatest King*, London: Head of Zeus, 2024, p. 23.
47. Castor, *The Eagle and the Hart*, loc. 4479.
48. Mortimer, *The Fears of Henry IV*, p. 147.
49. Ibid., p. 148.
50. Ibid., p. 152.
51. Ibid.
52. Ibid., p. 159.
53. Castor, *The Eagle and the Hart*, loc. 5087.
54. *The Chronicles of Froissart*, pp. 668–9, quoted in Mortimer, *The Fears of Henry IV*, p. 161.
55. Jones, *Henry V*, p. 60.
56. Mortimer, *The Fears of Henry IV*, pp. 172–174.
57. *Parliament Rolls*, 1399–1413, 25, quoted in Mortimer, *The Fears of Henry IV*, p. 191.
58. Mortimer, *The Fears of Henry IV*, p. 231.
59. Ibid.
60. Castor, *The Eagle and the Hart*, loc. 5882.
61. Mortimer, *The Fears of Henry IV*, p. 244.
62. Sharon Bennett Connolly, *Ladies of Magna Carta: Women of Influence in Thirteenth Century England*, South Yorkshire: Pen and Sword History, 2020, p. 215.
63. Green, *Lives of the Princesses of England,* Vol. 3, pp. 316–328.
64. Jones, *Henry V*, p. 132.
65. fmg.ac/Projects/MedLands/PALATINATE.
66. Mortimer, *The Fears of Henry IV*, p. 326.
67. Castor, *The Eagle and the Hart*, loc. 6926.
68. Ibid., and Mortimer, *The Fears of Henry IV*, p. 326.
69. Ibid.
70. A.L. Brown, and Henry Summerson, 'Henry IV [known as Henry Bolingbroke]' *Oxford Dictionary of National Biography*, Oxford University Press, online edition, 2023.
71. *Diplomatarium Norvegicum*, 19. 2, no. 650, pp. 791–5, from BL, MS Cotton Nero B III, fol. 13, quoted in Robert Bartlett, *Blood Royal: Dynastic Politics in Medieval Europe*, Cambridge: Cambridge University Press, 2020, pp. 397–398.
72. Mortimer, *The Fears of Henry IV,* p. 309.
73. 'Henry IV: March 1406', in *Parliament Rolls of Medieval England,* Chris Given-Wilson, Paul Brand, Seymour Phillips, Mark Ormrod, Geoffrey Martin, Anne Curry, Rosemary Horrox (eds.) (Woodbridge, 2005) *British History Online*, https://www.british-history.ac.uk/no-series/parliament-rolls-medieval/march-1406, accessed 21 October 2024.

74. Jones, *Henry V*, p. 215.
75. Castor, *The Eagle and the Hart*, loc. 6657.
76. Liam Foley, 'May 4, 1394: Birth of Philippa of England, Queen Consort of Denmark, Norway and Sweden,' europeanroyalhistory.com, 2020.
77. Anna Belfrage, 'The Bride who wore white for the first time ever. Meet a 15th century trendsetter,' annabelfrage.com, 2020.
78. Marie-Louise Flemberg, 'Queen Philippa as a benefactor of the Birgittines', http://www.sanctabirgitta.com/underniva/forska/, 2003.
79. Jones, *Henry V*, p. 224.
80. Flemberg, 'Queen Philippa as a benefactor of the Birgittines',
81. Ibid.
82. Foley, 'May 4, 1394: Birth of Philippa of England, Queen Consort of Denmark, Norway and Sweden'.
83. Belfrage, 'The Bride who wore white for the first time ever…'
84. Foley, 'May 4, 1394: Birth of Philippa of England, Queen Consort of Denmark, Norway and Sweden'.
85. Ibid.
86. fmg.ac/Projects/MedLands/ENGLAND.

Chapter Six: Royal Daughters of the House of York

1. *Domenico Mancini: de occupatione regni Anglie*, edited and translated by Annette Carson, Horstead: Imprimis Imprimatur, 2021, p. 47.
2. Ibid.
3. David Baldwin, *Elizabeth Woodville, Mother of the Princes in the Tower*, Stroud: Sutton Publishing, 2002, p. 14.
4. *Ingulph's chronicle of the abbey of Croyland with the continuations by Peter of Blois and anonymous writers*, London: H. G. Bohn, 1854, p. 457.
5. Rosemary Horrox, 'Elizabeth [Elizabeth of York] 1466–1503', *Oxford Dictionary of National Biography,* online edition, 2004.
6. Amy Licence, *Elizabeth of York: The Forgotten Tudor Queen*, Stroud, Amberley, 2013, ebook, loc. 936.
7. Ibid., loc. 404.
8. Green, *Lives of the Princesses of England,* Vol. 3, p. 396.
9. Licence, *Elizabeth of York,* ebook, loc. 475.
10. Baldwin, *Elizabeth Woodville,* p. 47.
11. Licence, *Elizabeth of York,* ebook, loc. 799.
12. Horrox, 'Elizabeth [Elizabeth of York] 1466–1503', ODNB.
13. Licence, *Elizabeth of York,* ebook, loc. 1046.
14. Norton, *England's Queens*, p. 236.

15. Hilton, *Queens Consort*, p. 482.
16. Licence, *Elizabeth of York,* ebook, loc. 1019.
17. Bluemantle Pursuivant quoted in Baldwin, *Elizabeth Woodville,* p. 57.
18. Baldwin, *Elizabeth Woodville,* pp. 86–87.
19. *Ingulph's chronicle of the abbey of Croyland*, p. 481.
20. Licence, *Elizabeth of York,* ebook, loc. 2117.
21. Baldwin, *Elizabeth Woodville,* p. 97.
22. Pauline E. Routh, 'Princess Bridget', *The Ricardian*, June 1975, pp. 13–14.
23. Green, *Lives of the Princesses of England,* Vol. 3, p. 401.
24. Ibid.
25. Ibid., p. 402.
26. Ibid., pp. 402–403.
27. *Ingulph's chronicle of the abbey of Croyland*, p. 482.
28. Ibid.
29. Ibid.
30. Ibid.
31. Ibid., p. 487.
32. *Collectanea Topographica Genealogica*, Vol. I, XL, *Harleian MS* 1074, No. IX, p. 304 quoted in fmg.ac/Projects/MedLands/ENGLAND.
33. Baldwin, *Elizabeth Woodville,* p. 136.
34. Much ink has been expended over the fate of the Princes in the Tower over the centuries, and whether they were murdered, escaped or grew up in obscurity. Their fate is beyond the scope of this book, but it should be noted that it played a significant role in the events of the day.
35. *Ingulph's chronicle of the abbey of Croyland*, p. 491.
36. Norton, *England's Queens*, p. 237.
37. Ellis, Letters, 2nd series, Vol. i, p. 149. Harl. MS. , 433, quoted in Green, *Lives of the Princesses of England,* Vol. 3, p. 415.
38. Norton, *England's Queens*, p. 237.
39. ROTP, 6,278, quoted in Horrox, 'Elizabeth [Elizabeth of York] 1466–1503', ODNB.
40. *Hall's Chronicle* quoted in Norton, *England's Queens,* p. 238.
41. *Camden Miscellany* quoted in Lisa Hilton, *Queens Consort*, p. 472.
42. 'Historical Memoranda of John Stowe: The baptism of Prince Arthur, son of Henry VII', in *Three Fifteenth-Century Chronicles with Historical Memoranda by John Stowe*, James Gairdner (ed.) (London, 1880), pp. 104–105. *British History Online* http://www.british-history.ac.uk/camdenrecord-soc/vol28/pp104-105 [accessed 31 January 2023].
43. Lisa Hilton, *Queens Consort*, p. 473.
44. Green, *Lives of the Princesses of England,* Vol. 3, p. 419.
45. Horrox, 'Elizabeth [Elizabeth of York] 1466–1503', ODNB.

46. Lisa Hilton, *Queens Consort*, p. 475.
47. Ibid., p. 476.
48. Horrox, 'Elizabeth [Elizabeth of York] 1466–1503', ODNB.
49. Ibid.
50. Green, Lives of the Princesses of England, Vol. 3, p. 422.
51. Champion, Sharon. 'Appendix I: Will of John, Lord Welles', in '"Not So Fortunate As Fair": The Life of Princess Cecily Plantagenet', *Isle of Wight History*, archive.org.
52. Rosemary Horrox, 'Cecily, Viscountess Welles', *Oxford Dictionary of National Biography,* online edition, 23 September 2004.
53. Ibid.
54. Green, *Lives of the Princesses of England*, Vol. 3, p. 424.
55. Michael A .R Graves., 'Howard, Thomas, third duke of Norfolk', *Oxford Dictionary of National Biography,* online edition, 23 September 2004.
56. Ibid.
57. Margaret R. Westcott, 'Katherine, Countess of Devon', *Oxford Dictionary of National Biography,* online edition, 3 January 2008.
58. Ibid.
59. Ibid.
60. Ibid.
61. Ibid.
62. Ibid.
63. Pauline E., Routh, 'Princess Bridget', *The Ricardian*, June 1975, pp. 13–14.
64. Ibid., p. 14.
65. Susan Higginbotham, 'Bridget of York: A Royal Nun', susanhigginbotham.com, 16 February 2013.
66. Ibid.
67. John Weaver, *Ancient Funeral Monuments* (1631), p. 338, quoted in Routh, *Princess Bridget*, p. 14 and Margaret M. Condon (2022). 'Princess and Nun: Bridget (1480–c. 1507), the youngest daughter of Edward IV', *The Ricardian.* 32: pp. 89–126.
68. Green, *Lives of the Princesses of England*, Vol. 4, pp. 47–48.
69. TNA, E36/214, f. 111v [p. 222; original foliation 108v] quoted in Condon (2022) 'Princess and Nun'.
70. Norton, *England's Queens*, p. 240.
71. CSP Spain, 1485–1509, 164 quoted in Horrox, 'Elizabeth [Elizabeth of York] 1466–1503', ODNB.
72. Horrox, 'Elizabeth [Elizabeth of York] 1466–1503', ODNB.
73. Ibid.
74. Moriarty, pp. 80–1, quoted in Crawford (ed.), *Letters of the Queens of England*, p. 158.

75. Crawford, *Letters of the Queens of England*, p. 154.
76. 'July 1498' in CSPS pp. 167–180, quoted in Nathen Amin, *Henry VII and the Tudor Pretenders: Simnel, Warbeck and Warwick*, Stroud: Amberley Publishing, 2020, p. 286 and Lisa Hilton, *Queens Consort*, p. 479.
77. BL Egerton MS 616, fol. 7, Latin. Wood, Vol. I, letter xlvi quoted in Crawford, *Letters of the Queens of England*, p. 157.
78. Amin, *Henry VII and the Tudor Pretenders,* pp. 279–280.
79. Rodrigo de Puebla, Spanish Ambassador, quoted in Amin, *Henry VI and the Tudor Pretenders,* pp. 282–283.
80. Amin, *Henry VII and the Tudor Pretenders*, pp. 290.
81. Ibid., pp. 302–307.
82. Lisa Hilton, *Queens Consort*, p. 483.
83. *English Historical Documents 1485–1558* quoted in Lisa Hilton, *Queens Consort*, p. 486.
84. Thomas More quoted in Lisa Hilton, *Queens Consort*, p. 486.

Chapter Seven: The Last White Rose

1. Chris Skidmore, *Richard III: Brother, Protector, King*, London: Weidenfeld & Nicholson, 2017, p. 74.
2. Matthew Lewis, *Richard III: Loyalty Binds Me*, Stroud: Amberley, 2018, p. 368.
3. Rosemary Horrox, 'Richard III', *Oxford Dictionary of National Biography,* online edition, 2013.
4. Buck (1647), p. 105, citing 'Grafton & Chron. MS in quarto apud Dn Rob Cotton' quoted in https://fmg.ac/Projects/MedLands/ENGLAND.
5. Lewis, *Richard III*, p. 106.
6. Ibid.
7. Ibid., p. 364.
8. Transcribed by D.H. Thomas and quoted in Susan Higginbotham, *Katherine Plantagenet, Richard III's Illegitimate Daughter*, susanhigginbotham.com, 17 April 2013.
9. Peter Hammond, 'Katherine Plantagenet', https://richardiii.net/richard-iii-his-world/his-family/illegitimate-children/katherine-plantagenet/, 2025.
10. Ibid.
11. Ibid.
12. Ibid.
13. Higginbotham, *Katherine Plantagenet.*
14. Rosemary Horrox, 'Richard III', Oxford Dictionary of National Biography, online edition, 2013.
15. Dr Christian Steer, *The King's Daughter in Late Medieval London: An Archival Discovery of Monumental Proportions*, yorkisthistorytrust.org, 2022.

Bibliography

Primary Sources

Adam of Usk, *Chronicon Adae de Usk, A.D. 1377–1421*, with translation and notes by Sir Edward Maunde Thompson (ed.), K.C.B., Oxford: Oxford University Press, 1904.

Barlow, Frank (ed.), *Vita Aedwardi Regis: the Life of King Edward Who Rests at Westminster*, London: Nelson, 1962.

Berners, John Bourchier, Lord (trans.) and Macauley, G. C. (ed.), Froissart, Jean, *The Chronicles of Froissart*, London: MacMillan & Co., 1899.

Bower, Walter, *Scotichronicon,* Vol. 5, Books 9 & 10, open source, archive.org, 1440.

Brut y Tywysogyn or *The Chronicle of the Princes: Peniarth MS 20 Version*, T. Jones (ed.), Cardiff, 1952.

Calendar of Close Rolls, Henry V: Volume 1, 1413–1419, british-history.ac.uk.

Calendar of Close Rolls, Henry VI: Volume 1, 1422–1429, british-history.ac.uk.

Calendar of Close Rolls, Henry VI: Volume 3, 1435–1441, british-history.ac.uk.

Calendar of Close Rolls, Henry VI: Volume 4, 1441–1447, british-history.ac.uk.

Calendar of Close Rolls, Henry VI: Volume 5, 1447–1454, british-history.ac.uk.

Calendar of the Charter Rolls preserved in the Public Record Office, Vol. IV, 1–14, Edward III, AD 1327–1341, London, 1912.

Calendar of the Fine rolls Preserved in the Public Record Office, London: HMSO, 1912.

Carlin, Martha and David Crouch (eds. and trans.), *Lost Letters of Medieval Life: English Society, 1200–1250,* Pennsylvania: University of Pennsylvania Press, 2013.

Chaucer, Geoffrey, *The Canterbury Tales*, D. Laing Purves (ed.), MacMay, e-book, 2007.

Chaucer, Geoffrey, *The Complete Works of Geoffrey Chaucer*, Thomas Thynne (ed.), Kindle edition, 2014.

Chronicle of Melrose 731–1270, A. O. Anderson and M. M. Anderson (eds.), 1936.

Chronicle of Melrose 731–1270, MS Cotton Faustina B ix, British Library.

Chronicles of the Reigns of Stephen, Henry II and Richard I, Nabu Press, 2012.

Crawford, Anne (ed. and trans.), *Letters of Medieval Women,* Stroud: Sutton Publishing, 2002.

Crawford, Anne (ed. and trans.), *Letters of the Queens of England*, Stroud: Sutton Publishing, 2002.

Crouch, David and Holden, Anthony J., *History of William Marshal: Text & translation (II. 10032–end)* Anglo-Norman text society from Birkbeck College, 2002.

Darlington, R. R. (ed.), *Vita Wulfstani of William of Malmesbury*, PR new series 40, 1928.

Darlington, R. R., and McGurk, P. (eds.), *The Chronicle of John of Worcester*, 2 Vols., Oxford: OMT, 1995, 1998.

Davis, R. H. C., and Chibnall, Marjorie (eds.), *The Gesta Guillielmi of William of Poitiers*, Oxford: OMT, 1998.

Domenico Mancini: de occupatione regni Anglie, Annette Carson (ed. and trans.), Horstead: Imprimis Imprimatur, 2021.

Dronke, Peter, *Medieval Testimonies*, Glasgow: University of Glasgow Press, 1976.

Eadmer of Canterbury, *Historia Novorum in Anglia,* Longman, 1884.

Eadmer of Canterbury, *The Life of St Anselm, Archbishop of Canterbury,* London: T. Nelson, 1962.

Florentii Wigorniensis monachi chronicon ex chronicis, B. Thorpe (ed.), 2, English Historical Society, 10, 1849.

Forester, Thomas, (trans. and ed.), *The Chronicle of John Florence of Worcester with the two continuations*, London: H. G. Bohn, 1854.

Froissart, Jean, *Chronicles*, dhi.ac.uk/onlinefroissart/.

Froissart, Jean, *Chronicles*, G. Brereton (trans.), London: Penguin Classics, 1968, revised edition 1978.

Froissart, Jean, *Chronicles*, London: Macmillan and Co., 1895.

Gallagher, Eric and Lesley Boatwright, (eds.), *The Great Roll of the Pipe for the Tenth Year of the Reign of King Henry III, Michaelmas 1226*, Woodbridge: The Boydell Press, 2022.

Gervase of Canterbury, *The Deeds of Kings,* W. Stubbs (ed.) in *The Historical Works of Gervase of Canterbury*, Rolls Series, 1880.

Gesta Regis Henrici Secundi Benedicti Abbatis: The Chronicle of the Reigns of Henry II and Richard I A. D. 1169–1192: Known Commonly Under the Name of Benedict of Peterborough, William Stubbs (ed.), Longmans, 1867.

Gesta Stephani, K. R. Potter (trans.), London: Thomas Nelson and Sons, 1955.

Guy, Bishop of Amiens, *Carmen de Haestingae Proelio*, Frank Barlow (ed. and trans.), Oxford: Clarendon Press, 1999.

Henry III Fine Rolls, *finerollshenry3.org.uk.*

Henry of Huntingdon, *The Chronicle of Henry of Huntingdon,* London: H. G. Bohn, 1853.

Henry of Huntingdon, *The History of the English People 1000–1154*, Diana Greenway (trans.), Oxford: Oxford University Press, 2002.

Ingram, James (trans.), *The Anglo-Saxon Chronicle*, London, 1823, reprinted by Dodo Press.

Ingulph's Chronicle of the Abbey of Croyland with the Continuations by Peter of Blois and Anonymous Writers, London: H. G. Bohn, 1854.

John of Fordun's Chronicle of the Scottish nation, W. F. Skene (ed.), Edinburgh: Edmonston and Douglas, 1872.

John of Salisbury, *The Letters of John of Salisbury*, W. J. Miller, S. J. Butler, H. E. Butler (eds.) and revised by C. N. L. Brooke, London: Thomas Nelson and Sons, 1955.

King James I, *The Poetical Remains of James I*, Edinburgh: J. and E. Balfour, 1793.

Liber Eliensis: A History of the Isle of Ely from the Seventh Century to the Twelfth, Janet Fairweather (trans.), Woodbridge: Boydell Press, 2005.

Luard, H. R. (ed.), *Matthaei Parisiensis, monachi sancti Albani, Chronica majora,* 7 Vols., RS, 57, 1872–83.

Mackay, A. J. G. (ed.), *The Historie and Cronicles of Scotland ... by Robert Lindesay of Pitscottie,* 3 Vols., Scottish Text Society, 42–3, 60, 1899–1911.

Magna Carta, British Library, transcript from bl.uk.

Magna Carta, nationalarchives.gov.uk/education/resources/magnacarta/charter-forest-1225-westminster/.

Maxwell, Herbert, *The Chronicle of Lanercost, 1272–1346*, Glasgow: J. Maclehose, 1913.

Mediaeval Chronicles of Scotland: the Chronicles of Melrose and Holyrood, Joseph Stephenson (trans.), London: Seeleys, 1850.

Morton, Catherine and Hope Muntz, (eds.), *The Carmen de Hastingi Proelio of Guy, Bishop of Amiens*, London, 1972.

Nicolas, N. H. (ed.), *Testamenta Vetusta: being illustrations from wills*, 2 Vols., (1826).

Ordericus Vitalis, *Histoire de Normandie, seconde partie*, L. F. Dubois (trans.), 1826, archive.org.

Ordericus Vitalis, *Historiae ecclesiasticae libri tredecem*, Auguste Le Prévost (trans.), Société de l'histoire de France, 1838, archive.org.

Ordericus Vitalis, *The Ecclesiastical History of England and Normandy*, London: H. G. Bohn, 1853.

Ordericus Vitalis, *The Ecclesiastical History of England and Normandy*, Vol. 6, Oxford: Clarendon Press, 1969.

Paris, Matthew, Robert de Reading and others, *Flores Historiarum*, Vol. III, Henry Richards Luard (ed.), HMSO, 1890.

Peter the Venerable, *The Letters of Peter the Venerable*, Giles Constable (ed.), Cambridge, MA: 2v Harvard University Press, 1967.

Ralph of Coggeshall *The English Chronicle,* J. Stevenson (ed.) in *Chronicon Anglicanum,* Rolls Series, 1875.

Ralph of Diceto, *Images of History*, W. Stubbs (ed.) in *The Historical Works of Master Ralph of Diceto*, Rolls Series, 1876.

Richard of Devizes, *The Chronicle of Richard of Devizes: Concerning the Deeds of Richard the First King of England also Richard of Cirencester's Description of Britain,* J. A. Giles (trans. and ed.), London, 1841.

Roger of Wendover, *Roger of Wendover's Flowers of History, Comprising the History of England from the Descent of the Saxons to A.D. 1235*, Vol. II, J. A. Giles (ed.), London: H. G. Bohn, 1849.

Rymer, T. (ed.), *Foedera, conventions, literae,* London: Record Commission, 1816–69.

Sawyer, P. H. *Anglo-Saxon Charters: An Annotated List and Bibliography, Royal Historical Society Guides and Handbooks* (1968).

Scottish Annals from English Chroniclers A.D. 500 to 1286, Alan Orr Anderson (ed.), London: Nutt, 1908.

Sharpe, J. (trans.), *The History of the Kings of England and of his Own Times by William Malmesbury*, Seeleys, 1854.

Shirley, W. W. (ed.), *Royal and Other Historical Letters*, London: Rolls Series, Chronicles and Memorials, 1862–6.

Stow, John, *The Annales of England, 'The race of the Kings of Brytaine after the received opinion since Brute, &c'*, London: G. Bishop and T. Adams, 1605.

Strachey, J (ed.), *Rotuli parliamentorum ut et petitiones, et placita in parliamento*, 6 Vols., 1767–77.

Swanton, Michael, (ed. and trans.) *The Anglo-Saxon Chronicles*, London: Phoenix Press, 2000.

Syllabus (in English) of the documents relating to England and other kingdoms contained in the collection known as 'Rymer's Foedera', Sir Thomas Duffus Hardy (ed.), London: Longmans, Green, 1869.

Symeon of Durham, *Vita Sanctae Margaretae Scotorum reginae, Symeonis Dunelmensis opera et collectanea*, J. H. Hinde (ed.), Surtees Society, 1868.

The Annals of Roger de Hoveden: Comprising the History of England and of other Countries of Europe from A.D. 732 to A.D. 1201, Henry T. Riley (ed. and trans.), H. G. Bohn, London, 1853.

The Autobiography of Giraldus Cambrensis, H. E. Butler (ed. and trans.), 1937, archive.org.

The 'Barnwell' Annals (anon.), W. Stubbs (ed.), in *The Historical Collections of Walter of Coventry*, Rolls Series, 1873.

The Letters of Hildegard of Bingen, Joseph L. Baird and Radd K. Ehrman (trans.), Oxford University, 1994, 1998, 2004.

The Life of the Black Prince by the Herald of Sir John Chandos, Mildred K. Pope (ed.), Oxford: Clarendon Press, 1910.

The Publications of the Pipe Roll Society, Pipe Roll Society, London, 1884–1925.

The Register of Henry Chichele, Archbishop of Canterbury, 1414–1443, E. F. Jacob (ed.), Oxford: Oxford University Press, 1937–47.

Thomas of Walsingham, *Thomae Walsingham Historia Anglicana* (in part one of *Chronica Monasterii Sancti Albani*) H. T. Riley (ed.) in Rolls Series 1863–4, Vol. 1.

Trivet, Nicholas, *Annales Sex Regum Angliae,* T. Hog (ed.), 1845.

Turgot, Bishop of St Andrews, *Life of St. Margaret Queen of Scotland*, Forgotten Books, 2012.

Turgot, *Vita Sanctae Margaretae Scotorum reginae, Symeonis Dunelmensis opera et collectanea*, J. H. Hinde (ed.), Surtees Society, 1868.

Van Houts, E. M. C. (ed.), *The Gesta Normannorum Ducum of William of Jumièges, Orderic Vitalis and Robert of Torigni*, 2 Vols., Oxford, 1992–5.

Van Houts, Elisabeth M. C. and Rosalind C. Love, (eds. and trans.), *The Warenne (Hyde) Chronicle*, Oxford: Clarendon Press, 2013.

Wace, Robert, *Le Roman de Rou*, Glyn S. Burgess (trans.), Woodbridge: Boydell Press, 2004.

Whitelock, D., Douglas, D. C. and Tucker, S. I. (eds. and trans.), *The Anglo-Saxon Chronicle: a Revised Translation*, 1961.

Wilkinson, Louise, *The Household Roll of Eleanor de Montfort, Countess of Leicester and Pembroke*, Woodbridge: The Boydell Press, 2020.

William of Malmesbury, *Chronicles of the Kings of England, From the Earliest Period to the Reign of King Stephen, c.1090–1143*, Perennial Press, 2016.

William of Malmesbury, *Chronicles of the Kings of England, From the Earliest Period to the Reign of King Stephen, c. 1090–1143*, John Sharpe and J. A. Giles (eds.), London: H. G. Bohn, 1847.

Secondary Sources

A History of the County of Rutland: Vol. 2, London: Victoria County History, 1935.

Abernethy, Susan, *Eleanor of Woodstock, Duchess of Guelders*, thefreelancehistorywriter.com, 4 March 2022.

Abernethy, Susan, *Margaret of England, Queen of Scots*, thefreelancehistorywriter.com, 26 October 2012.

Alio, Jacqueline, 'Betrothal of Joanna of England to William II of Sicily' (article), academia.edu, 2016, accessed January 2020.

Andrews, J. F., *Lost Heirs of the Medieval Crown: The Kings and Queens who Never were*, Barnsley, Yorkshire: Pen and Sword Books, 2019.

Andrews, J. F., *The Families of Eleanor of Aquitaine: A Female Network of Power in the Middle Ages*, Cheltenham: The History Press, 2023.

Bibliography

Asbridge, Thomas, *The Greatest Knight: The Remarkable Life of William Marshal, the Power Behind Five English Thrones*, London: Simon & Schuster, 2015.

Asch, T. D., *The Century of Calamity: England in the Long Eleventh Century*, Stroud: Amberley Publishing, 2021.

Ashley, Mike, *British Kings & Queens,* London: Constable & Robinson Ltd, 2014.

Ashley, Mike, *The Mammoth Book of British Kings & Queens,* London,: Robinson, 1998.

Baker, Darren, *The Two Eleanors of Henry III: The Lives of Eleanor of Provence and Eleanor de Montfort*, Barnsley, Yorkshire: Pen and Sword Books, 2019.

Baker, Darren, *With All For All: The Life of Simon de Montfort*, Stroud: Amberley Publishing, 2015.

Baldwin, David, *Elizabeth Woodville, Mother of the Princes in the Tower*, Stroud: Sutton Publishing, 2002.

Barrow, G. W. S., 'Margaret [St Margaret] (d. 1093), Queen of Scots, consort of Malcolm III', *Oxford Dictionary of National Biography*, Oxford University Press, online edition, 2004.

Bartlett, Robert, *Blood Royal: Dynastic Politics in Medieval Europe*, Cambridge: Cambridge University Press, 2020.

Bartlett, Robert, *England Under the Norman and Angevin Kings, 1075–1225,* Oxford: Oxford University Press, 2000.

Bartlett, W. B., *Richard the Lionheart: The Crusader King of England*, Stroud: Amberley Publishing, 2018.

Belfrage, Anna, 'The Bride wore white for the first time ever. Meet a 15th-century trendsetter', annabelfrage.com, 2020.

Bémont, Charles, *Medieval Europe, 395–1270*, Lecturable, e-book, 2012.

Bennett Connolly, Sharon, *Defenders of the Norman Crown: Rise and Fall of the Warenne Earls of Surrey*, Barnsley, Yorkshire: Pen and Sword Books, 2021.

Bennett Connolly, Sharon, *Heroines of the Medieval World,* Stroud: Amberley Publishing, 2017.

Bennett Connolly, Sharon, *Ladies of Magna Carta: Women of Influence in Thirteenth Century England*, Barnsley, Yorkshire: Pen and Sword Books, 2020.

Bennett Connolly, Sharon, *Women of the Anarchy*, Stroud: Amberley Publishing, 2024.

Bicheno, Hugh, *Battle Royal: The Wars of Lancaster and York, 1440–1462,* Croydon: Head of Zeus Ltd, 2016.

Borman, Tracy, *Crown and Sceptre: A New History of the British Monarchy from William the Conqueror to Elizabeth II,* London: Hodder & Stoughton Ltd, 2021.

Borman, Tracy, *Matilda, Wife of the Conqueror, First Queen of England*, London: Vintage Books, 2012.

Boyd, Douglas, *Eleanor, April Queen of Aquitaine*, Stroud: Sutton Publishing, 2004.

Boyd, Douglas, *Plantagenet Princesses: The Daughters of Henry II and Eleanor of Aquitaine*, Barnsley, Yorkshire: Pen and Sword Books, 2020.

Brindle, Steven and Agnieszka Sadraei, *Conisbrough Castle, English Heritage Guidebook*, London: English Heritage, 2015.

Brooks, Richard, *The Knight Who Saved England, William Marshal and the French Invasion, 1217*, Oxford: Osprey Publishing, 2014.

Brown, M. H., 'Margaret (1424–1445)', *Oxford Dictionary of National Biography*, Oxford University Press, online edition, 2004.

Brown, A. L., and Henry Summerson, 'Henry IV [known as Henry Bolingbroke]', *Oxford Dictionary of National Biography*, Oxford University Press, online edition, 2023.

Burghart, Alex, 'Æthelflæd, Iron Lady of Mercia', *BBC History Magazine*, Vol. 12, No. 8, August 2011.

Campbell, Bruce, 'Britain 1300', *History Today*, Vol. 50 (6), June 2000.

Cannon, John (ed.), *The Oxford Companion to British History*, Oxford: Oxford University Press, 1997.

Carol, *Eleanor of Leicester: A Broken Vow of Chastity* (article), historyofroyalwomen.com, 28 February 2017.

Carpenter, David, *Henry III: The Rise to Power and Personal Rule 1207–1258*, London: Yale University Press, 2021.

Castor, Helen, *She-Wolves: The Women who Ruled England Before Elizabeth*, London: Faber and Faber, 2010.

Castor, Helen, *The Eagle and the Hart: The Tragedy of Richard II and Henry IV*, London: Penguin, 2024.

Chibnall, Marjorie, *The Empress Matilda: Queen Consort, Queen Mother and Lady of the English*, Oxford: Blackwell Publishers, 1992.

Church, Stephen, *King John: England, Magna Carta and the Making of a Tyrant*, London: Pan Books, 2016.

Clark, K. L., *The Nevills of Middleham: England's Most Powerful Family in the Wars of the Roses*, Stroud: The History Press, 2016.

Cockayne, G. E., *The complete peerage of England, Scotland, Ireland, Great Britain and the United Kingdom, extant, extinct, or dormant*, G. H. White (ed.), London: The St Catherine Press, 1910.

Cockerill, Sara, *Eleanor of Aquitaine; Queen of France and England, Mother of Empires,* Stroud: Amberley Publishing, 2018.

Cockerill, Sara, *Eleanor of Castile: The Shadow Queen*, Stroud: Amberley Publishing, 2014.

Cole, Teresa, *After the Conquest: The Divided Realm 1066–1135*, Stroud: Amberley Publishing, 2018.

Cole, Teresa, *The Anarchy: The Darkest Days of Medieval England*, Stroud: Amberley Publishing, 2019.

Cole, Teresa, *The Norman Conquest: William the Conqueror's Subjugation of England,* Stroud: Amberley Publishing, 2016.

Cole, Teresa, *Women of Power: Formidable Females of the Medieval World*, Stroud: Amberley Publishing, 2023.

Condon, Margaret M., 'Princess and Nun: Bridget (1480–*c.*1507), the youngest daughter of Edward IV', *The Ricardian.* 32, (2022): pp. 89–126.

Corvi, Steven J., *Plantagenet Queens and Consorts*, Stroud: Amberley Publishing, 2018.

Crawford, Anne, (ed. and trans.), *Letters of Medieval Women*, Stroud: Sutton Publishing, 2002.

Crouch, David, *The Reign of King Stephen 1135–1154*, Harlow: Pearson Education Ltd, 2000.

Danziger, Danny and Gillingham, John, *1215 The Year of Magna Carta,* London: Hodder & Stoughton, 2004.

Davis, John Paul, *King John, Henry III and England's Lost Civil War*, Barnsley, Yorkshire: Pen and Sword Books, 2021.

Davis, William Stearns, *A History of France from the Earliest Times to the Treaty of Versailles*, Cambridge Massachusetts: The Riverside Press, 1919.

Dean, Kristie, *On the Trail of the Yorks*, Stroud: Amberley Publishing, 2016.

Doherty, Paul, *Isabella and the Strange Death of Edward II*, London: Constable, 2003.

Dougherty, Martin J., *The Wars of the Roses, The Conflict that Inspired Game of Thrones*, London: Amber Books, 2015.

Duckett, George Floyd, *Observations on the Parentage of Gundreda, the Daughter of William Duke of Normandy, and Wife of William de Warenne*, reprinted by Kessinger Legacy Reprints, originally published in Vol. III of the *Cumberland and Westmoreland Archaeological Society*, Kessinger Legacy Reprints, 1878.

Duducu, Jem, *Forgotten History: Unbelievable Moments from the Past,* Stroud: Amberley Publishing, 2016.

Dugdale, William, *Monasticon Anglicanum: a History of the Abbies and Other Monasteries, Hospitals, Frieries, and Cathedral and Collegiate Churches, with their dependencies, in England and Wales*, London: H. G. Bohn, 1840.

Duruy, Victor, *History of the Middle Ages*, Lecturable, e-book, 2012.

Englishmonarchs.co.uk; 'Joan, Lady of Wales (*c.*1191–1237)' (article), 2004.

Epistolae.ccnmtl.columbia.edu, *Marie of Boulogne and Blois* (article), accessed 4 December 2024.

Fairbank, F. Royston, 'The Last Earl of Warenne and Surrey, and the Distribution of his Possessions', *The Yorkshire Archaeological Journal*, Vol. XIX, (1907), pp. 193–266.

Farrer, William and Charles Travis Clay (eds.), *Early Yorkshire Charters, Vol. 8: The Honour of Warenne*, Cambridge: Cambridge University Press, 2013 edition, first published 1949.

Flemberg, Marie-Louise, 'Queen Philippa as a benefactor of the Birgittines', http://www.sanctabirgitta.com/underniva/forska/, 2003.

Foley, Liam, 'May 4, 1394: Birth of Philippa of England, Queen Consort of Denmark, Norway and Sweden', europeanroyalhistory.com, 2020.

Fraser, Antonia, *The Warrior Queens: Boadicea's Chariot,* London: George Weidenfeld & Nicolson Ltd, 1993.

Gardiner, Juliet and Neil Wenborn (eds.), *History Today Companion to British History,* London: Collins & Brown, 1995.

Gillingham, John, *The Wars of the Roses, Peace & Conflict in 15th Century England*, London: Phoenix Press, 1988.

Given-Wilson, C, 'Perrers, Alice (d. 1400/01)', *Oxford Dictionary of National Biography*, Oxford University Press, online edition, January 2008.

Goodman, Anthony, *John of Gaunt: The Exercise of Princely Power in Fourteenth-Century Europe*, London: Routledge, 1992.

Goodman, Anthony, 'Katherine (1372–1418)', *Oxford Dictionary of National Biography*, Oxford University Press, online edition, 2004.

Goubert, Pierre, *The Course of French History,* London: Routledge, 1991.

Grant, Lindy, 'Eleanor of Aquitaine', *BBC History Magazine*, August 2016.

Graves, Michael A. R., 'Howard, Thomas, third duke of Norfolk', *Oxford Dictionary of National Biography*, Oxford University Press, online edition, September 2004.

Green, Mary Anne Everett, *Lives of the Princesses of England from the Norman Conquest*, Vols. 1 to 3, London: Longman, Brown, Green, Longman, & Roberts, 1857.

h2g2.com/approved_entry/A2503298, *Philippa of Lancaster (1360–1415) – A tale from the History of Portugal* (article), 15 June 2004, updated 2008.

Hallam, Elizabeth (ed.), *Chronicles of the Age of Chivalry,* Twickenham: Tiger Books, 1995.

Hallam, Elizabeth (ed.), *The Plantagenet Chronicles,* Twickenham: Tiger Books, 1995.

Hallam, Elizabeth, 'Eleanor, Countess of Pembroke and Leicester (1215?–1275)', *Oxford Dictionary of National Biography*, Oxford University Press, online edition, 23 September 2004.

Hammond, Peter, *Katherine Plantagenet*, https://richardiii.net/richard-iii-his-world/his-family/illegitimate-children/katherine-plantagenet/, 2025.

Hanley, Catherine, *Matilda: Empress, Queen, Warrior*, London: Yale University Press, 2019.

Hickey, Julia A., *Medieval Royal Mistresses: Mischievous Women who Slept with Kings and Princes*, Barnsley, Yorkshire: Pen and Sword Books, 2022.

Hicks, Michael, *The Family of Richard III*, Stroud: Amberley Publishing, 2017.

Higginbotham, Susan, *A Royal Christening: Bridget of York, November 11, 1480*, susanhigginbotham.com, 11 November 2012.

Higginbotham, Susan, *Bridget of York: A Royal Nun*, susanhigginbotham.com, 16 February 2013.

Higginbotham, Susan, *Katherine Plantagenet, Richard III's Illegitimate Daughter*, susanhigginbotham.com, 17 April 2013.

Higginbotham, Susan, *The Woodvilles: The Wars of the Roses and England's Most Infamous Family,* Stroud: The History Press, 2013.

Hilliam, David, *Kings, Queens, Bones and Bastards: Who's Who in the English Monarchy from Egbert to Elizabeth II,* Stroud: The History Press, 2008 (first published 1998).

Hilton, Lisa, *Queens Consort: England's Medieval Queens*, London: Phoenix, 2009.

Historyofroyalwomen.com.

Hollman, Gemma, *The Queen and the Mistress: The Women of Edward III*, Cheltenham, The History Press, 2022.

Horrox, Rosemary, 'Cecily, Viscountess Welles', *Oxford Dictionary of National Biography,* Oxford University Press, online edition, 23 September 2004.

Horrox, Rosemary, 'Elizabeth [Elizabeth of York] 1466-1503', *Oxford Dictionary of National Biography,* Oxford University Press, online edition, 2004.

Horrox, Rosemary, *Richard III, Oxford Dictionary of National Biography,* online edition, 2013.

Huneycutt, Lois L., 'Adela, Countess of Blois (*c.*1067–1137)', *Oxford Dictionary of National Biography*, Oxford University Press, online edition, 2004.

Hunt, Tony, 'Marie (fl. *c.*1180–*c.*1189)', *Oxford Dictionary of National Biography*, Oxford University Press, online edition, 2004.

Huscroft, Richard, *Tales from the Long Twelfth Century*, London: Yale University Press, 2017.

James, Jeffrey, *Edward IV: Glorious Son of York*, Stroud: Amberley Publishing, 2015.

James, Jeffrey, *The Bastard's Sons: Robert, William and Henry of Normandy,* Stroud: Amberley Publishing, 2020.

Jobson, Adrian (ed.), *English Government in the Thirteenth Century*, Woodbridge: The Boydell Press, 2004.

Johns, Susan M., 'Warenne, Isabel de, suo jure Countess of Surrey (d. 1203)', *Oxford Dictionary of National Biography*, Oxford University Press, online edition, 2004.

Johns, Susan M., *Noblewomen, Aristocracy and Power in the Twelfth-Century Anglo-Norman Realm*, Manchester: Manchester University Press, 2007.

Johnson, Paul, *The Life and Times of Edward III,* London: Wiedenfeld and Nicolson and Book Club Associates, 1984.

Jones, Dan, *Henry V: The Astonishing Rise of England's Greatest King*, London: Head of Zeus, 2024.

Jones, Dan, *The Plantagenets, The Kings Who Made England*, Kindle edition, London: Harper Collins, 2013.

Jones, Terry, *Terry Jones' Medieval Lives*, London: BBC Books, 2005.

King, Edmund, *King Stephen*, London: Yale University Press, 2010

Koenigsberger, H. G., *Medieval Europe 400–1500,* New York: Longman, 1987.

Lacey, Robert, *Great Tales from English History*, London: Abacus, 2007.

Laffin, John, *Brassey's Battles: 3,500 Years of Conflict, Campaigns and Wars from A–Z*, London: Brassey's, 1995.

Lawless, Erin, *Forgotten Royal Women: The King and I*, Barnsley, Yorkshire: Pen and Sword Books, 2019.

Lewis, C. P., 'Warenne, Warenne, Gundrada de(d. 1085)' (d. 1088)', *Oxford Dictionary of National Biography*, Oxford University Press, online edition, 2004.

Lewis, Matthew, *Henry II and Eleanor of Aquitaine: Founding an Empire*, Stroud: Amberley Publishing, 2021.

Lewis, Matthew, *Henry III: the Son of Magna Carta*, Stroud: Amberley Publishing, 2016.

Lewis, Matthew, *Richard Duke of York: King by Right*, Stroud: Amberley Publishing, 2016.

Lewis, Matthew, *Richard III: Loyalty Binds Me*, Stroud: Amberley, 2018.

Lewis, Matthew, *Richard III's Illegitimate Children – Katherine Plantagenet*, Made by History (Substack), 2025.

Lewis, Matthew, *Stephen and Matilda's Civil War: Cousins of Anarchy*, Barnsley, Yorkshire: Pen and Sword Books, 2019.

Leyser, Henrietta, *Medieval Women, A Social History of Women in England 450–1500*, Phoenix, e-book, 2013.

Licence, Amy, *Edward IV and Elizabeth Wydeville: A True Romance*, Stroud: Amberley Publishing, 2016.

Licence, Amy, *Elizabeth of York: The Forgotten Tudor Queen*, Stroud: Amberley Publishing, 2013.

Licence, Amy, *Red Roses: Blanche of Gaunt to Margaret Beaufort*, Stroud: The History Press, 2016.

Lucraft, Jane, 'Missing From History: Katherine Swynford', *History Today*, Vol. 52 (5), May 2002.

Maddicott, J. R., 'Montfort, Simon de, eighth earl of Leicester (1208–1265)', *Oxford Dictionary of National Biography*, Oxford University Press, online edition, 3 January 2008.

Maddicott, J. R., 'Thomas of Lancaster, Second Earl of Lancaster, Second Earl of Leicester, and Earl of Lincoln (*c*.1278–1322)', *Oxford Dictionary of National Biography*, Oxford University Press, online edition, January 2008.

Marlow, Joyce, *Kings & Queens of Britain*, (sixth edition) London: Artus Publishing, 1979.

Marshall, Rosalind K. *Scottish Queens 1034-1714,* Edinburgh: Birlinn Ltd, 2019.

Martindale, Jane, 'Eleanor, suo jure Duchess of Aquitaine (*c*.1122–1204)', *Oxford Dictionary of National Biography*, Oxford University Press, online edition, May 2006.

Matthews, Helen, *The Legitimacy of Bastards*, Barnsley, Yorkshire: Pen and Sword Books, 2019.

Mcglynn, Sean, 'King John and the French Invasion of England', *BBC History Magazine*, Vol. 11, No. 6, June 2010.

Messer, Danna, *Joan, Lady of Wales: Power and Politics of King John's Daughter*, Barnsley, Yorkshire: Pen and Sword Books, 2020.

Morris, Marc, 'From Friendly Neighbours to Bitter Enemies', *BBC History Magazine*, Vol. 9 No. 3, March 2008.

Morris, Marc, *A Great and Terrible King: Edward I and the Forging of Britain*, London: Windmill Books, 2009.

Morris, Marc, *King John: Treachery, Tyranny and the Road to Magna Carta,* London: Windmill Books, 2015.

Morris, Marc, *William I: England's Conqueror*, London: Penguin Books, 2016.

Morrison, Susan Signe, 'Six Trailblazing Medieval Women' (article), historyextra.com, 2 June 2016.

Mortimer, Ian, *The Fears of Henry IV: The Life of England's Self-Made King*, London: Vintage Books, 2008.

Mortimer, Ian, *The Perfect King, the Life of Edward III*, Kindle edition, London: Jonathan Cape, 2006.

Mount, Toni, *A Year in the Life of Medieval England*, Stroud: Amberley Publishing, 2016.

Mundy, John H., *The High Middle Ages 1150–1309*, London: The Folio Society, 1998.

Norgate, Kate and Rev. A. D. Carr, 'Joan, d. 1237', *Oxford Dictionary of National Biography*, Oxford University Press, online edition, 2004.

Norton, Elizabeth, *England's Queens: From Boudica to Elizabeth of York*, Stroud: Amberley Publishing, 2015.

Norton, Elizabeth, *She Wolves: The Notorious Queens of England*, Stroud: The History Press, 2009.

Oram, Richard (ed.), *The Kings & Queens of Scotland*, Cheltenham: The History Press, 2021.

Ormrod, W. M., "Alice Perrers and John Salisbury", English Historical Review, volume 20, December 2015, p. 134.

Ormrod, W. M., *The Reign of Edward III*, Stroud: Tempus, 2000.

Pain, Nesta, *Empress Matilda: Uncrowned Queen of England*, London: Book Club Associates, 1978.

Royston Fairbank, F., 'Possessions', *The Yorkshire Archaeological Journal*, Vol. XIX, (1907), pp. 193–266.

Power, Eileen, *Medieval English Nunneries c. 1275–1535*, London: Cambridge University Press, 1922.

Rawcliffe, C., *The Staffords, Earls of Stafford and Dukes of Buckingham, 1394–1521*, Cambridge Studies in Medieval Life and Thought, 3rd ser., 11, 1978.

Reid, Norman H., 'Alexander III (1241–1286)', *Oxford Dictionary of National Biography*, Oxford University Press, online edition, revised 19 May 2011.

Rex, Peter, *William the Conqueror: The Bastard of Normandy,* (third edition), Stroud: Amberley Publishing, 2016.

Ross, David, *Scotland: History of a Nation*, Broxburn: Lomond Books Ltd, 2014.

Routh, Pauline E., 'Princess Bridget', *The Ricardian*, June 1975.

Santuiste, David, *Edward IV and the Wars of the Roses,* Yorkshire: Pen & Sword, 2010.

Seward, Desmond, *Richard III: England's Black Legend*, London: Penguin Books, 1997.

Seward, Desmond, *The Demon's Brood,* London: Constable, 2014.

Sharpe, Richard, 'King Harold's Daughter', *Haskins Society Journal*, Vol. 19, Stephen Morillo and William North (eds.), Woodbridge: The Boydell Press, 2008.

Skidmore, Chris, *Richard III: Brother, Protector, King*, London: Weidenfeld & Nicholson, 2017.

Southern, R. W., *The Making of the Middle Ages*, 4th edition, London: The Folio Society, 1998.

Spinks, Stephen, *Edward II the Man: A Doomed Inheritance*, Stroud: Amberley Publishing, 2017.

Stacey, R. C., 'Divorce, Medieval Welsh Style', *Speculum*, Vol. 77, Issue 4, October 2002, University of Chicago Press.

Stansfield, M. M. N., 'Holland, Thomas, Earl of Kent (*c*.1315–1360)', *Oxford Dictionary of National Biography*, Oxford University Press, online edition, Jan. 2008.

Steer, Dr Christian, *The King's Daughter in Late Medieval London:An Archival Discovery of Monumental Proportions*, yorkisthistorytrust.org, 2022.

Stringer, Keith, 'Joan (1210–1237)', *Oxford Dictionary of National Biography*, Oxford University Press, online edition, 2004.

Telford, Lynda, *Women in Medieval England*, Stroud: Amberley Publishing, 2021.

Thompson, S. P., 'Mary [Mary of Blois], suo jure Countess of Boulogne (d. 1182), Princess and abbess of Romsey', *Oxford Dictionary of National Biography*, Oxford University Press, online edition, May 2014.

Tranter, Nigel, *The Story of Scotland*, e-book, 4th edition, Neil Wilson Publishing, 2011.

Trow, M. J., *Richard III in the North*, Barnsley, Yorkshire: Pen and Sword Books, 2020.

Turner, Ralph V., 'The Children of Anglo-Norman Royalty and their Upbringing', *Medieval Porsopography*, Vol. II, No. 2 (Autumn 1990), pp. 17–52, jstor.org/stable/45048108.

Van Houts, Elisabeth, 'Adelida [Adeliza]', *Oxford Dictionary of National Biography*, Oxford University Press, online edition, September 2004.

Van Houts, Elisabeth, 'Matilda of Flanders (d. 1083) Queen of England, consort of William I', *Oxford Dictionary of National Biography*, Oxford University Press, online edition, May 2008.

Van Houts, Elisabeth, 'The Warenne View of the Past', in *Proceedings of the Battle Conference 2003,* John Gillingham (ed.), Suffolk: Boydell Press, 2004.

Walker, Simon, 'Katherine Roelt (1350?–1403)', *Oxford Dictionary of National Biography*, Oxford University Press, online edition, January 2008.

Warner, Kathryn, *Daughters of Edward I*, Barnsley, Yorkshire: Pen and Sword Books, 2021.

Warner, Kathryn, *Edward II: The Unconventional King*, Stroud: Amberley Publishing, 2017.

Warner, Kathryn, *Isabella of France, The Rebel Queen,* Stroud: Amberley Publishing, 2016.

Warner, Kathryn, *Philippa of Hainault: Mother of the English Nation*, Stroud: Amberley Publishing, 2019.

Warren, W. L., *Henry II* (New edition), London: Yale University Press, 2000.

Watt, D., 'The Minority of Alexander III of Scotland', *Transactions of the Royal Historical Society, 21* (1971), pp. 1–23. doi:10.2307/3678917.

Weir, Alison, *Britain's Royal Families: the Complete Genealogy,* London: Pimlico, 1996 (second edition).

Weir, Alison, *Eleanor of Aquitaine; By the Wrath of God, Queen of England,* London: Jonathan Cape, 1999.

Weir, Alison, *Elizabeth of York: The First Tudor Queen*, London: Jonathan Cape, 2013.

Weir, Alison, *Queens of the Conquest: England's Medieval Queens, 1066–1167*, London: Vintage, 2017.

Weir, Alison, *The Wars of the Roses*, London: Jonathan Cape, 1995.

Westcott, Margaret R., 'Katherine, Countess of Devon', *Oxford Dictionary of National Biography,* Oxford University Press, online edition, 3 January 2008.

Wilkinson, Louise, (ed. and trans.), *The Household Roll of Eleanor de Montfort, Countess of Leicester and Pembroke, 1265*, Suffolk: The Pipe Roll Society, 2020.

Wilkinson, Louise, 'Joan, Daughter of King John' (article), magnacarta800th.com 2016.

Wilkinson, Louise, *Women in Thirteenth-Century Lincolnshire,* Suffolk: Boydell, 2007.

Williamson, David, *Brewer's British Royalty,* London: Cassell, 1996.

Wilson, Derek, *The Plantagenets*, London: Quercus, 2011.

Wilson-Lee, Kelcey, *Daughters of Chivalry: The Forgotten Children of Edward I*, London: Picador, 2019.

Wright, James, *A Palace for Our Kings: The History and Archaeology of a Mediaeval Royal Palace in the Heart of Sherwood Forest,* London: Triskele Publishing, 2016.

Yonge, Charlotte M., *History of France*, New York: D. Appleton and Company, 1882.

Index